D0447216

SAT* MATH LEVEL 2 SUBJECT TEST

CRASH COURSE™

By Linda Hardman
and
Virginia Ogozalek, Ph.D.

Research & Education Association
Visit our website at: www.rea.com

Research & Education Association
61 Ethel Road West
Piscataway, New Jersey 08854
E-mail: info@rea.com

SAT MATH LEVEL 2 SUBJECT TEST CRASH COURSE™

Library of Congress Control Number 2012932839

ISBN-13: 978-0-7386-1032-0
ISBN-10: 0-7386-1032-1

SAT MATH LEVEL 2 SUBJECT TEST CRASH COURSE™
TABLE OF CONTENTS

PART I

Introduction

PART II

Numbers and Operations

PART III

Algebra and Functions

PART IV

Geometry and Measurement

PART V

Data Analysis, Statistics, and Probability

ONLINE PRACTICE EXAM .... *www.rea.com/studycenter*

ABOUT THIS BOOK

REA's *SAT Math Level 2 Subject Test Crash Course* is the first book of its kind for the last-minute studier or any student who wants a quick refresher on the subject. The book will provide you with an accurate and complete representation of the SAT Mathematics Level 2 Subject Test.

Written by experts skilled in mathematics and test prep development, our easy-to-read format gives students a crash course in mathematics. The targeted review chapters prepare students for the exam by focusing only on the important topics that will be tested on the SAT Math Level 2 Subject Test.

Unlike other test preps, REA's *SAT Math Level 2 Subject Test Crash Course* gives you a review specifically focused on what you really need to study in order to ace the exam. The review chapters provide a concise way to learn all the important facts, terms, and key topics before the exam.

The introduction discusses the keys to your success on the SAT Math Level 2 Subject Test and shows you strategies to help build your overall score. Also included is an overview of the different types of questions you will encounter on the test.

Each review chapter presents the essential information you need to know about math. Interspersed throughout the review chapters are Test Tips written to help you attain the highest score on the SAT Math Level 2 Subject Test.

To check your test readiness, either before or after studying this *Crash Course*, take REA's **FREE online practice exam**. To access your practice exam, visit the online REA Study Center at *www.rea.com/studycenter* and follow the on-screen instructions. Our true-to-format test features automatic scoring, enforced time conditions, and a detailed score report that pinpoints your strengths and weaknesses so you'll be ready on test day!

No matter how or when you prepare for the SAT Math Level 2 Subject Test, REA's *Crash Course* will show you how to study efficiently and strategically, so you can boost your score.

Good luck on your SAT Math Level 2 Subject Test!

ABOUT OUR AUTHORS

Linda Hardman

Linda Hardman has over 25 years of educational publishing experience, including such positions as Vice President of Math Product Development for Harcourt Achieve, Vice President and Publisher (Science, Technology, Mathematics, and Medical) for ProQuest, Vice President of Business Development & Special Projects for Cogito Learning Media, and Vice President of Educational Technology for Prentice Hall. As an author, Ms. Hardman is an award-winning leader in content development and assessment strategies. Her experience includes serving as lead author of six computer literacy textbooks with 96 supplementary products; as project manager, writer, and editor of K–14 mathematics products, including test-prep materials, basal pupil editions, basal teacher editions, online products, assessments, and tutorials; as author of end-of-course assessments for algebra; and as project manager, writer, and editor of an elementary and middle school math ELL online and special education mathematics program, funded by the U.S. Department of Education.

Virginia Ogozalek, Ph.D.

Dr. Virginia Ogozalek is a freelance mathematics writer with extensive experience in developing preparation materials for standardized tests including the SAT, GRE, and GMAT. Dr. Ogozalek is a Professor Emeritus at Worcester State University in Worcester, Massachusetts, where she has taught courses in developmental mathematics and served as principal investigator on the Goals 2000 and Project PALMS (Partnerships Advancing the Learning of Math and Science) grants, which established collaborative partnerships between university faculty and teachers of high school mathematics. Dr. Ogozalek holds advanced degrees from the University of Southern Maine, Worcester Polytechnic Institute, Northeastern University, and Harvard University, where she won the Crite Prize, which is awarded for "singular dedication to learning and the arts."

ACKNOWLEDGMENTS

In addition to our author, we would like to thank Larry B. Kling, Vice President, Editorial, for his overall guidance, which brought this publication to completion; Pam Weston, Publisher, for setting the quality standards for production integrity and managing the publication to completion; Alice Leonard, Senior Editor, for editorial project management; Diane Goldschmidt, Managing Editor, for preflight editorial review; and Mel Friedman, Lead Math Editor, for developing Practice Test content, and for technical review of the manuscript.

We also extend our special thanks to S4Carlisle Publishing Services for production services.

PART I:

INTRODUCTION

KEYS TO SUCCESS ON THE SAT MATH LEVEL 2 SUBJECT TEST

The SAT Math Level 2 Subject Test is intended for students who have taken college-preparatory mathematics for more than 3 years, including courses in algebra, geometry, trigonometry, and precalculus. If the exam covered every possible topic in all of these areas, the amount of studying you would need to earn a good score would be daunting.

But don't panic...relax. This *Crash Course* is going to guide you to success on the exam. The book's outline format was designed to streamline your study by focusing only on the topics you really need to know to do well on the exam. By studying efficiently and strategically, you can earn a high score on the exam. The keys to success on the exam also include knowing the following, so let's get started.

CONTENT OF THE SAT MATH LEVEL 2 SUBJECT TEST

The SAT Math Level 2 Subject Test is a one-hour test containing 50 multiple-choice questions that cover the following areas:

I. Numbers and Operations, 10–14%
II. Algebra and Functions, 48–52%
III. Geometry and Measurement, 28–32%
IV. Data Analysis, Statistics, and Probability, 8–12%

A good way to glean information about the content of the SAT Math Level 2 test is to compare it to the Math Level 1 test. Because new mathematical knowledge builds upon previous mathematical knowledge, it is reasonable to assume that students taking the Level 2 test will already be proficient in the topics covered at Level 1. The recommended preparation for the Level 1 exam is 2 years of algebra and 1 year of geometry. For the Level 2 exam, recommendations are also for 2 years of algebra and 1 year of geometry, with additional study in precalculus (elementary functions) and/or trigonometry as well. The following table shows topics included in both tests, as well as additional content in Math Level 2.

Content of the SAT Subject Tests: Math Levels 1 and 2

Content	Both Level 1 and Level 2	Level 2 Additional Content
Number and operations	Operations, ratio and proportion, arithmetic of complex numbers, counting, elementary number theory, matrices, sequences	Graphical and other properties of complex numbers, series, vectors
Algebra and functions	Expressions, equations, inequalities representation and modeling, properties of functions (linear, polynomial, rational, exponential)	Advanced equations, properties of functions (logarithmic, trigonometric, inverse trigonometric, periodic, piecewise, recursive, parametric)
Geometry and Measurement		
Coordinate	Lines, parabolas, circles, symmetry, transformations	Ellipses, hyperbolas, polar coordinates
Three-dimensional	Solids, surface area, and volume (cylinders, cones, spheres, pyramids, prisms)	Coordinates in three dimensions
Trigonometry	Right triangles, identities	Radian measure, law of cosines, law of sines, equations, double-angle formulas
Data analysis, statistics, and probability	Mean, median, mode, range, interquartile range, graphs and plots, least squares regression (linear), probability	Standard deviation, least squares regression (quadratic, exponential)

Source: The College Board, 2012

The numbers of questions for each topic also differ in the Math Level 1 and Level 2 tests, as shown in the following table.

Math Levels 1 and 2: Number of Questions by Topic

Topic	Approximate Number of Questions	
	Math Level 1	Math Level 2
Number and operations	5–7	5–7
Algebra and functions	19–21	24–26
Geometry and measurement	19–21	14–16
• **Plane Euclidean**	9–11	0
• **Coordinate**	4–6	5–7
• **Three-dimensional**	2–3	2–3
• **Trigonometry**	3–4	6–8
Data analysis, statistics, and probability	3–5	3–5

Source: The College Board

As you can see, the SAT Mathematics Level 2 test contains more questions covering algebra and functions, coordinate geometry, and trigonometry. Although plane geometry is not directly tested on the Level 2 exam, concepts learned in that area provide a foundation for questions in more advanced topics of coordinate geometry and three-dimensional geometry.

It is important to note that you can do very well on the Math Level 2 Subject Test even if you have not studied every subject that is covered. In fact, you may actually do better on the Math Level 2 exam than you would on Math Level 1 if you have recently studied the advanced mathematical topics covered in Math Level 2 and the content is more accessible in your mind!

TEST STRUCTURE

Knowing beforehand how a test is structured can help save you valuable time and also reduce anxiety. The SAT Math Level 2 test will be similar to many tests you have taken before, but there are also significant differences. You will feel more confident and relaxed going into the test if you already know what to expect. This section will give you some information about the test itself, as well as test-taking procedures.

The SAT Math Level 2 test contains 50 multiple-choice questions arranged from easier to harder. You will have 1 hour to answer all 50 questions. Each correct answer is worth 1 point, regardless of question difficulty. This means you do not get more points for answering the harder questions correctly, even if they take much more time to complete!

You can move around in the Math Level 2 test, answering questions in any order you want. If you don't know the answer to a question, you can skip it and then go back to answer it later. It's a good idea to check off questions as you complete them. This will help you when you go back to find the questions you previously skipped and also to avoid accidentally leaving questions unanswered.

If you try to answer a question on the Math Level 2 test but get it wrong, a fraction of a point ($-\frac{1}{4}$ point for each five-choice question) is subtracted from the total number of correct answers. If you do not answer a question, no points are added or subtracted. As a general rule, if you do not know the answer to a question but can make an educated guess, it's probably worth filling in an answer. Otherwise, if you are totally clueless, it's probably better to leave the question unanswered.

The questions themselves are given in a test booklet, but you'll be filling in answer circles with a No. 2 pencil on a separate answer sheet. Although it may sound silly to say, be careful that you fill in the correct circles as you go along. Keep your answer sheet neat and clean—it's scored by a machine that can't tell the difference between answers and doodles, resulting in the possibility that any random pencil marks could cause questions to be scored as unanswered or wrong. The test booklet itself contains ample designated space to use as scrap paper, so you can write in that area freely. (Unfortunately, although you'll be turning in the test booklet along with your answer sheet, no partial credit is given for work shown.)

TYPES OF QUESTIONS

All the questions on the SAT Math Level 2 test are multiple-choice, so you don't have to worry about writing essays or coming up with answers on your own. With that said, there are strategies you can use to increase your chances of answering multiple-choice questions correctly, even when you are not quite sure how to solve a given problem.

Using the process of elimination is probably the most common strategy for answering multiple-choice questions when you are not quite sure of the answer. Each question on the Math Level 2 test has five answer choices, designated by letters A through E, and you are instructed to choose the BEST answer. If you can identify and eliminate all the wrong choices, then the remaining answer choice must be correct. Let's look at a typical test question to see how that works.

Which of the following is an equation of a line perpendicular to $y = -4x + 5$?

(A) $y = 5x - 4$

(B) $y = 4x - 5$

(C) $y = \dfrac{1}{4}x + 5$

(D) $y = -\dfrac{1}{4}x + 5$

(E) $y = \dfrac{1}{-4x + 5}$

When answering this question, you might recall that if the equation of one of two perpendicular lines is in slope-intercept form, $y = mx + b$, then the x-coefficient in the equation of the other perpendicular line is the negative reciprocal of the x-coefficient in the first. This is because the first equation would have a slope of m, then the perpendicular line equation would have a slope of $-\dfrac{1}{m}$. Because m is -4 for the given equation $y = -4x + 5$, you can eliminate any answer where m is not $-\dfrac{1}{(-4)}$, or $\dfrac{1}{4}$. The correct answer is (C).

Although this question seems fairly straightforward, it provides an opportunity to look at a standard technique used to perplex multiple-choice test takers. When multiple-choice questions are created, the incorrect answer choices are not merely random, but instead are designed to resemble answers resulting from commonly made errors. These purposefully wrong answers are called *distractors* because they are intended to distract you from getting the right answer. For example, in the sample question provided earlier, choices (A) and (B) would result from being aware that changes in signs and coefficients take place, but omitting any changes involving the reciprocal. Choice (D) is correct except for the sign of the reciprocal, and choice (E) involves incorrect placement of the variable and constant, as well.

Although the majority of multiple-choice questions require you to simply identify a correct answer, you will encounter one or two questions of the following type:

The intersection of a right circular cylinder with a plane could be which of the following?

  I. A circle
  II. A square
  III. A triangle

  (A) I only
  (B) II only
  (C) I and II only
  (D) I and III only
  (E) I, II, and III

These questions are a bit trickier because you must first determine which items in the Roman numeral list are correct and then choose the correct corresponding answer. Again, the process of elimination can help. For example, you probably know that a triangle cannot be the intersection of a cylinder and a plane, allowing you to eliminate Roman numeral III and therefore choices (D) and (E) as well. You probably also know that a circle can be the intersection of a cylinder and a plane, allowing you to eliminate answer choice (B). This leaves a decision between choices (A) and (C), which depends on whether or not a square can be the intersection of a cylinder and a plane. If you realize that a square can be the intersection if the diameter and the height of the cylinder are equal, you eliminate choice (A) and determine the correct answer is (C).

For some questions, the exact numerical answer may not be among the answer choices. In this case, you should choose the answer that is closest to the correct value. Here's an example of this situation:

If cos x = 0.3895, then sec x =

  (A) 2.5674
  (B) 2.3646
  (C) 1.0858
  (D) 0.9210
  (E) 0.4229

Because the secant of an angle is the reciprocal of the cosine, you need to calculate $\frac{1}{0.3895}$, resulting in an answer that looks something like 2.567394095. This answer does not appear among the answer choices, but 2.5674 is what you get rounding to the nearest ten thousandth and so the correct answer is (A). This example now brings us to one of the most important issues to be addressed about the Math Level 2 test: calculator use.

Here's what the College Board says about the Subject Tests in Math and calculators: **"Students who take the test without a calculator will be at a disadvantage."** (Yes, boldface is used.) This statement is followed by an extensive amount of information and advice about calculator use on the test, including very specific rules for which types of calculators are permitted and which are not. To be on the safe side, you are advised to visit collegeboard.org to get the latest and most in-depth information on calculator usage on the SAT Math Level 2 Subject Test.

Here's the scoop: For about 35% to 45% of the questions on the Level 2 test, there's no need to use a calculator. In fact, using a calculator for those questions might actually cost you valuable time. However, for the other 55% to 65% of the questions, using a calculator will be really useful or even necessary, and a graphing calculator is highly recommended. Throughout the rest of this *Crash Course*, you'll be reviewing ways to use your calculator to answer all kinds of Math Level 2 questions easily, quickly, and correctly so you can score high on the test.

TEST SCORING

The first step in scoring the SAT Math Level 2 Subject Test is calculating the raw score as follows: +1 point for correct answers, $-\frac{1}{4}$ point for incorrect answers (5-choice questions), and 0 points for omitted questions. After the raw score is calculated, it is converted to a scaled score by a statistical process called "equating." This scale is from 200–800 and is the score you will see when your Math Level 2 test results are reported.

The following table shows some percentile ranks for 2011 college-bound seniors who took the SAT Math Level 2 Subject Test.

**Percentile Ranks for SAT Math Level 2
Subject Test, 2011 Test Takers**

Math Level 2 Score	Percentile
800	87
750	73
700	61
650	47
600	31
550	18
500	8

Source: The College Board

For each given score, the percentile rank shows the percentage of test takers who scored lower on the test than someone with that given score. So, if a particular test taker scored 700, this means that 61% of the other 2011 college-bound seniors who took the SAT Math Level 2 test scored lower than that test taker.

HOW TO SUPPLEMENT THIS *CRASH COURSE*

This *Crash Course* book and online practice test contain everything you need to do well on the SAT Math Level 2 Subject Test, but for this important step in your life you will want to make use of everything that can help. The College Board's website has a wealth of useful information to help you prepare for the exam, including test dates and locations, calculator guidelines, and past test questions.

PART II:

NUMBERS AND OPERATIONS

OPERATIONS

KEY VOCABULARY

Associative property For addition, $a + (b + c) = (a + b) + c$; for multiplication, $a \bullet (b \bullet c) = (a \bullet b) \bullet c$.

Binary operation An operation that requires two numbers. Addition is a binary operation.

Commutative property For addition, $a + b = b + a$; for multiplication, $a \bullet b = b \bullet a$.

Distributive property For multiplication distributed over addition, $a(b + c) = a(b) + a(c)$.

Identity A special number that when combined with another number using an operation leaves the other number unchanged. Zero is the additive identity and 1 is the multiplicative identity.

Operation A process that works on numbers.

Order of operations A set of rules that determines the order in which operations are performed. A popular mnemonic is **PEMDAS**, which stands for **P**arentheses, **E**xponents, **M**ultiplication, **D**ivision, **A**ddition, and **S**ubtraction.

 ## I. BASIC PROPERTIES

A. COMMUTATIVE PROPERTY

1. The rule for the commutative property of addition is "$a + b = b + a$"; this means that you can add numbers in any order. For example, $3 + 4 = 4 + 3$.

2. The rule for the commutative property of multiplication is "$a \cdot b = b \cdot a$"; this means that you can multiply numbers in any order. For example, $3 \cdot 4 = 4 \cdot 3$.

B. ASSOCIATIVE PROPERTY

1. The rule for the associative property of addition is "$a + (b + c) = (a + b) + c$"; this means that you can group numbers in any way when adding. For example, $2 + (3 + 4) = (2 + 3) + 4$.
2. The rule for the associative property of multiplication is "$a \cdot (b \cdot c) = (a \cdot b) \cdot c$"; this means that you can group numbers in any way when multiplying. For example, $2 \cdot (3 \cdot 4) = (2 \cdot 3) \cdot 4$.

C. DISTRIBUTIVE PROPERTY

1. The rule for the distributive property is "$a(b + c) = ab + ac$"; it is often described by saying that "multiplication is distributed over addition." For example, $2(3 + 4) = 2(3) + 2(4)$.
2. You can also distribute multiplication over subtraction. For example, $2(3 - 4) = 2(3) - 2(4)$.
3. However, you cannot distribute all operations. For example, you cannot distribute division over addition:

$$2 \div (3 + 4) = 2 \div 7 = \frac{2}{7}, \text{ but } 2 \div 3 + 2 \div 4 = \frac{2}{3} + \frac{2}{4} = 1\frac{1}{6}.$$

D. IDENTITY

1. An identity is a number such that when you use an operation to combine the identity with another number, the other number stays the same.
2. The additive identity is zero, because $0 + a = a$ and $a = a + 0$.
3. The multiplicative identity is 1, because $1 \cdot a = a$ and $a = a \cdot 1$.

E. INVERSE PROPERTY

1. The rule for the inverse property of addition is "$a + -a = 0$"; this means that when you add a number to its additive inverse, the result is 0. The additive inverse of a number is often called its negative or opposite. For example, the additive

inverse of 24 is −24 and 24 + −24 = 0. The additive inverse of −8 is 8 and −8 + 8 = 0.

2. The rule for the inverse property of multiplication is

$a\left(\dfrac{1}{a}\right) = 1$, except for 0; this means that any number

times its reciprocal, or multiplicative inverse, equals 1. A multiplicative inverse or reciprocal of a real number a

represented as $\dfrac{a}{1}$, except 0, can be created by interchanging

the numerator and denominator. So, the reciprocal of

$\dfrac{a}{1}$ is $\dfrac{1}{a}$. For example, the reciprocal of 4 is $\dfrac{1}{4}$ and the

reciprocal of $-\dfrac{2}{3}$ is $-\dfrac{3}{2}$ because $-\dfrac{2}{3}\left(-\dfrac{3}{2}\right) = 1$. Following are

some additional examples using the inverse property of multiplication.

Inverse Property of Multiplication Examples

Real Number	Reciprocal	Equation
5	$\dfrac{1}{5}$	$5\left(\dfrac{1}{5}\right) = 1$
−5	$-\dfrac{1}{5}$	$-5\left(-\dfrac{1}{5}\right) = 1$
$\dfrac{3}{4}$	$\dfrac{4}{3}$	$\dfrac{3}{4}\left(\dfrac{4}{3}\right) = 1$
$-\dfrac{5}{6}$	$-\dfrac{6}{5}$	$-\dfrac{5}{6}\left(-\dfrac{6}{5}\right) = 1$

II. **ORDER OF OPERATIONS**

A. MULTIPLICATION, DIVISION, ADDITION, AND SUBTRACTION

1. Evaluate multiplication and division *as they appear left to right* before addition and subtraction *as they appear left to right*: $1 + 2 \cdot 3 + 4 = 11$.

2. Evaluate terms inside parentheses or other grouping symbols first, then evaluate multiplication and division *as they appear left to right* before addition and subtraction *as they appear left to right*: $(1 + 2) \cdot 3 + 4 = 13$, $1 + 2 \cdot (3 + 4) = 15$, and $(1 + 2) \cdot (3 + 4) = 21$.

B. THE DIVISION BAR

1. The division bar is a grouping symbol: $\dfrac{1+2}{3+4}$ means the sum of 1 plus 2 is divided by the sum of 3 plus 4.

2. Parentheses must be used so that expressions with division bars are evaluated correctly: $\dfrac{1+2}{3+4} = (1+2) \div (3+4) = \dfrac{3}{7}$.

Calculators and Order of Operations Use parentheses to ensure that operations are performed in the correct order. Here are correct and incorrect ways to enter $\dfrac{1+2}{3+4}$.

CORRECT
press (1 + 2) ÷ (3 + 4) **ENTER**
(1+2)/(3+4)
                .4285714286

INCORRECT
press 1 + 2 ÷ 3 + 4 **ENTER**
1+2/3+4
                5.666666667

C. PEMDAS

1. Remember **PEMDAS** (**P**arentheses, **E**xponents, **M**ultiplication, **D**ivision, **A**ddition, and **S**ubtraction)!

2. Evaluate operations in this order:
   P   **P**arentheses
   E   **E**xponents (powers, roots)
   M   **M**ultiplication and **D**ivision
   D   *as they appear left to right*
   A   **A**ddition and **S**ubtraction
   S   *as they appear left to right*

D. EXPRESSIONS WITH EXPONENTS (POWERS AND ROOTS)

1. Use parentheses to ensure that operations are performed in the intended manner. For example, $(xy)^2 = x^2 \bullet y^2$, but $xy^2 = x \bullet y^2$.

2. Be able to write roots using exponents.

   For example, $\sqrt[3]{27} = 27^{\left(\frac{1}{3}\right)} = 3$.

Calculators and Exponents *Use parentheses to ensure that operations are performed in the correct order. For example, here's how to input* $\sqrt[3]{27}$ *(the cube root of 27) into the calculator.*

press 27^(1 ÷ 3) **ENTER**

Here's what happens if you leave out the parentheses.

press 27^1 ÷ 3 **ENTER**

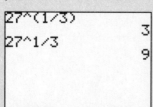

RATIO AND PROPORTION

KEY VOCABULARY

Cross multiplication When each side of an equation consists of a fraction/ratio, cross multiplication is a technique used to simplify the equation by multiplying the denominator of one fraction by the numerator of the other, and vice versa, setting the products equal to each other. For example, the equation $\frac{a}{b} = \frac{c}{d}$ can be simplified using cross multiplication: $\frac{a}{b} = \frac{c}{d} \rightarrow ad = bc$. For the equation $\frac{2}{3} = \frac{x}{5}$, we can solve for x using cross multiplication:

$\frac{2}{3} = \frac{x}{5} \rightarrow (2)(5) = (3)(x)$ and $x = \frac{10}{3}$ or $x = 3\frac{1}{3}$.

Proportion An equation with a ratio on each side that shows two ratios are equivalent. For example, $\frac{2}{3} = \frac{4}{6}$.

Ratio A comparison of two numbers, usually written with a colon or as a fraction. For example, the ratio of 2 to 3 can be written as 2:3 or $\frac{2}{3}$.

I. RATIOS

A. WRITING RATIOS

1. A ratio is a comparison of two numbers, usually written with a colon or as a fraction.
2. The ratio of 3 to 4 can be written as 3:4 or $\frac{3}{4}$.

B. FRACTION, DECIMAL, AND PERCENT EQUIVALENCIES

1. Know common fraction, decimal, and percent equivalencies:
$\frac{1}{2} = 0.5 = 50\%$, $\frac{1}{4} = 0.25 = 25\%$, $\frac{1}{5} = 0.2 = 20\%$, $\frac{2}{5} = 0.4 = 40\%$, $\frac{1}{8} = 0.125 = 12.5\%$, and $\frac{1}{10} = 0.1 = 10\%$.

2. Round values for ratios as close to the final answer as possible. For example, suppose you need to find the number of $\frac{1}{3}$-ounce servings in a 64-ounce container of milk. Rounding $\frac{1}{3}$ to 0.3 early on in the problem gives a different answer than rounding does later on, as shown in the following tip.

Calculators and Ratios *Round ratios to decimal equivalents as close to the final answer as possible.*

APPROACH #1	APPROACH #2
press 1 ÷ 3 **ENTER**	press 1 ÷ 3 **ENTER**
round 0.3333333333 to 0.3	use result for next calculation
press 64 ÷ 0.3 **ENTER**	press 64 ÷ ANS **ENTER**

```
1/3
          .3333333333
64/0.3
          213.3333333
```

```
1/3
          .3333333333
64/Ans
                   192
```

APPROACH #3

press 64 ÷ (1 ÷ 3) **ENTER**

```
64/(1/3)
                   192
■
```

In the first approach, $\frac{1}{3}$ is rounded to a decimal before being divided into 64, with a different and less accurate quotient as the result.

II. PROPORTIONS

A. WRITING PROPORTIONS WITH PERCENTS

1. What number is 50% of 150? $\dfrac{x}{150} = \dfrac{50}{100}$

2. The number 75 is 50% of what number? $\dfrac{75}{x} = \dfrac{50}{100}$

3. The number 75 is what percent of 150? $\dfrac{75}{150} = \dfrac{x}{100}$

B. SOLVING PROPORTIONS

1. You can solve a proportion as you would solve an equation. For example, to solve the proportion $\dfrac{x}{150} = \dfrac{50}{100}$, multiply both sides by 150: $\dfrac{x}{150}(150) = \dfrac{50}{100}(150)$ and $x = 75$.

2. You can solve a proportion by cross multiplying. For example, to solve the proportion $\dfrac{x}{150} = \dfrac{50}{100}$, cross multiply to get $100x = 150(50)$, and $x = 75$.

C. MODELING REAL-WORLD SITUATIONS WITH PROPORTIONS

1. Understand the problem: Two thirds of the marbles in a jar are yellow. If there are 12 yellow marbles in the jar, how many marbles are in the jar altogether?

2. Use a proportion to model the situation: Let n be the total number of marbles in the jar. The proportion $\dfrac{2}{3} = \dfrac{12}{n}$ models the situation, where 2 is to 3 as 12 is to n.

3. Cross multiply to solve the proportion:

$$\dfrac{2}{3} = \dfrac{12}{n}$$
$$2n = 3(12)$$
$$2n = 36$$
$$n = 18$$

There are 18 marbles altogether in the jar.

Cross Multiplying If you are familiar with cross multiplication, it can be a great timesaver when simplifying and solving proportions.

$$\frac{a}{b} = \frac{c}{d} \rightarrow ad = bc$$

Caution: Cross multiplication cannot be used if either of the denominators are equal to zero, because dividing by zero is undefined.

If you are not familiar with cross multiplication, you can also solve a proportion using the same techniques as for solving an equation.

COMPLEX NUMBERS

KEY VOCABULARY

Absolute value of a complex number The distance of the complex number from zero in the complex plane.

Argand plane An alternative name for the complex plane.

Complex conjugates Two complex numbers of the form $a + bi$ and $a - bi$. The product of complex conjugates is always a real number.

Complex number A number of the form $a + bi$, where a and b are real numbers and i is the imaginary unit. Either part can be 0.

Complex plane The plane in which complex numbers are located. The horizontal axis represents the real part of the complex number, and the vertical axis represents the imaginary part of the complex number.

Imaginary part In a complex number of the form $a + bi$, b is the imaginary part.

Imaginary unit i The unit that represents the square root of -1, such that $i^2 = -1$ and $i = \sqrt{(-1)}$.

Pure imaginary number A complex number with no real part; for example, $3i$ has no real part.

Radical An expression containing a root, such as $\sqrt{2}$ and $\sqrt[3]{27}$.

Real part In a complex number of the form $a + bi$, a is the real part.

Square root The square root of a number when multiplied by itself gives you the original number, for example $(\sqrt{13})(\sqrt{13}) = 13$.

I. PROPERTIES OF SQUARE ROOTS

A. PRODUCT PROPERTIES OF SQUARE ROOTS

1. For all nonnegative real numbers a and b, $\sqrt{ab} = (\sqrt{a})(\sqrt{b})$.
2. You can use the product property to simplify square roots. For example,

$$\sqrt{18} = \sqrt{9 \bullet 2}$$
$$= \sqrt{9} \bullet \sqrt{2}$$
$$= 3\sqrt{2}$$

B. QUOTIENT PROPERTIES OF SQUARE ROOTS

1. For all nonnegative real numbers a and b,

$$\sqrt{\frac{a}{b}} = \frac{\sqrt{a}}{\sqrt{b}}, \ b \neq 0.$$

2. You can use the quotient property to simplify square roots. For example:

$$\sqrt{\frac{1}{9}} = \frac{\sqrt{1}}{\sqrt{9}}$$
$$= \frac{1}{3}$$

C. THE SQUARE ROOT PROPERTY

1. For any real number n, if $x^2 = n$, then $x = \pm\sqrt{n}$.
2. If you are solving an equation such as $x^2 = 9$, the solution is $x = \pm 3$.

D. SIMPLIFYING SQUARE ROOTS

1. Do not leave radicals in the denominator. For example, you can simplify $\sqrt{\frac{1}{2}}$ as $\sqrt{\frac{1}{2}} = \frac{\sqrt{1}}{\sqrt{2}} = \frac{1}{\sqrt{2}}$, but you are not done

yet because there is still a radical in the denominator. Here's a simple technique you can use to remove radicals from the denominator:

$$\frac{1}{\sqrt{2}} = \frac{1}{\sqrt{2}} \cdot \frac{\sqrt{2}}{\sqrt{2}}$$ Multiply by 1, in the form $\frac{\sqrt{2}}{\sqrt{2}}$.

$$= \frac{\sqrt{2}}{\sqrt{2 \cdot 2}}$$ Product property of square roots

$$= \frac{\sqrt{2}}{\sqrt{4}}$$ Multiply.

$$= \frac{\sqrt{2}}{2}$$ Simplify.

So, the simplified form of $\sqrt{\frac{1}{2}}$ is $\frac{\sqrt{2}}{2}$.

2. Do not leave numbers under the radical sign if they have any square factors other than 1.

    i. For example, when simplifying $\sqrt{24}$, note that 24 has the square factor 4. This means that $\sqrt{24}$ is not in simplest form. Continue to simplify as follows.

$$\sqrt{24} = \sqrt{4 \cdot 6}$$
$$= \sqrt{4} \cdot \sqrt{6}$$
$$= 2\sqrt{6}$$

II. SQUARE ROOTS OF NEGATIVE NUMBERS

A. THE IMAGINARY UNIT *i*

1. $i^2 = -1$
2. $i = \sqrt{(-1)}$
3. The powers of *i* form a pattern.

Powers of *i*

i^1	$i^1 = i$
i^2	$i^2 = -1$
i^3	$i^3 = i^2 \bullet i = -1 \bullet i = -i$
i^4	$i^4 = i^2 \bullet i^2 = -1 \bullet -1 = 1$
i^5	$i^5 = i^4 \bullet i^1 = 1 \bullet i = i$
i^6	$i^6 = i^4 \bullet i^2 = 1 \bullet -1 = -1$
i^7	$i^7 = i^4 \bullet i^3 = 1 \bullet -i = -i$
i^8	$i^8 = i^4 \bullet i^4 = 1 \bullet 1 = 1$

In general, to find i^n, divide *n* by 4 and look at the remainder *R*. If $R = 0$, then $i^n = 1$; if $R = 1$, then $i^n = i$; if $R = 2$, then $i^n = -1$; if $R = 3$, then $i^n = -i$.

B. WRITING SQUARE ROOTS OF NEGATIVE NUMBERS

1. For all positive real numbers *b*, $\sqrt{-b^2} = \sqrt{b^2} \bullet \sqrt{-1} = bi$.

2. To simplify $\sqrt{-9}$, write $\sqrt{-9} = \sqrt{-3^2} = \sqrt{3^2} \bullet \sqrt{-1} = 3i$.

3. To simplify $\sqrt{-12}$, write:

$$\sqrt{-12} = \sqrt{-1 \bullet 2^2 \bullet 3}$$
$$= \sqrt{-1} \bullet \sqrt{2^2} \bullet \sqrt{3}$$
$$= i \bullet 2 \bullet \sqrt{3}$$
$$= 2i\sqrt{3}$$

Test Tip

Writing the Imaginary Unit *The imaginary unit i is written before a radical symbol. For example, write $i\sqrt{2}$, not $\sqrt{2}i$. This way, the i will not be placed under the radical symbol by mistake.*

III. COMPLEX NUMBERS

A. THE FORM OF COMPLEX NUMBERS

1. Complex numbers are of the form $a + bi$, where *a* and *b* are real numbers and *i* is the imaginary unit.

2. In a complex number of the form $a + bi$, a is the real part and b is the imaginary part.

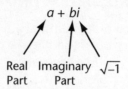

$a + bi$

Real Part · Imaginary Part · $\sqrt{-1}$

Complex Number Examples

Complex Number	Real Part	Imaginary Part
$4 + 3i$	4	3
4	4	0
$-2i$	0	-2

3. Two complex numbers are equal when their real parts are equal and their imaginary parts are equal. For example, $a + bi = c + di$ if $a = c$ and $b = d$.

B. PURE IMAGINARY NUMBERS

1. Pure imaginary numbers have no real part, only an imaginary part.
2. Examples of pure imaginary numbers include $2i$, $-3i$, and $i\sqrt{3}$.
3. The set of pure imaginary numbers is a subset of the set of complex numbers.

C. REAL NUMBERS

1. Real numbers have only a real part, with no imaginary part.
2. The set of real numbers is a subset of the set of complex numbers.
3. Although real numbers are also complex, the term "complex number" usually refers to a number that is not a real number.

IV. OPERATIONS ON COMPLEX NUMBERS

A. ADDING AND SUBTRACTING COMPLEX NUMBERS

1. To add complex numbers, add real parts to real parts and imaginary parts to imaginary parts. Write the sum in the form $a + bi$. For example:

$$(2 + 7i) + (4 - 2i) = (2 + 4) + (7i - 2i)$$
$$= 6 + 5i$$

2. To subtract complex numbers, subtract real parts from real parts and imaginary parts from imaginary parts. Write the difference in the form $a + bi$. For example,

$$(2 + 7i) - (4 - 2i) = (2 - 4) + (7i - (-2i))$$
$$= -2 + 9i$$

B. MULTIPLYING COMPLEX NUMBERS

1. Remember that $i^2 = -1$. This means, for example, that $2i \bullet 3i = 6i^2 = -6$ and $-2i \bullet 3i = -6i^2 = -6(-1) = 6$.

2. Use the FOIL technique (**First, Outer, Inner, Last**) to multiply two complex numbers of the form $a + bi$. For example:

$$(3 + 2i)(5 - 4i) = 3(5) + 3(-4i)$$
$$+ 2i(5) + 2i(-4i)$$
$$= 15 - 12i + 10i - 8i^2$$
$$= 15 - 2i - 8(-1)$$
$$= 23 - 2i$$

FOIL Method
First: $3(5)$
Outer: $3(-4i)$
Inner: $2i(5)$
Last: $2i(-4i)$

3. Complex conjugates are two complex numbers of the form $a + bi$ and $a - bi$. The product of complex conjugates is always a real number. For example, using the FOIL method:

$$(5 + 2i)(5 - 2i) = 5(5) + 5(-2i) + 2i(5) + 2i(-2i)$$
$$= 25 - 10i + 10i - 4i^2$$
$$= 25 - 4(-1)$$
$$= 29$$

C. DIVIDING COMPLEX NUMBERS

1. Write the quotient in fraction form. For example, write

   $2i \div (4 + 3i)$ as $\dfrac{2i}{4+3i}$.

2. Use the complex conjugate of the denominator to simplify the quotient. For example, simplify the quotient $\dfrac{2i}{4+3i}$ as follows:

   $$\dfrac{2i}{4+3i} = \dfrac{2i}{4+3i} \cdot \dfrac{4-3i}{4-3i}$$ Multiplying by $\dfrac{4-3i}{4-3i}$ is the same as multiplying by 1.

   $$= \dfrac{8i - 6i^2}{16 - 9i^2}$$ Multiplying by the conjugate simplifies the denominator.

   $$= \dfrac{8i + 6}{16 + 9}$$ Simplify.

   $$= \dfrac{6}{25} + \dfrac{8}{25}i$$ Write in standard form.

3. To simplify some quotients, you can simply multiply by $\dfrac{i}{i}$. For example, you can simplify the quotient $\dfrac{4+2i}{3i}$ as follows:

   $$\dfrac{4+2i}{3i} = \dfrac{4+2i}{3i} \cdot \dfrac{i}{i}$$ Multiplying by $\dfrac{i}{i}$ is the same as multiplying by 1.

   $$= \dfrac{4i + 2i^2}{3i^2}$$ Multiplying by $\dfrac{i}{i}$ simplifies the denominator.

   $$= \dfrac{4i - 2}{-3}$$ Simplify.

   $$= \dfrac{2}{3} - \dfrac{4}{3}i$$ Write in standard form.

Complex Numbers on Your Calculator *To work with complex numbers on your calculator, select the display mode to show the numbers in a + bi form. Press [MODE], [↓ 6 times], [>], and [ENTER].*

Test
Tip

To enter complex numbers and expressions with complex numbers, enter numbers and signs just as you see them. To enter the imaginary unit i, press [2ND][.]

V GRAPHING COMPLEX NUMBERS

A. THE COMPLEX PLANE

1. Complex numbers can be graphed on the complex plane. The horizontal axis represents the real part of the complex number, and the vertical axis represents the imaginary part of the complex number.

The Complex Plane

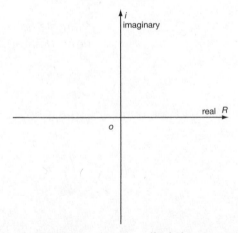

2. The complex plane is sometimes called the Argand plane.

B. LOCATING COMPLEX NUMBERS IN THE COMPLEX PLANE

1. The location of complex numbers in the complex plane tells you about the values of a and b. For example, the complex number p is equal to $a + bi$ and is located in Quadrant I, where $a > 0$ and $b > 0$; q is located in Quadrant II, where $a < 0$ and $b > 0$; s is located in Quadrant III, where $a < 0$ and $b < 0$; and t is located in Quadrant IV, where $a > 0$ and $b < 0$.

Points in the Complex Plane

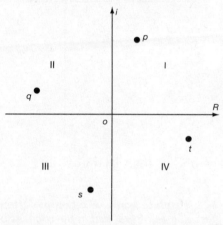

2. You can also determine how complex numbers are related to each other by their locations in the complex plane. For example, in the preceding Points in the Complex Plane figure, which point could be $-iq$? Think: The complex number q is equal to $a + bi$ and is located in Quadrant II, where $a < 0$ and $b > 0$. Multiplying $a + bi$ by $-i$ gives $-ai - bi^2 = b - ai$. Because $a < 0$ in q and a is negated when q is multiplied by $-i$, this means that $a > 0$ for $-iq$. Also, because $b > 0$ in q and b stays positive when q is multiplied by $-i$, this means that $b > 0$ for $-iq$. Finally, because b is now the coefficient for the real part of the number and a is now the coefficient for the imaginary part, $-iq$ is located in Quadrant I and could only be point p.

C. ABSOLUTE VALUE OF COMPLEX NUMBERS

1. The absolute value of a complex number is its distance from 0 in the complex plane.

Absolute Value: Complex Numbers in the Complex Plane

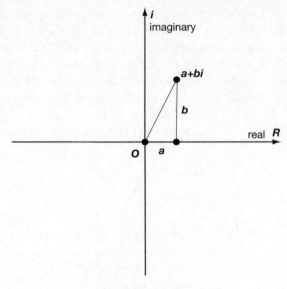

2. If $z = a + bi$, then $|z| = \sqrt{a^2 + b^2}$.

Absolute Value of a Complex Number *When a complex number is graphed in the complex plane, you can use the Pythagorean theorem to find its absolute value.* ($a^2 + b^2 = c^2$) *For example, the absolute value of 2 + 4i can be found by using the Pythagorean theorem to find the distance from zero:*

$$\sqrt{2^2 + 4^2} = \sqrt{20} = 2\sqrt{5}.$$

Absolute Value in the Complex Plane

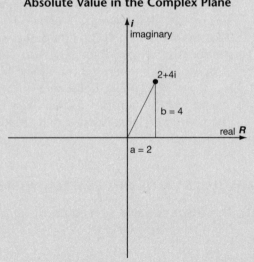

D. ADDING TWO COMPLEX NUMBERS BY GRAPHING

1. First, graph the two complex numbers you want to add in the complex plane. For example, to add $(-3 + i) + (1 + 2i)$ by graphing, first graph $-3 + i$ and $1 + 2i$.

Adding Two Complex Numbers

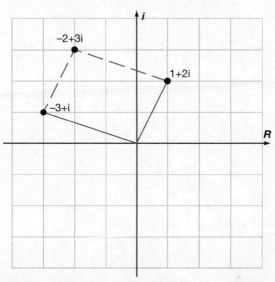

2. The two points combined with the origin form three vertices of a parallelogram. Draw the fourth vertex to complete the parallelogram.

3. The fourth vertex of the parallelogram is the sum! For example, in the preceding Adding Two Complex Numbers graph, $(-3 + i) + (1 + 2i) = -2 + 3i$.

COUNTING

KEY VOCABULARY

Combination A rearrangement of items in a list or set in which the order of the items does not matter. The number of combinations of

n distinct items taken k at a time is $C(n,k) = \dfrac{n!}{(n-k)!\,k!}$. You could use

the formula to find how many groups of three different letter tiles can be made from a total of 8 different letter tiles when order does not matter:

$C(8,3) = \dfrac{8!}{5!\,3!} = 56 \cdot$

Factorial Factorials are special kinds of products, indicated by an exclamation point. In general, $n!$ is the product of all whole numbers from 1 to n. To compute $n!$, multiply $1 \times 2 \times 3 \times 4 \times \ldots \times n$. For example, $5! = 1 \times 2 \times 3 \times 4 \times 5 = 120$.

Fundamental counting principle If event P can occur in p different ways and event Q can occur in q different ways, then event P followed by event Q can occur in $p \bullet q$ different ways. For example, if you can choose one flavor from 8 flavors and 1 topping from 12 toppings, you can choose from a total of 8 × 12 = 96 flavor-topping combinations.

Permutation A rearrangement of items in a list or set in which the order of the items matters. The number of permutations of n distinct items

taken k at a time is $P(n,k) = \dfrac{n!}{(n-k)!}$. You could use the formula to find

how many arrangements of 3 different letter tiles can be made from a

total of 8 different letter tiles when order matters: $P(8,3) = \dfrac{8!}{5!} = 336$.

FUNDAMENTAL COUNTING PRINCIPLE

A. RULE FOR THE FUNDAMENTAL COUNTING PRINCIPLE

1. If event P can occur in p different ways and event Q can occur in q different ways, then event P followed by event Q can occur in $p \bullet q$ different ways.

2. For example, suppose you are choosing a two-character alphanumeric code. The code has one letter followed by one digit. You can choose from 26 letters and 10 digits. Using the fundamental counting principle, there are $26 \bullet 10$ or 260 different two-character codes.

3. The fundamental counting principle can be extended to more than two events. For example, suppose you are choosing a five-character alphanumeric code for a security system where the first three characters are digits and the last two characters are letters. Using the fundamental counting principle, there are $10 \bullet 10 \bullet 10 \bullet 26 \bullet 26 = 676,000$ different five-character codes.

B. INDEPENDENT AND DEPENDENT EVENTS

1. In the example of choosing a two-character alphanumeric code, choosing a letter is one event and choosing a digit is a second event. The events are independent because the choice of a letter does not affect the choice of a number.

2. If the code is two alphabetic characters with no repeats allowed, choosing the first letter is one event and choosing the second letter is the second event. The events are dependent because the choice of the first letter affects the choice of the second letter. When playing a game with a deck of 52 playing cards, selecting a card from the deck and not replacing it and then selecting another card is another example of dependent events because the selection of the second card is dependent upon the selection of the first card.

3. The fundamental counting principle works with both independent and dependent events. With dependent events, the number of choices is reduced at each step to reflect the number of choices currently available. For example, when choosing a two-letter code without repeats, there are 26 choices when the first letter is chosen and 25 choices after the first letter is chosen, for a total of $26 \bullet 25$ or 650 possible choices.

II. PERMUTATIONS AND COMBINATIONS

A. PERMUTATIONS

1. A permutation is an ordered arrangement. If you want to find how many ways there are to arrange some items and order matters, you are finding the number of permutations. For example, the PIN code to a banking account is 5746. It does matter if the same digits are used in a different order because 7564 would not allow access to the account.

2. The number of permutations of *n* distinct items is *n*! For example, to find how many different ordered lines 5 people can arrange themselves in, find 5! Note that order matters.

3. For example, how many different ways could you arrange 4 different pictures on a shelf?

   $4! = 4 \cdot 3 \cdot 2 \cdot 1 = 24$ different ways

4. The notation $P(n, k)$ or $_nP_k$ represents the number of permutations of *n* distinct items taken *k* at a time.

5. The formula to find the number of permutations of *n* distinct items taken *k* at a time is $P(n,k) = \dfrac{n!}{(n-k)!}$.

6. For example, how many different ways can a 20-member team select a first, second, and third place, assuming that the same person cannot be selected for more than one of the places? Because order is important, we can solve this problem using the permutations formula: $P(n,k) = \dfrac{n!}{(n-k)!}$. The number of members on the team, 20, is the number we have to choose from. So, *n* is equal to 20. The number of members we are selecting for the places is 3. So, *k* is equal to 3.

$$P(20,3) = \frac{20!}{(20-3)!}$$

$$= \frac{20!}{17!}$$

$$= 6840$$

So, there are 6,840 ways for a 20-member team to select a first, second, and third place.

7. The formula to find the number of permutations of *n* items of which *p* are alike is $\frac{n!}{p!}$. To find the number of permutations of *n* items of which *p* are alike and *q* are alike is $\frac{n!}{p!q!}$. If more items are alike, more variables can be added to the denominator.

B. COMBINATIONS

1. If you want to find how many ways there are to arrange some items and order does not matter, you are finding the number of combinations. For example, if four employees out of 250 were selected to receive a $50 gift certificate, the order in which they were selected would not matter.

2. The notation $C(n, k)$ or $_nC_k$ represents the number of combinations of *n* distinct items taken *k* at a time.

3. The formula to find the number of combinations of *n* distinct items taken *k* at a time is $C(n,k) = \frac{n!}{(n-k)!k!}$.

4. For example, in a state lottery, 6 balls are chosen from 54 numbered balls. You win if you pick the 6 balls. What is the probability of you winning this lottery? Because the order that the balls are selected by the lottery machine does not matter, using the combinations formula will be appropriate.

$$C(n,k) = \frac{n!}{(n-k)!k!}$$

$$C(54,6) = \frac{54!}{(54-6)!6!}$$

$$= \frac{5!}{48!6!}$$

$$= 25,827,165$$

Thus, the probability that you will win is $\frac{1}{25,827,165}$

So for this lottery, your odds for winning are very low.

C. PERMUTATION OR COMBINATION?

1. Usually, the choice of counting method depends on whether or not order is important.

2. Permutation or combination? Suppose you want to find how many different ordered lines 5 people can arrange themselves in. Note that order matters, so you want to find permutations: find $5! = 120$ different arrangements.

3. Permutation or combination? Suppose you want to find how many different, ordered, 3-person lines 5 people can arrange themselves in. Again, order matters, so again you want to find permutations. This time, you want to count the number of permutations for n objects taken k at a time, where $n = 5$ and $k = 3$. Use the formula $P(n,k) = \dfrac{n!}{(n-k)!}$ to find $P(5,3) = \dfrac{5!}{(5-3)!} = 60$ different lines.

4. Permutation or combination? Suppose you want to know how many different 6-person groups can be made from a larger group of 10 people. This time order does not matter, so you are counting the number of combinations. To count the number of combinations for n objects taken k at a time, use the formula $C(n,k) = \dfrac{n!}{(n-k)!k!}$, substituting $n = 10$ and $k = 6$.

   There are $C(10,6) = \dfrac{10!}{(10-6)!6!} = 210$ different 6-person groups that can be made from a larger group of 10 people.

5. Permutation or combination? Suppose you want to know how many different ways 10 people can be divided into two groups, one with 6 people and the other with 4 people. Again, order does not matter, so again you are counting the number of combinations. You can answer this question by finding either the number of 6-person groups or the number of 4-person groups, which are equivalent. You have already found that there are 210 different 6-person groups. You can check the number of 4-person groups as well: $C(10,4) = \dfrac{10!}{(10-4)!4!} = 210$ different 4-person groups that can be made from a larger group of 10 people.

III. FACTORIALS

A. COMPUTING FACTORIALS

1. Factorials are special kinds of products, indicated by an exclamation point. In general, *n*! is the product of all whole numbers from 1 to *n*. To compute *n*! multiply $1 \times 2 \times 3 \times 4 \times \ldots \times n$.

2. By definition, 0! = 1.

3. Factorials quickly become too lengthy to compute by hand.

> **Factorials** *Most calculators will compute factorials for you. Here's how to access the factorial command on the TI-84. First, type the number you want the factorial of: in this example, 6. Then press [MATH][PRB][4:!] to access the factorial function. Finally, press ENTER to calculate 6!.*

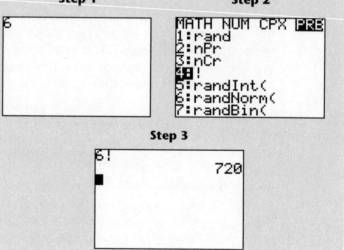

B. EXPRESSIONS CONTAINING FACTORIALS

1. Using the formulas for both permutations and combinations will require you to use shortcuts when computing factorials. For example, let's look at the formula for a combination of *n* objects taken *k* at a time,

where $n = 10$ and $k = 6$: $C(n,k) = \dfrac{n!}{(n-k)!k!} = \dfrac{10!}{4!6!}$.

Writing out the factorials gives the following:

$$C(10,6) = \frac{10 \times 9 \times 8 \times 7 \times 6 \times 5 \times 4 \times 3 \times 2 \times 1}{(4 \times 3 \times 2 \times 1)(6 \times 5 \times 4 \times 3 \times 2 \times 1)}$$

At first glance, this looks like a lot of calculations, even with a calculator.

2. Fortunately, you can use canceling to simplify expressions containing factorials. For example,

$$C(10,6) = \frac{10 \times \cancel{9}^3 \times \cancel{8}^2 \times 7 \times \cancel{6 \times 5 \times 4 \times 3 \times 2 \times 1}^1}{(\cancel{4}_1 \times \cancel{3}_1 \times \cancel{2}_1 \times 1)(\cancel{6 \times 5 \times 4 \times 3 \times 2 \times 1})_1} = 10 \times 3 \times 7 = 210$$

Factorial Expressions Your calculator will not only compute factorials for you, but will also do the calculations necessary to simplify the factorial expressions used to count permutations and combinations. Here's how to compute $C(10,4) = \dfrac{10!}{(10-4)!4!}$ on the TI-84.

Enter 10. Make it 10! Enter the rest of the expression using the same method. Compute.

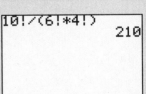

ELEMENTARY NUMBER THEORY

KEY VOCABULARY

Complex numbers Numbers of the form $a + bi$ where a and b are real numbers, and i is the imaginary unit that represents the square root of negative one.

Counting numbers The numbers 1, 2, 3, . . . , used for counting.

Divisors Numbers that divide evenly into other numbers are divisors. Divisors are also factors.

Factors When integers are multiplied, each of the multiplied integers is a factor of the product.

Integers The set of whole numbers and their opposites. For example, −3, −2, −1, 0, 1, 2, and 3 are all integers.

Irrational numbers A number that cannot be expressed as a repeating or terminating decimal. Irrational numbers cannot be written in the form $\frac{a}{b}$, where a and b are integers with $b \neq 0$. For example: $\sqrt{2}$ and π are both irrational numbers.

Multiple The product of a whole number and an integer.

Natural numbers The natural numbers are 1, 2, 3, ...

Prime factor A factor that is a prime number. For example, factors of 24 include 1, 2, 3, 4, 6, 8, 12, and 24. The prime factors of 24 are 2 and 3.

Prime number A whole number greater than 1 whose only factors are 1 and itself. For example, 2, 3, 5, 7, 11, 13, 17, 19, 23, 29, 31, 37, 41, 43, 47, 53, 59, 61, 67, 71, 73, 79, 83, 89, and 97 are prime numbers less than 100.

Rational numbers Rational numbers can be expressed as fractions of the form $\frac{m}{n}$, where m and n are integers and n is not zero. For example, 1, 1.2, -5, 0, $\frac{1}{6}$, and $-\frac{5}{9}$ are all rational numbers.

Real numbers Numbers that can be expressed as decimals, including rational and irrational numbers. For example, 1, 5.6, -55.999, $-\frac{2}{3}$, 0, $\sqrt{2}$, and π are all real numbers.

Whole numbers The whole numbers are 0, 1, 2, 3, ... They have no fractional or decimal part and no negative numbers.

I. TYPES OF NUMBERS

A. NUMBER SETS

1. The natural numbers, also called the *counting numbers*, are 1, 2, 3, ...
2. The whole numbers are 0, 1, 2, 3, ...
3. The integers are . . . -3, -2, -1, 0, 1, 2, 3, ...
    ▸ *The sum of a positive integer and its corresponding negative integer is zero.*
    ▸ *When integers are added, subtracted, or multiplied, the result is always another integer. This is not always the case when integers are divided.*
4. Rational numbers can be expressed as fractions of the form $\frac{m}{n}$, where m and n are integers and n is not zero.
5. Real numbers are numbers that can be expressed as decimals, including rational numbers (terminating decimals and decimals that have a repeating pattern) and irrational numbers (decimals with an infinite nonrepeating expansion).

6. Complex numbers are numbers of the form $a + bi$ where a and b are real numbers, and i is the imaginary unit that represents the square root of negative one, $i = \sqrt{-1}$.

II. POSITIVE AND NEGATIVE

A. RULES FOR INTEGERS

1. The integer 0 is neither positive nor negative.
2. When integers are added and subtracted, the result can be a positive integer, a negative integer, or zero, depending on the signs and absolute values of the integers involved.
3. When integers are multiplied, the product of two positive integers is a positive integer, the product of two negative integers is a positive integer, and the product of one negative integer and one positive integer is a negative integer.
4. When integers are divided, the quotient of two positive integers is positive, the quotient of two negative integers is positive, and the quotient of one negative integer and one positive integer is negative.
5. The absolute value of an integer is always zero or positive. For example, $|-645| = 645$ and $|654| = 654$.

B. ROOTS AND POWERS

1. Every positive number n has two square roots, one positive and one negative. However, the expression $\sqrt{n}$ refers to the positive number whose square is n. For example, $\sqrt{16} = 4$ and $4^2 = 16$. The number $-\sqrt{16}$ is equal to -4.
2. A square root is "a root of order 2." Higher-order roots for a positive number n include cube roots ("roots of order 3") and fourth roots ("roots of order 4"), designated by $\sqrt[3]{n}$ and $\sqrt[4]{n}$, respectively. For example, $\sqrt[3]{8} = 2$ and $2^3 = 8$.
3. Even-order roots have exactly two roots when n is positive and no roots when n is negative. If $n^2 = 9$, then n is the number whose square is 9. So, 9 has two square roots, namely $\sqrt{9} = 3$ and $-\sqrt{9} = -3$.

4. Odd-order roots have exactly one root, whether n is positive or negative. The $\sqrt[3]{64} = 4$ and $4^3 = 64$. However $\sqrt[3]{-64} = -4$ and $(-4)^3 = -64$.

5. If $a > 1$, then $a^2 > a$. For example, if a is 3, then 3^2 is 9, which is greater than 3. If $0 < b < 1$, then $b^2 < b$. For example, if b is $\frac{1}{3}$, then $\left(\frac{1}{3}\right)^2 = \frac{1}{9}$, which is less than $\frac{1}{3}$.

III. ODD AND EVEN

A. RULES FOR INTEGERS

1. Integers that are divisible by 2 are even. The even integers are . . . , $-4, -2, 0, 2, 4, \ldots$.

2. Integers that are not divisible by 2 are odd. The odd integers are . . . , $-5, -3, -1, 1, 3, 5, \ldots$.

3. The sum or difference of two even integers is always an even integer. For example, $4 + 2 = 6$ and $4 - 2 = 2$, both even integers.

4. The sum or difference of two odd integers is always an even integer. For example, $5 + 3 = 8$ and $5 - 3 = 2$.

5. The sum or difference of one even integer and one odd integer is always an odd integer. For example, $7 + 2 = 9$ and $7 - 2 = 5$.

6. The product of two even integers is always an even integer.

7. The product of two odd integers is always an odd integer.

8. The product of one even integer and one odd integer is always an even integer.

9. When a positive odd integer is divided by 2, the remainder is always 1.

Positive or Negative? Odd or Even? When a question asks whether the value of a variable expression is positive or negative, or even or odd, try substituting actual values for the variables to test if your logical conclusions are correct.

IV. FACTORS AND MULTIPLES

A. FACTORS

1. When integers are multiplied, each of the multiplied integers is a factor of the product. For example, 6•7 = 42 and both 6 and 7 are factors of 42.
2. Factors are also called *divisors*.
3. Negative numbers can be factors and divisors.
4. The number 1 is a factor of every integer; 0 is not a factor of any integer except 0.
5. Common factors of two nonzero integers *a* and *b* are integers that are factors of both *a* and *b*. The greatest common factor (GCF) of two nonzero integers *a* and *b* is the greatest positive integer that is a factor of both *a* and *b*. For example, 6 has factors 1, 2, 3 and 6. Factors of 12 include 1, 2, 3, 4, 6, and 12. The greatest common factor of 6 and 12 is 6. The greatest common factor is also called the greatest common divisor (GCD).

B. MULTIPLES

1. A product is said to be a multiple of its factors.
2. A product is also said to be divisible by its divisors.
3. Every nonzero integer has an infinite number of multiples.
4. The number 0 is a multiple of every integer; 1 is not a multiple of any integer except 1 and −1.
5. Common multiples of two nonzero integers *a* and *b* are integers that are multiples of both *a* and *b*. The least common multiple (LCM) of two nonzero integers *a* and *b* is the least positive integer that is a multiple of both *a* and *b*. For example, the multiples of 10 are: 10, 20, 30, 40, 50, . . . The multiples of 8 are: 8, 16, 24, 32, 40, . . . So, the LCM of 10 and 8 is 40.

Use Your Calculator to Find Factors *Use your calculator to save time if you need to determine if one number is a factor of another number. Remember that a number can be divided evenly by its factors. Do a quick check with your calculator to check divisibility.*

17 is a factor of 323.

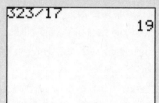

17 is not a factor of 326.

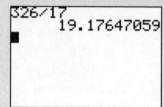

V. PRIME NUMBERS

A. DEFINITION

1. A prime number is a natural number greater than 1 that has only two positive divisors: 1 and itself.
2. The number 1 is not a prime number.
3. The number 2 is the only even prime number. Every other even number greater than 2 has at least three positive divisors: 1, itself, and 2.
4. The first 10 prime numbers in increasing order are 2, 3, 5, 7, 11, 13, 17, 19, 23, and 29.
5. The number 15, for example, is not prime because it has four positive divisors: 1, itself, 3, and 5.
6. A natural number greater than 1 that is not a prime number is a composite number. The numbers 4, 15, and 100, for example, are all composite numbers. Because 4, 15, and 100 can be divided evenly by numbers other than 1 and themselves, they are not prime numbers.

B. PRIME FACTORIZATION

1. Every natural number greater than 1 is either a prime number or can be expressed as the product of prime factors.

2. Following are some examples of prime factorizations:

$$8 = 2 \times 2 \times 2 = 2^3$$
$$12 = 2 \times 2 \times 3 = 2^2 \times 3$$
$$15 = 3 \times 5$$
$$17 = 17$$
$$30 = 2 \times 3 \times 5$$
$$63 = 3 \times 3 \times 7 = 3^2 \times 7$$
$$133 = 7 \times 19$$

3. If you know the only prime factors of some number n, you can also identify other numbers that cannot be factors. Suppose the only prime factors of n are 2, 5, and 11. This means that any number with a prime factor that is not 2, 5, or 11 cannot be a factor of n.

LOGIC AND PROOFS

KEY VOCABULARY

Conclusion The statement after the word "then" in a conditional statement.

Conditional statement An if-then statement.

Conjunction Two or more statements joined by the word "and."

Contrapositive Related conditional formed by interchanging and negating both the hypothesis and conclusion of a conditional statement.

Converse Related conditional formed by interchanging the hypothesis and conclusion of a conditional statement.

Deductive reasoning Type of reasoning that starts with facts and applies them to reach conclusions.

Disjunction Two or more statements joined by the word "or."

Hypothesis The statement after the word "if" in a conditional statement.

Indirect proof A proof that begins by assuming that the opposite of what is being proved is true and arrives at a false conclusion, based on the reasoning that if the opposite of the conjecture results in a false conclusion, then the conjecture must be true; also called a *proof by contradiction*.

Inductive reasoning Type of reasoning that starts with individual cases and ends up with a generalization.

Inverse Related conditional formed by negating both the hypothesis and conclusion of a conditional statement.

Negation The opposite of a statement.

Statement A sentence that is either true or false, but not both.

Truth tables Tables used to organize truth values of statements.

Truth value The assessment of whether a statement is true or false.

I. LOGIC

A. STATEMENTS

1. A statement is either true or false, but not both. For example, the sentence "Today is Tuesday" is a statement.
    ▶ *Statements are usually represented by variables such as p or q.*
    ▶ *The truth value of a statement is whether or not the statement is true.*
2. The negation of a statement is the opposite of the statement. For example, the negation of the statement "Today is Tuesday" is "Today is not Tuesday."
    ▶ *Negations are represented as ~ p or ~ q, read as "not p" or "not q."*
    ▶ *The truth value of the negation of a statement is the opposite of the truth value of the statement.*
3. A conjunction is formed by joining two or more statements by the word "and." For example, "Today is Tuesday and it is raining" is a conjunction.
    ▶ *Conjunctions are represented as $p \wedge q$, read as "p and q."*
    ▶ *Conjunctions are true only when both statements are true.*
4. A disjunction is formed by joining two or more statements by the word "or." For example, "Today is Tuesday or it is raining" is a disjunction.
    ▶ *Disjunctions are represented as $p \vee q$, read as "p or q."*
    ▶ *Disjunctions are true if at least one of the statements is true.*

5. Truth tables are used to organize the truth values of statements. Following are the truth tables for negations, conjunctions, and disjunctions:

p	$\sim p$
T	F
F	T

p	q	$p \wedge q$	$p \vee q$
T	T	T	T
T	F	F	T
F	T	F	T
F	F	F	F

B. CONDITIONAL STATEMENTS

1. Conditional statements are if-then statements. For example, "If today is Tuesday, then Kim has a piano lesson" is a conditional statement.

   ▸ *Conditional statements are represented as $p \rightarrow q$, read as "if p, then q."*

   ▸ *The part of the statement directly after the word "if" is called the hypothesis. The part of the statement directly after the word "then" is called the conclusion. For example, in the statement "If today is Tuesday, then Kim has a piano lesson," the hypothesis is "today is Tuesday" and the conclusion is "Kim has a piano lesson."*

   ▸ *A conditional statement is false only when its hypothesis is true and its conclusion is false.*

2. Related conditionals are new conditional statements formed by rearranging a conditional statement.

   ▸ *A converse is the resulting conditional statement when the hypothesis and conclusion are reversed. For example, the converse of the statement "If today is Tuesday, then Kim has a piano lesson" is "If Kim has a piano lesson, then today is Tuesday." If the conditional is represented as $p \rightarrow q$, then its converse is $q \rightarrow p$.*

▸ An inverse is the resulting conditional statement when the hypothesis and conclusion are both negated. For example, the inverse of the statement "If today is Tuesday, then Kim has a piano lesson" is "If today is not Tuesday, then Kim does not have a piano lesson. If the conditional is represented as $p \rightarrow q$, then its inverse is $\sim p \rightarrow \sim q$.

▸ A contrapositive is the resulting conditional statement when the hypothesis and conclusion are both negated and reversed. For example, the contrapositive of the statement "If today is Tuesday, then Kim has a piano lesson" is "If Kim does not have a piano lesson, then today is not Tuesday." If the conditional is represented as $p \rightarrow q$, then its contrapositive is $\sim q \rightarrow \sim p$.

3. Following is the truth table for conditionals statements and related conditionals:

p	q	$p \rightarrow q$	$q \rightarrow p$	$\sim p \rightarrow \sim q$	$\sim q \rightarrow \sim p$
T	T	T	T	T	T
T	F	F	T	T	F
F	T	T	F	F	T
F	F	T	T	T	T

Note that statements with the same truth values are considered to be logically equivalent.

True or False? *The truth values for conditional statements and related conditionals may not be intuitive. Note that a conditional statement is only false when the hypothesis is true and the conclusion is false. This means that the statement "If the sum of the measures of a rectangle is 180°, then a square has three sides" is true according to mathematical logic. If you encounter a question involving conditional statements and/or related conditionals on the SAT Math Level 2 test, it will probably be helpful to identify the hypothesis and conclusion, assess the truth value of each statement separately, and then apply the values in the truth table to determine whether the entire conditional statement is true or false.*

II. PROOFS

A. TYPES OF REASONING

1. Inductive reasoning is the type of reasoning that starts with individual cases and then uses them to make generalizations.

   ▸ *A conjecture is made when inductive reasoning is used to make a generalization. Basically, a conjecture is an educated guess. For example, if you know several left-handed people and they are all good at solving mathematical problems, you might make the conjecture that all left-handed people are good at solving math problems.*

   ▸ *A counterexample is an example of a case where a conjecture is not true. A single counterexample can show that a conjecture is false. For example, it only takes one left-handed person who is not good at solving math problems to show that your conjecture is false.*

2. Deductive reasoning is the type of reasoning that starts with facts and then applies them to reach conclusions.

   ▸ *You can use deductive reasoning to draw conclusions from true conditional statements. The law of detachment says that if p → q is true and p is true, then q is true.*

   ▸ *You can also use deductive reasoning to draw conclusions from true conditional statements that are related. The law of syllogism says that if p → q is true and q → r is true, then p → r is true.*

   ▸ *Deductive reasoning can also be used to prove conjectures.*

B. PROOF BASICS

1. A proof is a logical argument that shows the truth of a statement.

2. A proof is developed through a sequence of statements where each statement is true.

3. The steps of a proof are arranged in order so that each statement is related to an earlier statement.

4. Each step of a proof must be justified by a definition, property, postulate, or theorem.

   ▸ *A postulate, also called an axiom, is a statement that is simply accepted as true. For example, the idea that there is exactly one line through any two points is a postulate.*

> ▸ *A theorem is a statement that has already been shown to be true. A theorem can be used to justify the truth of other statements in the course of proving other theorems.*

5. A proof consists of the following components:

> ▸ *A statement of the conjecture or theorem to be proven*
> ▸ *A statement of the given information*
> ▸ *If appropriate, a diagram illustrating the given information*
> ▸ *Steps of the proof, with justifications for each step*
> ▸ *A concluding statement that proves the conjecture or theorem and completes the proof*

C. TYPES OF PROOFS

1. A direct proof consists of a straightforward flow of logical steps beginning with a statement of the conjecture or theorem to be proven and ending with a concluding statement that proves the conjecture or theorem.

2. An indirect proof or proof by contradiction begins by assuming that the opposite of what you are trying to prove is true. Based on the assumption, a series of logical steps are followed until a conclusion is reached that is known to be false because it contradicts known information. The reasoning behind an indirect proof is that if you can prove that the opposite of a conjecture is false, then the conjecture must be true.

D. PROOF FORMATS

1. A paragraph proof or informal proof is a paragraph that explains why a given conjecture is true.

2. A two-column proof shows statements in the left column and justifications in the right column.

3. A flowchart proof uses flowchart symbols and arrows to show the logical steps of a proof.

Test Tip

Prove It Backward *If you encounter a question involving proofs on the SAT Math Level 2 test and are having difficulty answering it, try starting with the conclusion and following the steps backward to the beginning.*

MATRICES

KEY VOCABULARY

Additive identity matrix The matrix that when added to a matrix does not change the sum. The additive identity matrix for an $m \times n$ matrix is the $m \times n$ zero matrix.

Column matrix A matrix with only one column.

Determinant A quantity associated with a square matrix that can be used when solving equations.

Double subscript notation The notation used to locate an element in a matrix. For example, a_{23} is the element in the second row and the third column.

Element One of the terms that comprise a matrix.

Matrix A rectangular array of elements arranged in rows and columns.

$m \times n$ matrix A matrix with m rows and n columns.

Row matrix A matrix with only one row.

Scalar The name for the number by which each element of a matrix is multiplied when finding a scalar product.

Scalar multiplication The process of multiplying each element of a matrix by a number called a *scalar*.

Scalar product The product of a scalar k and an $m \times n$ matrix called A is given by the notation kA. Each element in the matrix kA is the corresponding element from A multiplied by the scalar k.

Second-order determinant The determinant for a 2 × 2 matrix.

Square matrix A matrix with the same number of rows as columns.

Zero matrix A matrix whose elements are all zeros.

I. MATRIX BASICS

A. DEFINITION

1. A matrix is a rectangular array of elements arranged in rows and columns.
2. A matrix is usually written in square brackets, as shown in the following illustration:

$$\begin{bmatrix} 2 & 1 & 3 & 3 \\ 4 & 0 & 1 & 1 \\ 1 & 2 & 0 & 5 \end{bmatrix}$$

3. Elements can be any type of numbers or other information.
4. The plural of matrix is *matrices*.

B. MATRIX SIZE AND STRUCTURE

1. Matrices are often described by their size, given as their row-by-column dimensions. A matrix with *m* rows and *n* columns is an *m* × *n* matrix. Following are examples:

2 × 2 matrix   3 × 4 matrix   1 × 5 matrix

$$\begin{bmatrix} 2.1 & 0.35 \\ 13.3 & 4.0 \end{bmatrix} \quad \begin{bmatrix} 2 & 1 & 3 & 3 \\ 4 & 0 & 1 & 1 \\ 1 & 2 & 0 & 5 \end{bmatrix} \quad \begin{bmatrix} \dfrac{1}{2} & \dfrac{7}{8} & \dfrac{1}{4} & \dfrac{3}{2} & \dfrac{5}{3} \end{bmatrix}$$

Test Tip

Understanding Matrix Dimensions A 3 × 4 matrix is not the same as a 4 × 3 matrix. A 3 × 4 matrix has 3 rows and 4 columns, whereas a 4 × 3 matrix has 4 rows and 3 columns.

2. A row matrix has only one row. A column matrix has only one column.

Row Matrix **Column Matrix**

$$
\begin{bmatrix} \frac{1}{2} & \frac{7}{8} & \frac{1}{4} & \frac{3}{2} & \frac{5}{3} \end{bmatrix}
\qquad
\begin{bmatrix} 6 \\ 2 \\ 1 \\ 5 \end{bmatrix}
$$

3. A square matrix has the same number of rows as columns. A square matrix is sometimes called a *matrix of the nth order*, where *n* is the number of rows/columns.

Matrix of the 2nd order **Matrix of the 5th order**

$$
\begin{bmatrix} 2.1 & 0.35 \\ 13.3 & 4.0 \end{bmatrix}
\qquad
\begin{bmatrix}
1 & 0 & 0 & 2 & 1 \\
0 & 3 & 2 & 3 & 4 \\
2 & 2 & 1 & 0 & 3 \\
2 & 1 & 4 & 4 & 0 \\
1 & 2 & 3 & 1 & 1
\end{bmatrix}
$$

4. To name an element, use double subscript notation where the first subscript number is the row location and the second subscript number is the column location.

Double Subscript Notation

$$
\begin{bmatrix}
a_{11} & a_{12} & a_{13} & \cdots & a_{1n} \\
a_{21} & a_{22} & a_{23} & \cdots & a_{2n} \\
a_{31} & a_{32} & a_{33} & \cdots & a_{3n} \\
\vdots & \vdots & \vdots & \vdots & \vdots \\
a_{m1} & a_{m2} & a_{m3} & \cdots & a_{mn}
\end{bmatrix}
$$

a_{23} is the element in the second row and the third column.
a_{3n} is the element in the third row and the *n*th column.
a_{mn} is the element in the *m*th row and the *n*th column.

5. Matrices are usually named with capital letters and their elements are usually referenced with corresponding lowercase letters using double subscript notation. Variables may also be used for the subscripts in double subscript notation. For example, in matrix B, the element in the ith row and the jth column is referenced as b_{ij}.

II. MATRIX OPERATIONS

A. MATRIX EQUALITY

1. For two matrices to be equal, they must have the same dimensions and be identical, element by element.

Equal:
Same dimensions, same elements

$$\begin{bmatrix} 5 & 3 \\ 4 & 3 \\ 0 & 1 \end{bmatrix} = \begin{bmatrix} 5 & 3 \\ 4 & 3 \\ 0 & 1 \end{bmatrix}$$

Not equal:
Same dimensions, different elements

$$\begin{bmatrix} 5 & 3 \\ 4 & 3 \\ 0 & 1 \end{bmatrix} \neq \begin{bmatrix} 5 & 3 \\ 4 & 3 \\ 6 & 1 \end{bmatrix}$$

Not equal:
Different dimensions

$$\begin{bmatrix} 6 & 0 \\ 2 & 0 \\ 1 & 0 \\ 5 & 0 \end{bmatrix} \neq \begin{bmatrix} 6 \\ 2 \\ 1 \\ 5 \end{bmatrix}$$

2. You can use what you know about matrix equality to solve matrix equations. For example, solve

$$\begin{bmatrix} 3 & 2 \\ 4 & 0 \end{bmatrix} = \begin{bmatrix} 3 & y+1 \\ 2x & 0 \end{bmatrix}$$ for x and y. Because the

corresponding elements are equal, you can determine that $2x = 4$ and $y + 1 = 2$, so $x = 2$ and $y = 1$.

B. MATRIX ADDITION

1. Matrices must have the same dimensions in order to be added. To find the sum $A + B$ of two matrices, the two matrices A and B must have the same dimensions.

2. The sum of two $m \times n$ matrices is an $m \times n$ matrix whose elements are the sums of the corresponding elements in the matrices that were added. For example:

$$\begin{bmatrix} 3 & -1 & 5 \\ 2 & 0 & -2 \end{bmatrix} + \begin{bmatrix} 2 & 3 & -3 \\ -3 & -1 & 2 \end{bmatrix} = \begin{bmatrix} 5 & 2 & 2 \\ -1 & -1 & 0 \end{bmatrix}.$$

3. For any $m \times n$ matrix, the $m \times n$ zero matrix is the additive identity. For example, for a 2×2 matrix, the 2×2 zero matrix is the additive identity matrix:

$$\begin{bmatrix} 2 & 3 \\ 4 & 5 \end{bmatrix} + \begin{bmatrix} 0 & 0 \\ 0 & 0 \end{bmatrix} = \begin{bmatrix} 2 & 3 \\ 4 & 5 \end{bmatrix}$$

4. For any $m \times n$ matrix A, the matrix $-A$ is the additive inverse.

If $A = \begin{bmatrix} a_{11} & a_{12} \\ a_{21} & a_{22} \end{bmatrix}$, then $-A = \begin{bmatrix} -a_{11} & -a_{12} \\ -a_{21} & -a_{22} \end{bmatrix}.$

Adding A and $-A$ produces the $m \times n$ zero matrix. For example:

$$\begin{bmatrix} 2 & 3 \\ 4 & 5 \end{bmatrix} + \begin{bmatrix} -2 & -3 \\ -4 & -5 \end{bmatrix} = \begin{bmatrix} 0 & 0 \\ 0 & 0 \end{bmatrix}$$

C. MATRIX SUBTRACTION

1. Matrices must also have the same dimensions in order to be subtracted. To find the difference $A - B$ of two matrices, the two matrices A and B must have the same dimensions.

2. The difference of two $m \times n$ matrices is an $m \times n$ matrix whose elements are the differences of the corresponding elements in the matrices that were subtracted. For example:

$$\begin{bmatrix} 3 & -1 & 5 \\ 2 & 0 & -2 \end{bmatrix} - \begin{bmatrix} 2 & 3 & -3 \\ -3 & -1 & 2 \end{bmatrix} = \begin{bmatrix} 1 & -4 & 8 \\ 5 & 1 & -4 \end{bmatrix}.$$

D. SCALAR MULTIPLICATION

1. Scalar multiplication is the process of multiplying each element of a matrix by a number called a *scalar*.

2. The notation kA represents the scalar product of a scalar k and an $m \times n$ matrix called A. Each element in the matrix kA is the corresponding element from A multiplied by the scalar k.

   For example, if $A = \begin{bmatrix} 2 & 4 \\ -1 & 0 \end{bmatrix}$, then $3A = \begin{bmatrix} 6 & 12 \\ -3 & 0 \end{bmatrix}$.

E. MATRIX MULTIPLICATION

1. Two matrices A and B can only be multiplied if the number of columns in A is the same as the number of rows in B.

2. To find the product AB of matrices A and B, multiply one row of A by one column of B for each element in AB. For example, if $A = \begin{bmatrix} 2 & 4 \\ -1 & 0 \end{bmatrix}$ and $B = \begin{bmatrix} 3 & -1 & 5 \\ 2 & 0 & -2 \end{bmatrix}$, then to help calculate AB, show the two matrices next to each other like this: $\begin{bmatrix} 2 & 4 \\ -1 & 0 \end{bmatrix}\begin{bmatrix} 3 & -1 & 5 \\ 2 & 0 & -2 \end{bmatrix}$

$$AB = \begin{bmatrix} 2(3)+4(2) & 2(-1)+4(0) & 2(5)+4(-2) \\ -1(3)+0(2) & -1(-1)+0(0) & -1(5)+0(-2) \end{bmatrix}$$

$$= \begin{bmatrix} 14 & -2 & 2 \\ -3 & 1 & -5 \end{bmatrix}.$$)

3. Suppose that matrix $A = \begin{bmatrix} 2 & 4 \\ -1 & 0 \end{bmatrix}$ and matrix $B = \begin{bmatrix} 3 & 2 \\ -1 & 0 \\ 5 & -2 \end{bmatrix}$.

   The product AB does not exist because the number of columns in A does not equal the number of rows in B. However, the product BA does exist because the number of columns in B equals the number of rows in A.

4. The commutative property does not hold true for matrix multiplication. In matrix multiplication, order does matter. In most cases of matrix multiplication, the product AB is different from the product BA.

III. MODELING REAL-WORLD DATA WITH MATRICES

A. DATA REPRESENTATION

1. Matrices can be used to model many different kinds of data. For example, inventory for the number of T-shirts at a clothing store by color and size is modeled with the following 3 × 4 matrix:

Number of T-Shirts by Color and Size

	S	M	L	XL
Red	15	18	25	17
White	39	45	58	32
Blue	27	30	35	25

2. A similar matrix could also be used to model prices of T-shirts by color and size:

Price ($) of T-Shirts by Size and Color

	Red	White	Blue
S	12	8	15
M	12	8	15
L	14	8	15
XL	18	10	20

3. The price of a large red T-shirt is found in row 3, column 1 of the matrix. The element is represented by the notation a_{31}. The price of a large red T-shirt is $14.

Enter a Matrix into a Calculator Let's enter the 4 × 3 matrix for T-shirt prices into a calculator:

$$\begin{bmatrix} 12 & 8 & 15 \\ 12 & 8 & 15 \\ 14 & 8 & 15 \\ 18 & 10 & 20 \end{bmatrix}.$$

Here's how it works on a TI-84.

Press [2ND] [x^{-1}] to get to the MATRIX screen. Press [>][>] to get to EDIT, highlight MATRIX[A] and press ENTER, and then enter 4 for rows, 3 for columns, and press ENTER.

Go to the matrix screen.

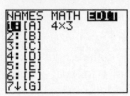

Create a 4 × 3 matrix.

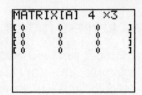

Enter the data.

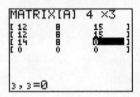

On your calculator, this matrix is now referred to by the letter A. To see matrix A, go to the matrix screen with NAMES highlighted, press the number 1, and then press ENTER.

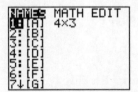

[A]

    [[12 8   15]
     [12 8   15]
     [14 8   15]
     [18 10 20]]

B. USING MATRIX OPERATIONS WITH REAL-WORLD DATA

1. Scalar multiplication can be used to multiply each element in the matrix by the same value. For example, if matrix *A* represents T-shirt prices by size and color, then 0.15*A* represents the amount of a 15% discount by T-shirt size and color.

$$A = \begin{bmatrix} 12 & 8 & 15 \\ 12 & 8 & 15 \\ 14 & 8 & 15 \\ 18 & 10 & 20 \end{bmatrix}$$

$$0.15A = \begin{bmatrix} 1.80 & 1.20 & 2.25 \\ 1.80 & 1.20 & 2.25 \\ 2.10 & 1.20 & 2.25 \\ 2.70 & 1.50 & 3.00 \end{bmatrix}$$

2. Matrices can also be added and subtracted to solve real-world problems. For example, the T-shirt sale prices with the 15% discount can be found by subtracting $A - 0.15A$:

$$A - 0.15A = \begin{bmatrix} 10.20 & 6.80 & 12.75 \\ 10.20 & 6.80 & 12.75 \\ 11.90 & 6.80 & 12.75 \\ 15.30 & 8.50 & 17.00 \end{bmatrix}$$

> **Matrix Operations with a Calculator** *You can use matrix operations on your calculator to compute the T-shirt sale prices with the 15% discount. The 4×3 matrix for T-shirt prices has already been entered into the TI-84 calculator as matrix A:*
>
> $$\begin{bmatrix} 12 & 8 & 15 \\ 12 & 8 & 15 \\ 14 & 8 & 15 \\ 18 & 10 & 20 \end{bmatrix}.$$

Press [2ND] [x^{-1}] to get to the MATRIX screen. Press 1 and Enter to show [A] (for matrix A) in the command line. Continue to enter the entire command line: [A] $-$ [A] $\times$ 0.15. Press ENTER.

Go to the matrix screen.

Press 1 and ENTER to reference matrix A in the command line.

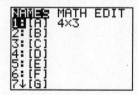

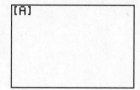

Use the matrix menu to enter [A] $-$ [A] $\times$ 0.15.

The discounted T-shirt prices are given in the resulting matrix.

IV. MATRICES AND EQUATIONS

A. DETERMINANTS

1. Every square matrix has a number that is called its *determinant*.
2. A second-order determinant is the determinant of a 2 × 2 matrix.
3. If the matrix is $\begin{bmatrix} a & b \\ c & d \end{bmatrix}$, its determinant can be represented

   as $\begin{vmatrix} a & b \\ c & d \end{vmatrix}$ or $\det\begin{bmatrix} a & b \\ c & d \end{bmatrix}$.

4. To find the value of a second-order determinant, calculate the difference of the products of the two diagonals. If the matrix is

   $\begin{bmatrix} a & b \\ c & d \end{bmatrix}$, then $\begin{vmatrix} a & b \\ c & d \end{vmatrix} = ad - bc$. For example, if the matrix

   is $\begin{bmatrix} 2 & -3 \\ -1 & 4 \end{bmatrix}$, then $\begin{vmatrix} 2 & -3 \\ -1 & 4 \end{vmatrix} = (2)(4) - (-3)(-1) = 5$.

5. The third-order determinant of a 3 × 3 matrix $\begin{bmatrix} a & b & c \\ d & e & f \\ g & h & i \end{bmatrix}$

   can be found by calculating the determinant as follows:

   $$\begin{vmatrix} a & b & c \\ d & e & f \\ g & h & i \end{vmatrix} = a\begin{vmatrix} e & f \\ h & i \end{vmatrix} - b\begin{vmatrix} d & f \\ g & i \end{vmatrix} + c\begin{vmatrix} d & e \\ g & h \end{vmatrix}.$$

6. Following is as third-order determinant of a 3 × 3 matrix example:

   $$\det\begin{bmatrix} 5 & 2 & 1 \\ 3 & 4 & 1 \\ 6 & 1 & 3 \end{bmatrix} = 5\begin{vmatrix} 4 & 1 \\ 1 & 3 \end{vmatrix} - 2\begin{vmatrix} 3 & 1 \\ 6 & 3 \end{vmatrix} + 1\begin{vmatrix} 3 & 4 \\ 6 & 1 \end{vmatrix}$$

   $$= 5(12-1) - 2(9-6) + 1(3-24)$$
   $$= 55 - 6 - 21$$
   $$= 28$$

B. CRAMER'S RULE

1. Cramer's Rule can be used to solve systems of linear equations using matrices and determinants.

2. Consider a system of two linear equations $ax + by = e$ and $cx + dy = f$, where a, b, c, d, e, and f are constants. Cramer's rule says that the solution of the system is (x, y), where

$$x = \frac{\begin{vmatrix} e & b \\ f & d \end{vmatrix}}{\begin{vmatrix} a & b \\ c & d \end{vmatrix}}, \; y = \frac{\begin{vmatrix} a & e \\ c & f \end{vmatrix}}{\begin{vmatrix} a & b \\ c & d \end{vmatrix}}, \text{ and } \begin{vmatrix} a & b \\ c & d \end{vmatrix} \neq 0.$$

3. Here's an example of how Cramer's rule works. Suppose you want to solve the linear system $5x + 2y = 1$ and $3x - 3y = 9$. Substitute the constants $a = 5$, $b = 2$, $c = 3$, $d = -3$, $e = 1$, and $f = 9$ into the formulas:

$$x = \frac{\begin{vmatrix} e & b \\ f & d \end{vmatrix}}{\begin{vmatrix} a & b \\ c & d \end{vmatrix}} = \frac{\begin{vmatrix} 1 & 2 \\ 9 & -3 \end{vmatrix}}{\begin{vmatrix} 5 & 2 \\ 3 & -3 \end{vmatrix}} = \frac{-3-18}{-15-6} = \frac{-21}{-21} = 1$$

$$y = \frac{\begin{vmatrix} a & e \\ c & f \end{vmatrix}}{\begin{vmatrix} a & b \\ c & d \end{vmatrix}} = \frac{\begin{vmatrix} 5 & 1 \\ 3 & 9 \end{vmatrix}}{\begin{vmatrix} 5 & 2 \\ 3 & -3 \end{vmatrix}} = \frac{45-3}{-15-6} = \frac{42}{-21} = -2$$

Cramer's rule tells you the solution is $(1, -2)$. Check by substituting $(1, -2)$ for x and y in both equations in the linear system to check the results:

$$5x + 2y = 1 \qquad 3x - 3y = 9$$
$$5(1) + 2(-2) = 1 \qquad 3(1) - 3(-2) = 9$$
$$5 - 4 = 1 \qquad 3 - (-6) = 9$$

The solution is correct!

SEQUENCES
AND SERIES

KEY VOCABULARY

Arithmetic means Terms between any two nonconsecutive terms of an arithmetic sequence; for example, an arithmetic sequence with two arithmetic means between 3 and 12 is 3, 6, 9, 12, ... The arithmetic means between 3 and 12 in the sequence are 6 and 9.

Arithmetic sequence A sequence in which each term after the first term is equal to the sum of the preceding term and a constant called the *common difference*. The sequence -2, 5, 12, 19, . . . is an arithmetic sequence with a common difference of 7.

Arithmetic series The indicated sum of elements in an arithmetic sequence.

Common difference The constant added to each term in an arithmetic sequence.

Common ratio The ratio by which each term in a geometric sequence is multiplied.

Elements The terms in a sequence.

Geometric sequence A sequence in which each term after the first term is equal to the product of the preceding term and a constant called the *common ratio*. The sequence 3, 9, 27, 81, . . . is a geometric sequence with a common ratio of 3.

Geometric series The indicated sum of elements in a geometric sequence.

Infinite geometric series with a finite sum A series in which the common ratio *r* is between −1 and 1.

*n***th partial sum** The sum of the first *n* terms of a series.

Recursive formula A formula for a sequence in which terms are defined in terms of preceding terms.

Sequence An ordered list of numbers.

Series The indicated sum of elements in a sequence.

Terms Elements in a sequence.

I. ARITHMETIC SEQUENCES AND SERIES

A. ARITHMETIC SEQUENCES

1. A sequence is an ordered list of numbers. A sequence may also be called a *progression*.
2. The items that comprise a sequence are called *terms* or *elements*.
3. A sequence is a function whose domain is the set of natural numbers. The terms of the sequence are the range of the function.
4. The terms of a sequence are usually referenced by numbered subscripts as a_1, a_2, a_3, and so on. Variables are also used for subscripts, such as a_i and a_n, where variables *i* and *n* represent the index or the counter.
5. Sometimes sequences start with an index of 0 instead of 1. This would mean that the first term of the sequence is a_0, not a_1.

Start Numbering at 0 or 1? Because the value of the subscript variable may be used to generate sequence terms, it is important to know whether subscript numbering starts at 0 or 1 when working with sequences. "Start with 0 or 1?" is an important question when it comes to the mathematical process of counting.

6. In an arithmetic sequence, each term after the first term is equal to the sum of the preceding term and a constant called the *common difference*. If the first term is a_1 and the common difference is d, then the second term $a_2 = a_1 + d$, the third term $a_3 = a_2 + d$, and so on.

7. The terms of an arithmetic sequence are given by a_1, $a_1 + d$, $a_1 + 2d$, . . .

8. To find the next term in an arithmetic sequence, you must find the common difference by subtracting any term from the term that comes next. For example, to find the next term in the arithmetic sequence $-3, 1, 5, 9, . . .$, first determine that the common difference is 4 ($1 - (-3) = 4$, $5 - 1 = 4$, $9 - 5 = 4$) and then add $9 + 4 = 13$. The next term is 13.

9. An arithmetic sequence can be defined recursively as $a_n = a_{n-1} + d$. The definition is recursive because each term in the sequence is defined using the term that precedes it.

10. If you know the first term of an arithmetic sequence a_1 and the common difference d, you can find the nth term of the sequence a_n by using the formula $a_n = a_1 + (n - 1)d$. For example, if the first term of an arithmetic sequence is 2 and the common difference is 6, the 8th term of the sequence is given by $a_8 = 2 + (8 - 1)6 = 44$.

11. Terms between any two nonconsecutive terms of an arithmetic sequence are called *arithmetic means*. For example, an arithmetic sequence with two arithmetic means between 10 and 25 is 10, 15, 20, 25, ...The two arithmetic means in the sequence are 15 and 20.

B. ARITHMETIC SERIES

1. An arithmetic series is the sum of the terms in an arithmetic sequence. The term *indicated sum* is sometimes used because the terms that are to be included in the sum must be specified.

2. Sigma notation may be used to describe how terms are summed in an arithmetic sequence. Sigma is the Greek letter corresponding to capital *S*. For example, $\sum_{n=1}^{10} a_n$ means to find the sum of the a_n terms from $n = 1$ to $n = 10$. Written out in expanded form, $\sum_{n=1}^{10} a_n$ means $a_1 + a_2 + a_3 + a_4 + a_5 + a_6 + a_7 + a_8 + a_9 + a_{10}$.

3. Another representation of the sum of the first n terms of an arithmetic series is called the nth partial sum, symbolized S_n. The partial sum is the sum of a finite number of terms. The formula for the sum of the first n terms of an arithmetic series is $S_n = \dfrac{n}{2}(a_1 + a_n)$. For example, the sum of the first 50 terms in the arithmetic series $2 + 4 + 6 + 2 + 4 + 6 + \cdots + 100$ is given by $S_n = \dfrac{50}{2}(2 + 100) = 2550$.

4. If you do not know the nth term in the series for which you want the nth partial sum, use the formula $a_n = a_1 + (n - 1)d$ to find the nth term of an arithmetic sequence. For example, if you want to find the sum of the first 25 terms in the arithmetic series $2 + 5 + 8 + \cdots$, first find the 25th term of the arithmetic sequence with first term $a_1 = 2$ and common difference $d = 3$: $a_{25} = 2 + (25 - 1)3 = 74$. Then you can use the sum formula to find that the sum of the first 25 terms is $S_n = \dfrac{25}{2}(2 + 74) = 950$.

5. To find a partial sum between the ith and jth terms, find the partial sums S_i and S_j, and then subtract $S_j - S_i$.

Find the Sum of a Series on Your Calculator *To work with sequences and series on your calculator, you should first change your calculator to sequence mode. On a TI-84, press MODE, then [ˇ] 3 times and [>] 3 times to select SEQ mode.*

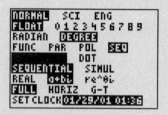

Test Tip

Suppose you want to find the sum of the first 50 terms of the arithmetic series with first term 2 and a common difference of 2. You can use the seq function on your calculator to define a sequence with first term 2 and common difference 2, and you can use the sum function to add the terms. Here's how to find a geometric sum on a TI-84:

(continued)

(continued)

> *Step 1: To get the sum function, press [2ND][STAT] to get the LIST menu, then select MATH and 5.*
>
> *Step 2: Continue the command by defining the sequence. Press [2ND][STAT] to get the LIST menu, then select OPS and 5 to get the seq function.*
>
> *Step 3: Complete the entries for the sequence: the sequence formula (2n), the index variable (n), the first index value (1), the last index value (50), and increment (1).*

Select the sum function.

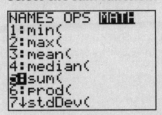

Select the sequence function.

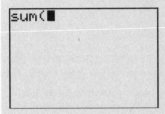 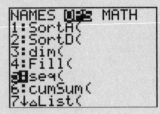

Define the sequence.

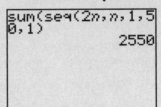

GEOMETRIC SEQUENCES AND SERIES

A. GEOMETRIC SEQUENCES

1. Like an arithmetic sequence, a geometric sequence or progression is an ordered list of numbers comprised of "terms"

or elements." A geometric sequence is a function whose domain is the set of natural numbers and whose range is the terms of the sequence. The terms of a geometric sequence are usually referenced by numbered subscripts as a_1, a_2, a_3, and so on. Recall that sometimes sequences start with an index of 0 instead of 1.

2. In a geometric sequence, each term after the first term is equal to the product of the preceding term and a constant called the *common ratio*. If the first term is a_1 and the common ratio is r, then the second term $a_2 = a_1 r$, the third term $a_3 = a_2 r$, and so on.

3. The terms of a geometric sequence are given by a_1, $a_1 r$, $a_1 r^2$, . . .

4. To find the next term in a geometric sequence, you must find the common ratio by dividing any term by the preceding term in the sequence. For example, to find the next term in the geometric sequence $-1, \dfrac{2}{3}, -\dfrac{4}{9}, \ldots$, first determine that the common ratio is $-\dfrac{2}{3} \left(\dfrac{2}{3} \div -1 = -\dfrac{2}{3}, -\dfrac{4}{9} \div \dfrac{2}{3} = -\dfrac{2}{3} \right)$ and then multiply $-\dfrac{4}{9} \left(-\dfrac{2}{3} \right) = \dfrac{8}{27}$. The next term is $\dfrac{8}{27}$.

5. As with arithmetic sequences, geometric sequences can be defined recursively. For a geometric sequence, $a_n = a_{n-1} r$. The definition is recursive because each term in the sequence is defined using the term that precedes it.

6. If you know the first term of a geometric sequence a_1 and the common ratio r, you can find the nth term of the sequence a_n by using the formula $a_n = a_1 r^{n-1}$. For example, if the first term of a geometric sequence is 6 and the common ratio is 2, the 7th term of the sequence is given by $a_7 = 6 (2^{7-1}) = 6(64) = 384$.

7. Terms between any two nonconsecutive terms of a geometric sequence are called *geometric means*. For example, a geometric sequence with two geometric means between 3 and 81 is 3, 9, 27, 81, ... The geometric means of the sequence are 9 and 27.

B. GEOMETRIC SERIES

1. A geometric series is the sum of the terms in a geometric sequence. The term *indicated sum* is sometimes used because the terms that are to be included in the sum must be specified.

2. You may use sigma notation to describe how terms are summed in a geometric series. For a geometric series with first term a_1 and common ratio r, the sum of the first n terms is given by $\sum_{i=1}^{n} a_i = \dfrac{a_1 - a_1 r^n}{1-r}$. For example, the sum of the first 4 terms in a geometric series with first term 2 and common ratio 2 is given by $\dfrac{a_1 - a_1 r^n}{1-r} = \dfrac{2 - 2(2^4)}{1-2} = 30$. Written out, the series is $2 + 4 + 8 + 16 + 32 + \cdots$, and the sum of the first 4 terms is 30.

3. Another representation of the sum of the first n terms of a geometric series is called the nth partial sum, symbolized S_n. The formula for the sum of the first n terms of a geometric series is $S_n = \dfrac{a_1 - a_1 r^n}{1-r}$. For example, the sum of the first 10 terms in the geometric series $2 + 4 + 8 + 16 + 32 + \cdots$ is given by $S_{10} = \dfrac{2 - 2(2^{10})}{1-2} = 2046$.

4. Geometric series are said to be *finite* or *infinite*. When you find the sum of a finite geometric series, you are finding the sum of a finite number of terms. For example, you can find the sum of the first 10 terms of the geometric series $2 + 4 + 8 + 16 + 32 + \cdots$. In a geometric series, when $|r| < 1$, an infinite sum also exists. For example, the geometric series $1 + \dfrac{1}{2} + \dfrac{1}{4} + \dfrac{1}{8} + \dfrac{1}{16} + \dfrac{1}{32} + \cdots$ has a common ratio of $\dfrac{1}{2}$ and is infinite. Yet because the common ratio is a fraction, the terms in the series get smaller and smaller, approaching zero.

5. The formula for finding the sum S of an infinite geometric series if $|r| < 1$, is $S = \dfrac{a_1}{1-r}$. So, the sum S of the infinite geometric series $1 + \dfrac{1}{2} + \dfrac{1}{4} + \dfrac{1}{8} + \dfrac{1}{16} + \dfrac{1}{32} + \cdots$ is $S = \dfrac{1}{1 - \dfrac{1}{2}} = 2$.

VECTORS

KEY VOCABULARY

Direction One part of the quantity of a vector; in a graphic representation of a vector, direction is shown by the arrowhead.

Initial point The point where a vector begins.

Magnitude One part of the quantity of a vector; in a graphic representation of a vector, magnitude is the length of the line segment.

Resultant The sum of two or more vectors.

Scalar quantity A quantity with only magnitude but not direction. For example, length and temperature are scalar quantities.

Terminal point The point where a vector ends.

Vector A quantity that has both magnitude and direction.

 I. VECTOR BASICS

A. REPRESENTING VECTORS

1. A vector is a quantity that has both magnitude and direction.
2. Geometrically, a vector is represented by a directed line segment, as shown in the following diagram. This vector can be named $\vec{v}$ or $\vec{AB}$. The length of the line segment represents the magnitude of this vector. The magnitude of $\vec{v}$ is $|\vec{v}|$.

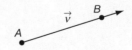

3. For two vectors to be equal, they must have the same direction and the same magnitude.

4. Two vectors are parallel if they have either the same or opposite directions.

B. ADDING AND SUBTRACTING VECTORS

1. The sum of two or more vectors is called the *resultant*.

2. There are two methods to add vectors: the parallelogram method and the triangle method.

   ▶ *For the parallelogram method, both vectors have the same initial point. The resultant is the diagonal from the corner of the parallelogram formed by the initial points of the vectors to the opposite corner of the parallelogram.*

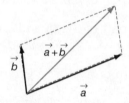

   ▶ *For the triangle method, the initial point of the second vector begins at the terminal point of the first vector. The resultant is the segment from the initial point of the first vector to the terminal point of the second vector.*

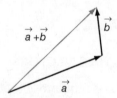

3. Opposite vectors have the same magnitude and opposite directions. The opposite of a vector $\vec{v}$ is $-\vec{v}$. Opposite vectors can be used for vector subtraction, with adding $-\vec{v}$ the same as subtracting $\vec{v}$.

Vectors and Triangles *The following diagram shows the sub-traction of vector a from vector b using the triangle method.*

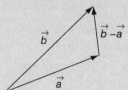

The triangle inequality rule states that the length of a side of a triangle must be less than the sum of the lengths of the other two sides and greater than the difference of the lengths of the other two sides. You can use this rule to describe relationships between vectors. For example, if the magnitudes of $\vec{a}$ and $\vec{b}$ are 7 and 10, respectively, then the magnitude of $\vec{b} - \vec{a}$ must be greater than 3 and less than 17.

II. VECTORS IN THE COORDINATE PLANE

A. REPRESENTATIONS OF VECTORS

1. In the coordinate plane, a vector is in standard position if its initial position is at the origin. The direction of the vector is the angle between the positive *x*-axis and the vector. In the following diagram, the direction of $\vec{v}$ is 60°.

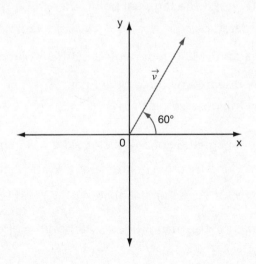

2. In the following coordinate plane, $\overrightarrow{OC}$ is in the standard position. The initial point of $\overrightarrow{OC}$ is (0, 0) and the terminal point is (3, 4). You can find the magnitude of $\overrightarrow{OC}$ by finding the length of the hypotenuse of the right triangle with vertices (0, 0), (3, 0), and (3, 4): $\sqrt{3^2 + 4^2} = 5$. Note that $\overrightarrow{OC}$, $\overrightarrow{AB}$, and $\overrightarrow{DE}$ are all equal because they have the same direction and magnitude.

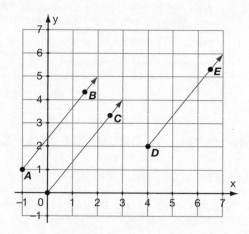

3. In the coordinate plane, vectors can be represented as ordered pairs. If $A(x_1, y_1)$ is the initial point of a vector and $B(x_2, y_2)$ is the terminal point, then $\overrightarrow{AB}$ is represented by the ordered pair $\langle x_2 - x_1, y_2 - y_1 \rangle$. For example, in the preceding diagram, $\overrightarrow{AB}$ is represented by the ordered pair $\langle 3, 4 \rangle$, $\overrightarrow{OC}$ is represented by the ordered pair $\langle 3, 4 \rangle$, and $\overrightarrow{DE}$ is represented by the ordered pair $\langle 3, 4 \rangle$.

4. The magnitude of any vector $\overrightarrow{AB}$ is $|\overrightarrow{AB}|$. This magnitude can be found by using coordinates and the Pythagorean theorem. If vector $\overrightarrow{AB}$ has initial point $A(x_1, y_1)$ and terminal point $B(x_2, y_2)$, the magnitude of $\overrightarrow{AB}$ is $|\overrightarrow{AB}| = \sqrt{(x_2 - x_1)^2 + (y_2 - y_1)^2}$.

5. The zero vector has both its head and tail at the origin. The zero vector can go in any direction and always has a magnitude of 0.

B. VECTOR OPERATIONS

1. To add vectors $\vec{A}\langle a_1, a_2 \rangle$ and $\vec{B}\langle b_1, b_2 \rangle$, add corresponding components. $\vec{A} + \vec{B} = \langle a_1 + b_1, a_2 + b_2 \rangle$.

2. To subtract vectors $\vec{A}\langle a_1, a_2 \rangle$ and $\vec{B}\langle b_1, b_2 \rangle$, subtract corresponding components. $\vec{A} - \vec{B} = \langle a_1 - b_1, a_2 - b_2 \rangle$.

3. You can also multiply a vector by a scalar. A scalar quantity has only magnitude. A vector can be multiplied by a scalar quantity, resulting in a product that is a vector. If a vector $\vec{v}$ is multiplied by a scalar k, the product will be a vector with a magnitude of $k|\vec{v}|$. If $k > 0$, the vector has the same direction as $\vec{v}$; if $k < 0$, the vector has the opposite direction as $\vec{v}$.

Test Tip

Vector Symbols Vectors are represented in a variety of different ways. Often, a symbol is placed over the vector name. Sometimes, the symbol is an arrow $(\vec{v})$ and sometimes it is a harpoon $(\vec{v})$. Although both symbols are commonly used, vectors have been shown with arrows in the released items on the College Board website.

PART III:
ALGEBRA AND FUNCTIONS

EXPRESSIONS

KEY VOCABULARY

Algebraic expression An algebraic statement that can contain variables, symbols, and numbers upon which are performed operations including addition, subtraction, multiplication, division, and exponents (powers and roots).

Binomial A polynomial with two terms.

Coefficient The numeric part of a term with variables.

Constant In a term that contains only a number, the number is called a *constant*.

Factors The factors of an expression are the numbers, variables, and/or terms for which the expression is their product.

Integral exponents Exponents that are integers.

Leading term The first term of a polynomial when written in standard form; the leading term has the highest degree of all terms in the polynomial.

Monomial A polynomial with one term.

Polynomial An expression with one monomial or the sum or difference of monomials.

Radical expression A radical sign and its radicand.

Radical sign The mathematical symbol that represents taking a root. The symbol $\sqrt{}$ represents a square root, the symbol $\sqrt[3]{}$ represents a cube root, and the symbol $\sqrt[n]{}$ represents an *n*th root.

Radicand The expression under the radical sign.

Rational exponent An exponent that is a rational number.

Rational expression An expression in which a polynomial is divided by another polynomial.

Rationalizing the denominator Writing an equivalent expression without any radicals in the denominator.

Terms The parts of an algebraic expression separated by addition or subtraction.

Trinomial A polynomial with three terms.

Variable A value, usually represented by a letter, that can change.

I. ALGEBRAIC EXPRESSIONS

A. EXPRESSION BASICS

1. In an algebraic expression, operations including addition, subtraction, multiplication, division, powers, and roots are performed upon combinations of numbers and/or variables.
2. Expressions are comprised of terms, which are those parts of an algebraic expression separated by addition or subtraction. For example, in the expression $3x^2 + x - 2$, the terms are $3x^2$, x, and -2.
3. A coefficient is the numeric part of a term. For terms with variables and no coefficients, the coefficient is understood to be 1. The coefficient of a constant term is the constant. For the terms $3x^2$, x, and -2, the coefficients are 3, 1, and -2, respectively.
4. The numbers and variables that are multiplied to comprise a term are called *factors* of the term. For example, the factors of $5x^2$ are 5 and x^2.

5. Terms that have the same variable factors are called *like terms*. For example, $5x^2$ and $6x^2$ are like terms with the common variable factor x^2.

B. SIMPLIFYING ALGEBRAIC EXPRESSIONS

1. The process of simplifying an algebraic expression involves writing an equivalent algebraic expression in which all grouping symbols have been removed and all like terms have been combined.

2. The commutative, associative, and distributive properties can be useful in the process of simplifying an algebraic expression. For example, to remove the parentheses from the expression $5(x + y)$, use the distributive property: $5(x + y) = 5x + 5y$.

3. You can evaluate an algebraic expression for a given value of a variable. For example, to evaluate $4(x - 3)^2$ for $x = 5$, substitute 5 for x in the expression and evaluate: $4(x - 3)^2 = 4(5 - 3)^2 = 4(2)^2 = 4(4) = 16$.

II. EXPRESSIONS WITH INTEGRAL EXPONENTS

A. RULES OF INTEGRAL EXPONENTS

1. The product rule: $(x^m)(x^n) = x^{m+n}$. If you are multiplying exponential expressions with the same base, you can add the exponents. Use the sum as the exponent of the common base. For example: $x^2 x^3 = x^{2+3} = x^5$.

2. The quotient rule: $\dfrac{x^m}{x^n} = x^{m-n}$. If you are dividing exponential expressions with the same nonzero base, you can subtract the exponents in the denominator from the exponents in the numerator. Use the difference as the exponent of the common base. For example: $\dfrac{x^5}{x^3} = x^{5-3} = x^2$.

3. The zero-exponent rule: $x^0 = 1$. This rule holds for all real numbers $x \neq 0$. For example: $4^0 = 1$ and $\left(-\dfrac{1}{3}\right)^0 = 1$.

4. The negative-exponent rule: $x^{-n} = \dfrac{1}{x^n}$ and $\dfrac{1}{x^{-n}} = x^n$. If x is a real number not equal to 0 and n is a natural number, this rule lets you rewrite a negative exponent so that it is positive.

For example: $x^{-1} = \dfrac{1}{x}$ and $\dfrac{1}{x^{-2}} = x^2$.

5. The power rule: $\left(x^m\right)^n = x^{mn}$. If a power is raised to a power, the base is raised to the product of the powers. For example: $\left(x^2\right)^3 = x^{2\times3} = x^6$.

6. The products-to-powers rule: $\left(xy\right)^n = x^n y^n$. If a product is raised to a power, each factor of the product is raised to the power. For example: $\left(xy\right)^2 = x^2 y^2$.

7. The quotients-to-powers rule: $\left(\dfrac{x}{y}\right)^n = \dfrac{x^n}{y^n}$. If a quotient is raised to a power, the numerator and denominator are each raised to the power. For example: $\left(\dfrac{x}{y}\right)^3 = \dfrac{x^3}{y^3}$.

B. SIMPLIFYING EXPRESSIONS WITH INTEGRAL EXPONENTS

1. When you are simplifying an exponential expression, there are often different paths that will arrive at the same simplified end destination.

2. Here is a checklist of some strategies for using the rules of exponents to simplify algebraic expressions.

    i. Remove parentheses by using the following rules:

        a) Product rule: $\left(x^m\right)\left(x^n\right) = x^{m+n}$

        b) Power rule: $\left(x^m\right)^n = x^{mn}$

        c) Products-to-powers rule: $\left(xy\right)^n = x^n y^n$

        d) Quotients-to-powers rule $\left(\dfrac{x}{y}\right)^n = \dfrac{x^n}{y^n}$

    ii. Combine like terms so that each base appears only once. For example: $2x^2 - 6x^2 + x - 3x - 6 - 8 = -4x^2 - 2x - 14$.

    iii. Rewrite negative exponents as positive exponents.

Rules of Exponents Quick Reference

Rule	Definition	Example
Product rule	$\left(x^{m}\right)\left(x^{n}\right)=x^{m+n}$	$\left(2^{2}\right)\left(2^{3}\right)=2^{2+3}=2^{5}=32$
Quotient rule	$\dfrac{x^{m}}{x^{n}}=x^{m-n}$	$\dfrac{2^{6}}{2^{4}}=2^{6-4}=2^{2}=4$
Zero-exponent rule	$x^{0}=1$ if $x\neq 0$	$2^{0}=1$
Negative-exponent rule	$x^{-n}=\dfrac{1}{x^{n}}$ and $\dfrac{1}{x^{-n}}=x^{n}$	$2^{-3}=\dfrac{1}{2^{3}}=\dfrac{1}{8}$ and $\dfrac{1}{2^{-3}}=2^{3}=8$
Power rule	$\left(x^{m}\right)^{n}=x^{mn}$	$\left(2^{2}\right)^{5}=2^{2\times5}=2^{10}=1024$
Products-to-powers rule	$\left(xy\right)^{n}=x^{n}y^{n}$	$\left(3\bullet4\right)^{2}=3^{2}4^{2}=9\bullet16=144$
Quotients-to-powers rule	$\left(\dfrac{x}{y}\right)^{n}=\dfrac{x^{n}}{y^{n}}$	$\left(\dfrac{2}{3}\right)^{4}=\dfrac{2^{4}}{3^{4}}=\dfrac{16}{81}$

Exponents on Your Calculator *You can enter exponents into your calculator by using the [^] key. The screens below show different exponents entered. Note the effect of parentheses.*

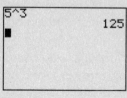

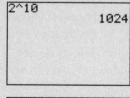

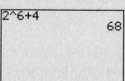

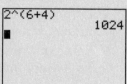

III. POLYNOMIAL EXPRESSIONS

A. POLYNOMIAL BASICS

1. A polynomial is either a monomial term or the sum of terms that contain only numbers and variables raised to whole-number exponents. Polynomials do not contain terms with fractional exponents, fractional terms with variables in the denominator, or terms with roots of variables.

Polynomial	Not a Polynomial
4	$x^{\frac{2}{3}}$
$4x^2$ $4x^2 + 3x + 5$	$\dfrac{1}{x-2}$
$3a^2b^3 - 4ab$	$3\sqrt{x} - 4x$
$2x + 1$	$\sqrt{2}$

2. A polynomial that contains one term is called a *monomial*. A polynomial that contains two terms is called a *binomial*. A polynomial that contains three terms is called a *trinomial*.

3. Polynomials are usually written with the variable exponents in decreasing order. This is called *standard form*. For example, $4x^2 + 7 + 3x^3 + x^6$ would be rewritten in standard form as $x^6 + 3x^3 + 4x^2 + 7$.

4. The first term of a polynomial when written in standard form is called the *leading term*. In the expression $x^6 + 3x^3 + 4x^2 + 7$, the leading term is x^6.

5. The exponent of a term tells you the degree of the term. The degree of the leading term of a polynomial, when written in standard form, is the degree of the polynomial. The degree of the polynomial $x^6 + 3x^3 + 4x^2 + 7$ is 6 because the leading term x^6 is degree 6.

6. Some polynomials have two or more variables. When a term has two or more variables, the degree of the term is the sum

of the variable exponents. The degree of the polynomial is the degree of the term with the greatest degree. For example, the degree of the term $3a^2b^3$ is $2 + 3 = 5$, the sum of the variable exponents 2 and 3. The degree of the term $4ab$ is $1 + 1 = 2$. The degree of the polynomial $3a^2b^3 - 4ab$ is 5, since 5 is the sum of the variable exponents 2 and 3.

B. OPERATIONS ON POLYNOMIALS

1. To add and subtract polynomials, combine like terms. For example: $(2x^2 + 7x + 5) + (6 - 3x) = 2x^2 + (7x - 3x) + (5 + 6) = 2x^2 + 4x + 11$.

2. To multiply monomials, multiply the coefficients and then multiply the variables using the product rule for exponents. For example: $2x^3 \cdot 4x^2 = (2)(4) \cdot x^{3+2} = 8x^5$.

3. To multiply a monomial and a polynomial, use the distributive property and multiply two monomials at a time. For example: $2x^3(4x^2 + 3) = 2x^3(4x^2) + 2x^3(3) = 8x^5 + 6x^3$.

4. To multiply two polynomials, find the product of each pair of terms and then combine like terms. For example: $(x + 1)(x^2 + 2x + 3) = x(x^2) + x(2x) + x(3) + 1(x^2) + 1(2x) + 1(3) = x^3 + 3x^2 + 5x + 3$.

5. To multiply two binomials, use FOIL (First, Outer, Inner, Last): $ac + ad + bc + bd$.

6. Special products are products that occur so regularly that it's worth memorizing how they work.

   i. The square of a binomial sum: $(A + B)^2 = A^2 + 2AB + B^2$

   ii. The square of a binomial difference: $(A - B)^2 = A^2 - 2AB + B^2$

   iii. The product of the sum and the difference of two terms: $(A + B)(A - B) = A^2 - B^2$

C. FACTORING POLYNOMIALS

1. To factor a polynomial expression that is the sum of monomials, write an equivalent expression that is a product. For example, the factored form of $x^2 + 5x + 6$ is $(x + 2)(x + 3)$.

2. Some strategies for factoring are the following:

    i. You can use the distributive property to factor out the greatest common factor (GCF) from a polynomial expression that is the sum of monomials. For example, to factor $12x^3 + 15x^2$, use the distributive property to factor out the GCF of $3x^2$ and write the factored form: $3x^2(4x + 5)$.

    ii. For some polynomials, you may be able to factor out a common binomial or other polynomial expression. For example, the factored form of

    $(x + 2)(x - 1)+(x - 3)(x + 2) = (x + 2)((x - 1)+(x - 3)) = $

    $(x + 2)(2x - 4)$.

    iii. You can factor out a common factor with a negative coefficient. For example, you can factor $-3x^2 - 6x$ as $-3x(x + 2)$, factoring out $-3x$.

    iv. You can factor by grouping, with the terms grouped by their common factors. For example, you can group the terms in the polynomial $12xy + 3x + 4y + 9x^2$:

    $$12xy + 3x + 4y + 9x^2 = 9x^2 + 3x + 12xy + 4y$$
    $$= 3x(3x + 1) + 4y(3x + 1)$$
    $$= (3x + 4y)(3x + 1)$$

    v. To factor trinomials of the form $x^2 + bx + c$, look for two numbers whose sum is b and whose product is c. Each of these numbers will be the second terms of two binomial factors whose first term is x. For example: $x^2 - 5x + 6 = (x - 2)(x - 3)$, where $-2 + (-3) = -5$ and $(-2)(-3) = 6$.

Factoring Trinomials *Being able to quickly factor trinomials will help you score higher on the SAT Math Level 2 Subject Test. Here's an example of how to factor $x^2 + 5x + 6$:*

$x^2 + 5x + 6$	*Write the trinomial you want to factor.*
$x^2 + 5x + 6$	*Identify b and c: b = 5 and c = 6* *What two numbers add to 5 and multiply to 6? 2 and 3*
$x^2 + 2x + 3x + 6$	*Write the expanded expression.*
$x(x+2) + 3(x+2)$	*Use the distributive property to pull commom factors from grouped terms.*
$(x+3)(x+2)$	*Simplify.*

3. There are special forms of polynomials that are always factored in the same way. These are worth memorizing:
   i. The difference of two squares: $A^2 - B^2 = (A + B)(A - B)$
   ii. Perfect square trinomials: $A^2 + 2AB + B^2 = (A + B)^2$ and $A^2 - 2AB + B^2 = (A - B)^2$
   iii. The sum of two cubes: $A^3 + B^3 = (A + B)(A^2 - AB + B^2)$
   iv. The difference of two cubes: $A^3 - B^3 = (A - B)(A^2 + AB + B^2)$

4. Dividing polynomials by monomials or by other polynomials can be done using different methods, including long division and synthetic division. For example, to divide $-4x^2 + 2x - 4$ by $x + 1$ using long division:

$$\begin{array}{r} -4x+6 \\ x+1{\overline{\smash{\big)}\,-4x^2+2x-4}} \\ \underline{4x^2+4x} \\ 6x-4 \\ \underline{-6x-6} \\ -10 \end{array}$$

IV. RATIONAL EXPRESSIONS

A. RATIONAL EXPRESSION BASICS

1. A rational expression is an expression in which a polynomial is divided by another polynomial. Some rational expressions are $\dfrac{1}{x+2}$, $\dfrac{x+2}{x-2}$, and $\dfrac{x+2}{2x^2-5x+3}$.

2. One of the most important things to know about rational expressions is that the expression in the denominator can never have a value of zero.

B. SIMPLIFYING RATIONAL EXPRESSIONS

1. A rational expression is considered to be simplified if its numerator and denominator have no common factors other than 1 and -1. A good strategy for simplifying a rational expression is to completely factor the numerator and the denominator, and then cancel out any common factors.

2. To multiply rational expressions, multiply numerators by numerators and denominators by denominators, as you would with fractions. To reduce the number of steps in the multiplication process, you can completely factor both numerators and denominators, and then cancel out any common factors before multiplying. For example, following is a product where the number of steps in the multiplication process was greatly reduced by factoring and canceling out common factors first:

$$\left(\frac{x+2}{x^2+x-12}\right)\left(\frac{x^2-9}{x^2+5x+6}\right)=\left(\frac{x+2}{(x-3)(x+4)}\right)\left(\frac{(x+3)(x-3)}{(x+2)(x+3)}\right)$$

$$=\left(\frac{\cancel{x+2}}{(\cancel{x-3})(x+4)}\right)\left(\frac{(\cancel{x+3})\,(\cancel{x-3})}{(\cancel{x+2})\,(\cancel{x+3})}\right)$$

$$=\frac{1}{x+4}$$

3. To divide rational expressions, first invert the divisor and then multiply numerators by numerators and denominators by denominators, again as you would with fractions. To reduce

the number of steps in the process, you can completely factor both numerators and denominators, and then cancel out any common factors before dividing and/or multiplying. Again, the expression in the denominator can never have a value of zero. For example:

$$\frac{\dfrac{x+2}{x^2+x-12}}{\dfrac{x^2+4x+4}{x^2-x-6}} = \left(\frac{x+2}{x^2+x-12}\right)\left(\frac{x^2-x-6}{x^2+4x+4}\right)$$

$$= \left(\frac{\cancel{x+2}}{\cancel{(x-3)}(x+4)}\right)\left(\frac{\cancel{(x+2)}\,\cancel{(x-3)}}{\cancel{(x+2)}\,\cancel{(x+2)}}\right)$$

$$= \frac{1}{x+4}$$

4. Adding and subtracting rational expressions is again very much like adding and subtracting fractions.

   i. If the expressions have the same denominator, the numerators can simply be added or subtracted, with the solution being the sum or difference over that same denominator. For example, $\dfrac{2}{x-3}-\dfrac{4-x}{x-3}$ can be simplified as $\dfrac{2}{x-3}-\dfrac{4-x}{x-3}=\dfrac{2-4+x}{x-3}=\dfrac{x-2}{x-3}$.

   ii. If the denominators are different, however, a least common denominator (LCD) must be found. Let's look at the process for adding $\dfrac{x+2}{x^2+x-12}+\dfrac{2}{x^2-9}$

   a) Completely factor both denominators: $x^2 + x - 12 = (x + 4)(x - 3)$, $x^2 - 9 = (x + 3)(x - 3)$

   b) Write the sum with the factored denominators:

   $$\frac{x+2}{(x+4)(x-3)}+\frac{2}{(x+3)(x-3)}$$

   c) After completely factoring both denominators, the LCD is the product of all the different factors, without repeats. So the LCD for this sum is $(x + 4)(x + 3)(x - 3)$. Note that the factor $(x - 3)$ was repeated.

d) Rewrite an equivalent expression for each rational expression so that the LCD is now the denominator:

$$\frac{(x+2)(x+3)}{(x+4)(x+3)(x-3)} + \frac{2(x+4)}{(x+4)(x+3)(x-3)}$$

e) Once all expressions have the same denominator (the LCD), add or subtract numerators, with the solution being the sum or difference over the LCD.

$$\frac{(x+2)(x+3)+2(x+4)}{(x+4)(x+3)(x-3)} = \frac{x^2+3x+2x+6+2x+8}{(x+4)(x+3)(x-3)}$$

$$= \frac{x^2+7x+14}{(x+4)(x+3)(x-3)}$$

V. RADICAL EXPRESSIONS

A. RADICAL EXPRESSION BASICS

1. The symbol $\sqrt{}$ is called a *radical sign*. The number under the radical sign is called a *radicand*. For roots greater than two, a number, called an *index*, is shown in the radical sign that tells which root to take. For example, $\sqrt[3]{x}$ means take the cube root of x. Together, the radical sign and the radicand form a *radical expression*.

2. Square root: The symbol $\sqrt{}$ is used to indicate a principal square root. The principal square root must be nonnegative. This means that even if $\sqrt{x}$, where x is a nonnegative real number, has two real square roots, only the nonnegative square root is indicated. For example: $\sqrt{4} = 2$, not -2. Also, for any real number a, $\sqrt{a^2} = |a|$.

3. Cube root: The symbol $\sqrt[3]{}$ is used to indicate a cube root. The cube root of x is written as $\sqrt[3]{x}$. This means that if $\sqrt[3]{x} = y$, then $y^3 = x$. Also, for any real number a, $\sqrt[3]{a^3} = a$. This means that a cube root can be simplified if any expressions in the radicand can be written as cubes. For example: $\sqrt[3]{9x \bullet 3x^2} = \sqrt[3]{27x^3} = \sqrt[3]{3^3 x^3} = 3x$.

4. *n*th roots: The symbol $\sqrt[n]{}$ is used to indicate an *n*th root. If *n* is even, then $\sqrt[n]{a^n} = |a|$ for any real number *a*. If *n* is odd, then $\sqrt[n]{a^n} = a$ for any real number *a*.

B. ROOTS AND RATIONAL EXPONENTS

1. Roots can be represented using rational exponents. For example, $\sqrt{a} = a^{\frac{1}{2}}$ and $\sqrt[3]{a} = a^{\frac{1}{3}}$. In general, $a^{\frac{1}{n}} = \sqrt[n]{a}$. If *a* is negative, then *n* must be odd. Otherwise, *n* can be any natural number (1, 2, 3, . . .).

2. Expressions containing roots and exponents can be represented using rational exponents of the form $a^{\frac{m}{n}}$, where $\sqrt[n]{a^m}$ is a real number, $n \geq 2$ is an integer, and $\dfrac{m}{n}$ is positive and reduced to lowest terms.

3. There are two ways to define $a^{\frac{m}{n}}$:

   i. $a^{\frac{m}{n}} = \sqrt[n]{a^m}$. This means that *a* is first raised to the *m*th power and then the *n*th root is taken.

   ii. $a^{\frac{m}{n}} = \left(\sqrt[n]{a}\right)^m$. This means that first the *n*th root of *a* is taken, and then the result is raised to the *m*th power.

   iii. Both ways can be used interchangeably depending on the requirements of the situation. The results are the same.

   iv. A negative rational exponent is handled in the same way as a negative integral exponent: $a^{-\frac{m}{n}} = \dfrac{1}{a^{\frac{m}{n}}}$

4. The same rules of exponents that apply to integral exponents also apply to rational exponents. These rules include the product, quotient, power, products-to-powers, and quotients-to-powers rules.

C. SIMPLIFYING RADICAL EXPRESSIONS

1. Radical expressions can be simplified by rewriting the expressions using rational exponents and then using the rules of exponents to simplify the expressions. Simplified

expressions can then be rewritten using radicals. For example:

$$\left(\sqrt{x}\right)\left(\sqrt[3]{x}\right)=\left(x^{\frac{1}{2}}\right)\left(x^{\frac{1}{3}}\right)=x^{\frac{1}{2}+\frac{1}{3}}=x^{\frac{5}{6}}=\sqrt[6]{x^5}\ .$$

2. Radical expressions can also be simplified by factoring.

    For example: $\sqrt{8}=\sqrt{4\bullet2}=\sqrt{2^2\bullet2}=\sqrt{2^2}\left(\sqrt{2}\right)=2\sqrt{2}$ and

    $\sqrt[3]{32x^5y^3z^2}=\sqrt[3]{8\bullet4\bullet x^3\bullet x^2\bullet y^3\bullet z^2}=2xy\sqrt[3]{4x^2z^2}$.

3. You can also multiply radical expressions. The product rule

    for radicals says that $\left(\sqrt[n]{a}\right)\left(\sqrt[n]{b}\right)=\sqrt[n]{ab}$ if $\sqrt[n]{a}$ and $\sqrt[n]{b}$ are real

    numbers. For example: $\left(\sqrt[3]{8}\right)\left(\sqrt[3]{27}\right)=\sqrt[3]{216}=6$.

4. To simplify some algebraic expressions, you may also have to add, subtract, and divide radical expressions.

    i. Radicals that have the same indices and radicands are called *like radicals*. Like radicals can be added and subtracted by combining them just as you would combine like terms. For example: $\sqrt{2}+2\sqrt{2}=3\sqrt{2}$ and $5\sqrt[3]{x}-2\sqrt[3]{x}=3\sqrt[3]{x}$.

    ii. Some radicals may require simplification before they can be added or subtracted. For example: $\sqrt{18}+\sqrt{50}=\sqrt{9\bullet2}+\sqrt{25\bullet2}=3\sqrt{2}+5\sqrt{2}=8\sqrt{2}$.

5. An expression that contains a radical expression in its denominator is not considered to be completely simplified. To completely simplify the expression, the denominator must be "rationalized," which means writing an equivalent expression without any radicals in the denominator. For example, to rationalize the denominator of $\dfrac{3}{\sqrt{2}}$, multiply both the denominator and the denominator by the radical that will produce a perfect square of the radicand: $\dfrac{3}{\sqrt{2}}\bullet\dfrac{\sqrt{2}}{\sqrt{2}}=\dfrac{3\sqrt{2}}{\sqrt{4}}=\dfrac{3\sqrt{2}}{2}$. Note that multiplying by $\dfrac{\sqrt{2}}{\sqrt{2}}$ is the same as multiplying by 1.

Roots and Radical Exponents on Your Calculator *Your calculator most likely has a key designated specifically for square roots. But suppose you want to find the 5th root of 32? Although there is no calculator key marked "5th root," you can use your calculator to find any root for which you can represent the expression with rational exponents.*

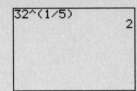

EQUATIONS

KEY VOCABULARY

Conditional equation An equation that is not an identity but is true for at least one real number.

Equation A statement of equality between algebraic expressions.

Equivalent equations Equations that have the same value or solution.

Identity An equation that is true for all real numbers for which both sides are defined, no matter what values are chosen.

Inconsistent equation An equation that is not true for any real numbers.

Linear equation An equation that can be written in the form $y = mx + b$.

Properties of equality The properties that say if you add, subtract, multiply, or divide both sides of an equation by the same value, the resulting equation is equivalent to the original equation.

System of equations A group of two or more equations containing two or more variables, whose solution is the set of values that satisfy all equations in the system.

I. EQUATIONS

A. EQUATION BASICS

1. An equation is a statement of equality between algebraic expressions. An equation contains an equal sign, but an expression does not!

2. Equivalent equations have the same value. For example, $x + 2 = 5$ and $2x + 4 = 10$ are equivalent, both having the solution $x = 3$.

B. SOLVING EQUATIONS

1. The process of solving an equation involves repeatedly transforming the original equation into equivalent equations, with the goal of isolating a variable and reaching an equation of the form "variable = a number."

2. Properties of equality are used to solve equations.

   i. The addition property of equality says that the same real number or algebraic expression can be added to both sides of an equation without changing the solution of the equation. Subtraction is included in this property of equality as the additive inverse. For example, add 3 to both sides the equation $x - 3 = 5$. Then, $x - 3 + 3 = 5 + 3$ has a solution of $x = 8$.

   ii. The multiplication property of equality says that both sides of an equation may be multiplied by the same real number or algebraic expression without changing the solution of the equation. Division is included in this property of equality as the multiplicative inverse. So, multiply both sides of the equation $\frac{1}{2}x = 6$ by 2: $2\left(\frac{1}{2}\right)x = 6 \cdot 2$ to get a solution of $x = 12$.

Test Tip

Check Your Solutions! Use Your Calculator! The last thing you want is a wrong answer due to a careless error. One of the most effective ways of eliminating errors is to check your solutions to equations: Just plug the solution into the original equation and check that the resulting equation is true. If you think checking answers will take too much valuable time, speed up the process by using your calculator to evaluate the expressions.

C. CATEGORIZING EQUATIONS

1. An identity is an equation that is true for all real numbers for which both sides are defined. An example of an identity is $a + 2 = a + 2$. This equation is true for all numbers.

2. A conditional equation is not an identity but is true for at least one real number. An example of a conditional equation is $a + 2 = 5$. This equation is true for $a = 3$.

3. An inconsistent equation is not true for any real numbers. An example of an inconsistent equation is $a = a + 1$. There is no real number that is equal to itself plus one.

II. LINEAR EQUATIONS IN ONE VARIABLE

A. LINEAR EQUATION BASICS

1. A linear equation in one variable can be written in the form $ax + b = 0$, where a and b are real numbers and $a \neq 0$.

B. SOLVING LINEAR EQUATIONS

1. Solving a linear equation in one variable is the process of identifying all values of the variable that, when substituted into the equation, make a true statement.

2. The process of solving a linear equation includes the following steps:
   i. Simplify the algebraic expressions on both sides. Make sure all grouping symbols are removed and all like terms are combined.
   ii. Transform the equation so that all variable terms are on one side of the equation and all constants are on the other.
   iii. Solve by isolating the variable.
   iv. Check the solution by substituting it for the variable in the original equation.

3. To solve a linear equation with fractions, you must follow some additional steps:
   i. Identify the lowest common denominator of the fractions in the equation.
   ii. Multiply both sides of the equation by that lowest common denominator.
   iii. Clear and simplify all the fractions.
   iv. Simplify the algebraic expressions on both sides. Make sure all grouping symbols are removed and all like terms are combined.

v. Transform the equation so that all variable terms are on one side of the equation and all constants are on the other.

vi. Solve by isolating the variable.

vii. Check the solution by substituting it for the variable in the original equation.

III. SYSTEMS OF LINEAR EQUATIONS IN TWO VARIABLES

A. SYSTEM-OF-LINEAR-EQUATIONS BASICS

1. A system of linear equations consists of multiple equations with multiple variables. The solution of a system of equations is a set or sets of numbers that, when substituted into the equations, will satisfy all the equations in the system.

2. A system of linear equations in two variables consists of two equations containing two variables. The solution of a system of linear equations in two variables is an ordered pair that, when substituted into both equations, will make both equations true.

3. A system of linear equations in two variables can have one solution, no solutions, or infinitely many solutions.

B. SOLVING SYSTEMS OF LINEAR EQUATIONS IN TWO VARIABLES

1. Solve by graphing: Graph both equations on the same coordinate plane. The intersection of the graphs represents the solution to the linear system.

Solve Linear Systems on Your Calculator! *You can use your calculator to solve linear systems by graphing. Here's how you can solve the following system:*

$$\begin{cases} y = 0.5x \\ 2 + y = x \end{cases}$$

▶ *Make sure both equations in your system have the y-variable isolated on one side. For example, rewrite 2 + y = x as y = x − 2.*

(continued)

(*continued*)

▶ *Enter both equations into your calculator: Press [Y=] and enter one equation for Y₁= and the other equation for Y₂=.*

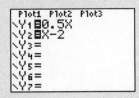

▶ *View the graphs of both equations: Press [GRAPH].*

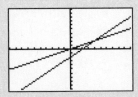

▶ *Identify the point of intersection: Press [2ᴺᴰ] [TRACE] to get the CALC menu. Then press 5 to launch to intersect function.*

▶ *Press ENTER to complete the prompts and get the solution, which is (4, 2).*

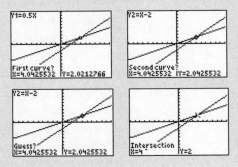

2. Solve by substitution: This strategy can be used to solve a system quickly if one equation already has one variable isolated on one side.

   i. The following steps can be followed to solve a linear system by substitution:

     a) Solve either equation so that one variable is isolated on one side. The expression on the other side is equal to this variable.

     b) Substitute the expression for the variable in step (a) for that same in the other equation.

     c) Solve the other equation.

     d) Substitute the solution for the other variable into either equation and solve for the first variable.

   ii. Here's how substitution can be used to solve the system $\begin{cases} y = 0.5x \\ 2+y = x \end{cases}$:

     a) Variables are already isolated on one side in both equations.

     b) Either variable could be substituted. Let's substitute $0.5x$ for y in the other equation: $2 + 0.5x = x$.

     c) Solve the other equation:

$$2+0.5x = x$$
$$2+0.5x-0.5x = x-0.5x$$
$$2 = 0.5x$$
$$2(2) = 2(0.5x)$$
$$4 = x$$

     d) Substitute the solution $x = 4$ for x in either equation and solve for y: $2 + y = 4$, so $y = 2$. The solution of the system is (4, 2).

3. Solve by addition: This system can be used to solve a system quickly if one variable has opposite coefficients in the two equations.

   i. The following steps can be followed to solve a linear system by addition:

     a) Rewrite both equations in the form $Ax + By = C$.

     b) Multiply one or both equations by numbers so that the coefficients of either the x-variables or the y-variables are opposites.

c) Add the equations. The variable with the opposite coefficients will be eliminated and the sum will be a linear equation in one variable.

d) Solve the equation.

e) Substitute the solution into either equation and solve for the other variable.

ii. Here's how addition can be used to solve the system $\begin{cases} 3x + 2y = -1 \\ -3x + y = -5 \end{cases}$:

a) Both equations are already in the form $Ax + By = C$.

b) The coefficients of the x-variables are opposites.

c) Add the equations:

$$\begin{array}{r} 3x + 2y = -1 \\ -3x + y = -5 \\ \hline 0x + 3y = -6 \end{array}$$

d) Solve the equation: $3y = -6$, so $y = -2$.

e) Substitute $y = -2$ into either equation and solve for x:

$$\begin{array}{r} 3x + 2y = -1 \\ 3x + 2(-2) = -1 \\ 3x - 4 = -1 \\ 3x = 3 \\ x = 1 \end{array}$$

f) The solution is $(1, -2)$.

4. Systems of equations can also be solved by using matrices. An example of how to solve a linear system in two variables using matrices and Kramer's rule is given in Chapter 8: Matrices.

IV. POLYNOMIAL EQUATIONS

A. SOLVING QUADRATIC EQUATIONS

1. The square root property: The square root property says that if $x^2 = k$, then $x = \pm\sqrt{k}$. For example, if you are solving the quadratic equation $x^2 - 2 = 7$, you can rewrite the equation as $x^2 = 9$ and use the square root property to determine that $x = \pm\sqrt{9} = \pm 3$.

2. Factoring: The zero-product principle says that if the product of two algebraic expressions is 0, then at least one of the factors is 0. So, you can write the quadratic equation in standard form as $ax^2 + bx + c = 0$, factor the left side completely, set each term containing a variable to 0, and solve. Here's an example of how it works when solving the equation:

$$0 = (x+3)(x-2)$$

   Then, $x + 3 = 0$ and $x = -3$. Also, $x - 2 = 0$ and $x = 2$. So, there are two solutions for x, -3 or 2.

3. Completing the square: If an equation cannot be solved by factoring, completing the square lets you write an equivalent equation that can be solved by applying the square root property. Here are the steps for completing the square:

   i. Isolate the binomial $x^2 + bx$ on the left side of the equation. If necessary, move the constant c to the right side.

   ii. Add $\left(\dfrac{b}{2}\right)^2$, which is the square of half the coefficient of x, to both sides of the equation. (Note that the addition property of equality keeps the equations equivalent before and after $\left(\dfrac{b}{2}\right)^2$ is added.)

   iii. The expression on the left side is now a perfect square trinomial. Factor the left side.

   iv. Solve the equation.

   v. For example, $0 = x^2 - 4x$ has a b-value of -4 and $\left(\dfrac{b}{2}\right)^2 = \left(\dfrac{-4}{2}\right)^2 = 4$. So, add 4

   to both sides of the equation:

$$0 = x^2 - 4x$$
$$4 = x^2 - 4x + 4$$
$$4 = (x-2)^2$$
$$4 = (x-2)^2$$
$$2 = x - 2 \text{ or } -2 = x - 2$$
$$4 = x \text{ or } 0 = x$$

4. The quadratic formula: The quadratic formula is $x = \dfrac{-b \pm \sqrt{b^2 - 4ac}}{2a}$. It's worth memorizing, because it always works. Simply identify the coefficients that correspond to *a*, *b*, and *c*, and then plug them into the formula. It's important to remember to always keep the plus-or-minus symbol in your calculations, so that solutions are not lost. The quadratic formula has the advantage that it will allow you to identify complex roots as well as real roots.

5. Example: Find the solution or solutions for $0 = x^2 + 2x - 8$. Using the quadratic formula: $a = 1$, $b = 2$, and $c = -8$:

$$x = \frac{-2 \pm \sqrt{2^2 - 4(1)(-8)}}{2(1)}$$

$$= \frac{-2 \pm \sqrt{4 + 32}}{2}$$

$$= \frac{-2 \pm 6}{2}$$

The solution is $x = -4$, $x = 2$.

Solve Quadratic Equations on Your Calculator! *When a quadratic equation is graphed, its solutions are the x-values that corresponds to y = 0 or where the graph crosses the x-axis. Because it is difficult to identify precise solutions by simply look-ing at a graph, graphing is not usually one of the recommended strategies for solving quadratic equations. However, simple solutions can be visualized, and graphing is also a good way to check if answers are reasonable. Here's how you can solve the quadratic equation x² + x − 6 = 0 on your calculator:*

▶ *Enter the equation into your calculator: Press [Y=] and enter the equation.*

```
Plot1 Plot2 Plot3
\Y1■X²+X-6■
\Y2=
\Y3=
\Y4=
\Y5=
\Y6=
\Y7=
```

(continued)

(continued)

> ▶ *View the graph of the equation: Press [GRAPH].*

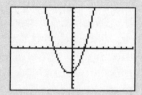

> ▶ *Identify the points where the graph intersect the x-axis: Press [2ᴺᴰ][TRACE] to get the CALC menu. Then press 2 to launch the zero function.*

> ▶ *Press ENTER and complete the prompts. Use the arrows to move the arrows to identify boundaries around each point where the graph intersects the x-axis. Get the solutions, which are x = −3 and x = 2.*

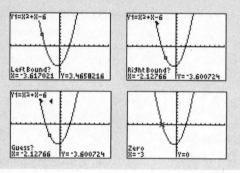

6. There are different ways you can gather information about the solutions of a quadratic equation.

   i. Graph the equation: If the graph intersects the x-axis in two places, the equation has two real solutions; if the graph is tangent to the x-axis (intersects in one place), the equation has one real solution; and if the graph does not intersect the *x*-axis, the equation has no real solutions.

   ii. The discriminant: The discriminant is determined by substituting corresponding variables for coefficients *a*, *b*, and *c* into the expression $b^2 - 4ac$. If the discriminant is positive, the equation has two real solutions; if the discriminant is zero, the equation has one real solution; and if the discriminant is negative, the equation has no real solutions.

B. SOLVING POLYNOMIAL EQUATIONS

1. Polynomial equations with more than two solutions can be solved by using a combination of strategies. For example, if a third-degree polynomial expression can be written as the product of a monomial and a quadratic equation, the monomial can be set to zero and solved for one solution, and the quadratic equation can be set to zero and solved for two solutions.

2. The number of unique real solutions of a polynomial equation is equal to the number of times its graph intersects the *x*-axis.

V. RATIONAL EQUATIONS

A. RATIONAL EQUATION BASICS

1. A rational equation contains one or more rational expressions.

2. An example of a rational equation is $\dfrac{1}{2-x} + \dfrac{5}{6} = \dfrac{1}{3}$.

B. SOLVING RATIONAL EQUATIONS

1. Just as the LCD was used to add and subtract rational expressions, it can be used to solve rational equations. When each side of a rational equation is multiplied by the LCD, the equation is cleared of fractions.

2. To solve the rational equation $\dfrac{1}{2-x}+\dfrac{5}{6}=\dfrac{1}{3}$, follow these steps:

   i. First determine that the lowest common denominator is $6(2-x)$.

   ii. Multiply both sides of the equation by the LCD $6(2-x)$ to clear the fractions and then solve the equation:

$$6(2-x)\left(\frac{1}{2-x}+\frac{5}{6}\right)=6(2-x)\left(\frac{1}{3}\right)$$

$$6(2-x)\left(\frac{1}{2-x}\right)+6(2-x)\left(\frac{5}{6}\right)=6(2-x)\left(\frac{1}{3}\right)$$

$$6(2-x)\left(\frac{1}{2-x}\right)+6(2-x)\left(\frac{5}{6}\right)=6(2-x)\left(\frac{1}{3}\right)$$

$$6+10-5x=4-2x$$
$$-3x=-12$$
$$x=4$$

 ## VI. EXPONENTIAL EQUATIONS

A. EXPONENTIAL EQUATION BASICS

1. An exponential equation contains a variable as an exponent.
2. Some examples of exponential equations are $3^x = 81$, $2^{4x-3} = 32$, and $5^x = 100$.

B. SOLVING EXPONENTIAL EQUATIONS

1. In an exponential equation, if $b^M = b^N$, then $M = N$. This means that if each side of the equation can be expressed as a power of the same base, then the equation can be solved by writing an equation that sets the powers equal to each other and then solving that equation.
2. To solve the exponential equation $2^{4x-3} = 32$, you can rewrite 32 as 2^5. The equation then becomes $2^{4x-3} = 2^5$, and you can solve it by solving $4x - 3 = 5$ for a solution of $x = 2$.

VII. RADICAL EQUATIONS

A. RADICAL EQUATION BASICS

1. A radical equation has a variable in a square root, a cube root, or an *n*th root.
2. An example of a radical equation is $\sqrt[4]{x} = 3$.

B. SOLVING RADICAL EQUATIONS

1. To solve a radical equation, first write the equation so the radical with the variable and index *n* is on one side. Raise both sides of the equation to the *n*th power to eliminate the radical. If necessary, repeat the process to eliminate all radicals. Then solve the equation.
2. To solve the radical equation $\sqrt[4]{x} = 3$, first raise both sides to the 4th power to eliminate the radical: $x = 3^4$. Since $3^4 = 81$, the solution is $x = 81$.

VIII. SOLVING A FORMULA FOR A VARIABLE

A. FORMULA AND VARIABLES

1. Formulas often contain multiple variables, as well as exponents, radicals, and other operations. A common challenge is to rewrite a formula in terms of one of its variables.
2. An example of a formula that has multiple variables is the formula for the area *A* of a circle, $A = \pi r^2$, where *r* is the radius of the circle.

B. SOLVING FOR A VARIABLE

1. When solving a linear equation in one variable, there is only one variable you need to solve for. Sometimes you will need to work with an equation or a formula that has more than one variable and solve for one of the variables. You can solve these problems using the same techniques you used to solve one-variable equations.

2. Use the addition and multiplication properties of equality to isolate the specified variable on one side of the equation. Note that the other side of the equation will most likely be an algebraic expression, not just a number.

3. To solve the formula $A = \pi r^2$ for r, follow these steps:

$$A = \pi r^2$$

$$\frac{A}{\pi} = \frac{\pi r^2}{\pi}$$

$$\frac{A}{\pi} = r^2$$

$$\sqrt{\frac{A}{\pi}} = \sqrt{r^2}$$

$$r = \sqrt{\frac{A}{\pi}}$$

INEQUALITIES

KEY VOCABULARY

Absolute inequality An inequality that is true for all values of a variable.

Compound inequality Inequalities joined by the words *and* or *or*.

Conditional inequality An inequality that is true for some but not all values of a variable.

Equivalent inequalities Inequalities that have the same solution set.

Inequality A comparison between algebraic expressions.

Interval notation A notation for representing solutions of inequalities. For example, the solution set that includes all real numbers greater than or equal to 2 is represented as $[2, \infty)$ in interval notation.

Linear inequality in one variable An inequality that can be written in the form $ax + b > 0$, $ax + b < 0$, $ax + b \geq 0$, or $ax + b \leq 0$.

Properties of inequality These properties say if you add or subtract the same value to both sides of an inequality, the resulting inequality is equivalent to the original inequality; if you multiply or divide both sides of an inequality by the same positive value, the resulting inequality is equivalent to the original inequality; and if you multiply or divide both sides of an inequality by the same negative value, the resulting inequality is equivalent to the original inequality as long as the direction of the inequality symbol is reversed.

Set-builder notation A notation for representing solutions of inequalities. For example, the solution set that includes all real numbers greater than or equal to 2 is represented as $\{x \mid x \geq 2\}$ in set-builder notation.

System of inequalities A group of two or more inequalities containing two or more variables, whose solution is the set of values that satisfy all inequalities in the system.

 I. INEQUALITIES

A. INEQUALITY BASICS

1. An inequality is a comparison of expressions. Comparisons are the following:
     i. < (less than)
     ii. > (greater than)
     iii. ≤ (less than or equal to)
     iv. ≥ (greater than or equal to)
2. Compound inequalities are inequalities joined by operators such as *and* and *or*. Inequalities can also be written with more than one inequality sign. For example, the conditions "*x* is greater than or equal to 3" and "*x* is less than 7" can be written as $3 \leq x < 7$.
3. Inequalities are said to have a "sense" indicated by the direction of the sign. Two inequalities have the "same sense" if their signs point in the same direction and the "opposite sense" if their signs point in opposite directions.

B. SOLUTIONS OF INEQUALITIES

1. The solution of an inequality is all the values of the variable in the inequality that make the inequality true.
2. Unlike equations, which usually have solutions that are single values, inequalities have solution sets of the form $x > 1$ or $y \leq 5$.
3. Inequalities are not defined for complex numbers. The solution sets of inequalities consist only of real numbers.
4. Equivalent inequalities have the same solution. For example, $4x > 8$ and $x + 3 > 5$ are equivalent, both having the solution $x > 2$.

5. Solutions of inequalities can be represented in different ways:
    i. Set-builder notation: $\{x \mid x \geq 2\}$
    ii. Interval notation: Interval notation translates set-builder notation into more compact forms. Here are some interval notation examples:
        a) $[2, \infty)$ represents $\{x \mid x \geq 2\}$
        b) $(-3,3]$ represents $\{x \mid -3 < x \leq 3\}$
        c) $(-\infty,100)$ represents $\{x \mid x < 100\}$
    iii. Graphs: Solutions of inequalities can also be represented graphically. Parentheses or open circles represent endpoints that are not included in the solution. Square brackets or closed circles represent endpoints that are included in the solution. Here are some examples:
        a) (a, ∞) represents $\{x \mid x > a\}$

        b) $[a,b)$ represents $\{x \mid a \leq x < b\}$

Test Tip

Interval Notation *Remember that in interval notation, parentheses indicate endpoints that are not included in the solution and square brackets indicate endpoints that are included in the solution. Parentheses are always used with ∞ or $-\infty$.*

C. SOLVING INEQUALITIES

1. The process of solving an inequality involves repeatedly transforming the original inequality into equivalent inequalities, with the goal of isolating a variable and reaching an inequality of a form such as "variable $<$ a number" or "a number $\geq$ variable."

2. Just as properties of equality are used to solve equations, properties of inequality are used to solve inequalities, but with one very important difference: When both sides of an inequality are multiplied or divided by a negative number, the direction of the inequality sign is reversed.

3. Here are the properties of inequality explained in more detail:

    i. The addition property of inequality says that the same real number or algebraic expression can be added to both sides of an inequality without changing the solution of the inequality. Subtraction is included in this property of inequality as the additive inverse.

    ii. The positive multiplication property of inequality says that both sides of an inequality may be multiplied by the same positive real number or algebraic expression without changing the solution of the inequality. Division by positive real numbers or algebraic expressions is included in this property of equality as the multiplicative inverse.

    iii. The negative multiplication property of inequality says that both sides of an inequality may be multiplied by the same negative real number or algebraic expression without changing the solution of the inequality as long as the direction of the inequality symbol is reversed. Division by negative real numbers or algebraic expressions is included in this property of equality as the multiplicative inverse.

Quick Reference: Properties of Inequality

Property	Rule
Addition property of inequality	If $a < b$, then $a + c < b + c$. If $a < b$, then $a - c < b - c$.
Positive multiplication property of inequality	If $a < b$ and c is positive, then $ac < bc$. If $a < b$ and c is positive, then $\frac{a}{c} < \frac{b}{c}$.
Negative multiplication property of inequality	If $a < b$ and c is negative, then $ac > bc$. If $a < b$ and c is negative, then $\frac{a}{c} > \frac{b}{c}$.

D. CATEGORIZING INEQUALITIES

1. A conditional inequality is true for some but not all values of the variable. An example of a conditional inequality is $x - 2 < 7$. This inequality is true for all real values of $x < 9$, but not true for $x \geq 9$.

2. An absolute inequality is true for all values of the variable. An example of an absolute inequality is $x < x + 1$. This inequality is true for all real values of x.

II. LINEAR INEQUALITIES IN ONE VARIABLE

A. LINEAR INEQUALITY BASICS

1. A linear inequality in one variable can be written in the forms $ax + b > 0$, $ax + b < 0$, $ax + b \geq 0$, and $ax + b \leq 0$, where a and b are real numbers and $a \neq 0$.
2. The solution of a linear inequality in one variable can be graphed on a number line.

B. SOLVING LINEAR INEQUALITIES

1. Solving a linear inequality in one variable is the process of identifying all values of the variable that, when substituted into the inequality, make a true statement.
2. The process of solving a linear inequality includes the following steps:
   i. Simplify the algebraic expressions on both sides. Make sure all grouping symbols are removed and all like terms are combined.
   ii. Use the addition property of inequality to transform the inequality so that all variable terms are on one side of the inequality and all constants are on the other.
   iii. Solve by isolating the variable. Use the multiplication property of inequality to isolate the variable. If both sides are multiplied or divided by a negative number, make sure to reverse the direction of the inequality symbol.
   iv. Represent the solution in set-builder notation, interval notation, or by graphing.
   v. Check the solution by testing values that are both included and not included in the solution. Values that are included in the solution should make the inequality true; values that are not included in the solution should make the inequality false.

III. COMPOUND INEQUALITIES

A. COMPOUND INEQUALITY BASICS

1. A compound inequality is formed when two inequalities are joined by the words *and* or *or*.

2. Solutions to compound inequalities are found by identifying the intersections or unions of the solution sets of the individual inequalities.

B. COMPOUND INEQUALITIES WITH *AND*

1. When two inequalities joined by the word *and* form a compound inequality, the solution set *only* includes values of the variable that make *both* inequalities true.

2. If *A* is the solution set of one inequality and *B* is the solution set of the other inequality in a compound inequality formed by the word *and*, then the solution set of the compound inequality is the intersection of *A* and *B*. The intersection of set *A* and set *B*, which is symbolized *A* ∩ *B*, is the set of all elements that are common to both *A* and *B*.

3. To solve a compound inequality joined by *and*, solve each inequality separately and then identify the intersection of the solution sets. By graphing the separate inequalities on a number line, the area of intersection can be identified visually. Represent the solution in set-builder notation or interval notation.

C. COMPOUND INEQUALITIES WITH *OR*

1. When two inequalities joined by the word *or* form a compound inequality, the solution set includes all values of the variable that make either of the inequalities true.

2. If *A* is the solution set of one inequality and *B* is the solution set of the other inequality in a compound inequality formed by the word *or*, then the solution set of the compound inequality is the union of *A* and *B*. The union of set *A* and set *B*, which is symbolized *A* ∪ *B*, is the set of all elements that are either in *A* or in *B*, or in both *A* and *B*.

3. To solve a compound inequality joined by *or*, solve each inequality separately and then identify the union of the solution sets. By graphing the separate inequalities on a number line, the area of union can be identified visually. Represent the solution in set-builder notation or interval notation.

IV. LINEAR INEQUALITIES IN TWO VARIABLES

A. LINEAR-INEQUALITIES-IN-TWO-VARIABLES BASICS

1. A system of linear inequalities in two variables is similar to an equation of the form $Ax + By = C$, except the $=$ symbol is changed to $<$, $>$, $\leq$, or $\geq$.
2. Examples of linear inequalities in two variables are $x + y > 5$ and $4x - 2y \leq -6$.

B. SOLUTIONS OF LINEAR INEQUALITIES IN TWO VARIABLES

1. A solution of a linear inequality in two variables is an ordered pair that makes the inequality true. A linear inequality in two variables may have infinitely many solutions.
2. Solutions of linear inequalities can be graphed in the coordinate plane, with a shaded area that represents all ordered pairs that satisfy the inequality.

C. GRAPHING LINEAR INEQUALITIES IN TWO VARIABLES

1. To graph a linear inequality, first replace the inequality symbol with an equal sign. Graph the corresponding equation in the coordinate plane. If the inequality symbol was $<$ or $>$, draw a dashed line. If the inequality symbol was $\leq$ or $\geq$, draw a solid line. The graph of the linear inequality $f(x) \geq x + 3$ is shown with a solid line and the graph of the linear inequality $f(x) > -x + 5$ is shown with a dotted line.

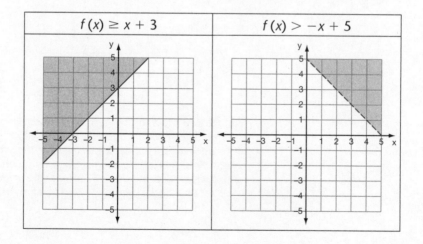

$f(x) \geq x + 3$	$f(x) > -x + 5$

2. The line that corresponds to the equation now divides the coordinate plane into two half-planes. The solution of the linear inequality will be represented by shading one of the half-planes to show that all the included ordered pairs, when substituted into the inequality, will make it true. You now have to decide which half-plane to shade.

3. To determine which half-plane to shade, choose a point in one of the planes and substitute the values into the inequality. If the values make the inequality true, then shade the half-plane that includes that point. If the values make the inequality false, then shade the other half-plane.

Graph Linear Inequalities in Two Variables on Your Calculator
Here's how to graph the solution of the linear inequality $x + y > 5$ on a calculator. After replacing the inequality symbol with an equal sign, make sure the equation is written in the "y =" form: $y = -x + 5$. Then follow these steps:

▶ *Press [Y=] and enter the equation.*

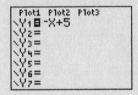

▶ *Press [GRAPH] to see the graph.*

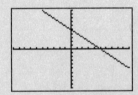

▶ *To add shading, return to the [Y=] screen and, on the line of your equation, press the left arrows to move the cursor to the backslash at the left of the Y. Press [ENTER] to change the shading and line options. Because the "y=" form of the inequality is $y > -x + 5$, the shading should be above the line of*

(continued)

(continued)

the equation. On the calculator, this type of shading is represented by a symbol that looks like the upper part of a diagonal half-plane.

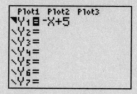

▶ *Press [GRAPH] to see the graph with shading.*

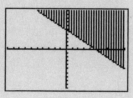

D. SYSTEMS OF LINEAR INEQUALITIES IN TWO VARIABLES

1. A system of linear inequalities in two variables consists of two inequalities with two variables. The solution of a system of linear inequalities in two variables is a set of ordered pairs that, when substituted into both inequalities, will make both inequalities true.

2. The solution of a system of linear equations in two variables is graphed on the coordinate plane. Each inequality is graphed and the solution of the system is given by the intersection of the half-planes that represent the solutions of each linear inequality. The solution set of the inequalities $y > -x + 5$ and $y \leq x + 2$ is shown as the intersection of these two inequalities on the graph.

A graph of the linear inequality $f(x) > -x + 5$ is shown with a dotted line.

$y > -x + 5$ and $y \leq x + 2$ showing both graphs and the intersection	$y > -x + 5$ and $y \leq x + 2$ showing only the intersection
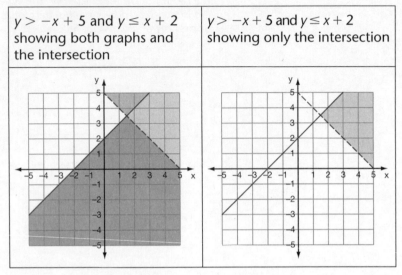	

E. NONLINEAR INEQUALITIES

1. Nonlinear inequalities include polynomial inequalities and rational inequalities. As with linear inequalities, the solutions of nonlinear inequalities are graphed.

2. As with linear inequalities, the first step in solving a nonlinear inequality is to replace the inequality symbol with an equal sign. The solution of the equation is graphed, and then a point is tested to see which half-plane should be shaded. Following is the graph of the quadratic inequality $f(x) \geq x^2$:

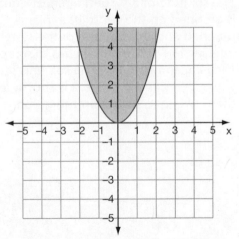

Graph Nonlinear Inequalities on Your Calculator *Here's how to graph the solution of the nonlinear inequality $x^2 + y \leq 5$ on a calculator. After replacing the inequality symbol with an equal sign, make sure the equation is written in the "y = " form: $y = -x^2 + 5$. Then follow these steps:*

▶ *Press [Y=] and enter the equation.*

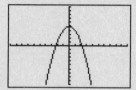

▶ *Press [GRAPH] to see the graph.*

▶ *To add shading, return to the [Y=] screen and, on the line of your equation, press the left arrows to move the cursor to the backslash at the left of the Y. Press [ENTER] to change the shading and line options. Because the "y = " form of the inequality is $y \leq -x^2 + 5$, the shading should be below the curve of the equation. On the calculator, this type of shading is represented by a symbol that looks like the lower part of a diagonal half-plane.*

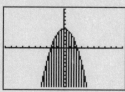

▶ *Press [GRAPH] to see the graph with shading.*

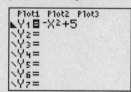

REPRESENTATION
AND MODELING

KEY VOCABULARY

Exponential decay A situation where a quantity decreases exponentially.

Exponential growth A situation where a quantity increases exponentially.

Mathematical model An equation or formula that represents a real-world situation by representing relationships between quantities represented as variables.

Rate of change The rate of change of the dependent variable based on the per unit change of the independent variable.

I. MODELING REAL-WORLD SITUATIONS MATHEMATICALLY

A. REPRESENTATION AND MODELING

1. A *mathematical model* is an equation or formula that represents a real-world situation by representing relationships between quantities represented as variables.

2. A mathematical model can be used by substituting values for the variables. For example, the equation $h = -16t^2 + 100$ gives the height h, after t seconds, of a ball dropped from a height of 100 feet (approximately a 10-story building). To find the height of the ball after 2 seconds, substitute 2 for t: $h = -16(2)^2 + 100 = 36$ feet.

Make Sure Your Model Is Valid If the mathematical model does not accurately represent the real-world situation, then even if there are correct mathematical solutions based on the model, the solutions will not be valid for the real-world situation. For example, if the $15 cost of a pizza is to be divided equally among n friends, then the equation $c = \dfrac{15}{n}$ will correctly model the cost per person c, but the equation $c = 15n$ will not.

B. DEVELOPING A MATHEMATICAL MODEL

1. Study the real-world situation. If the situation is presented as a word problem, read the problem carefully.
2. Choose variables to represent the unknown quantities. If possible, write expressions to represent all unknown quantities in terms of one variable.
3. Use the variable or variables to write an equation that models the word description of the situation.
4. Solve the equation to answer the question.
5. Here's an example of how you could develop a mathematical model for a simple word problem:

> Suppose you bought a hat, a jacket, and a sweater for a total of $77. The jacket cost $20 more than the hat, and the sweater cost $8 less than the jacket. What was the cost of each item?

> ▶ *First, study the situation carefully. Three different items were bought for a total of $77. You are given information about the costs of the three items, as well as information relating the cost of the jacket to the cost of the hat and the cost of the sweater to the cost of the jacket. If you can find the cost of one item, you can determine the costs of the other two items as well.*

> ▶ *Let the variable h represent the cost of the hat. The cost of the jacket, therefore, can be represented by the expression h + 20. The cost of the sweater can be represented by the expression h + (20 − 8) or h + 12.*

▶ *Since the total cost of the three items is $77, the situation can be represented by the equation h + (h + 20) + (h + 12) = 77.*

▶ *Solve the equation and answer the question:*

$$h + (h + 20) + (h + 12) = 77$$
$$3h + 32 = 77$$
$$3h = 45$$
$$h = 15$$

The cost of the hat is $15, the cost of the jacket is $15 + $20 = $35, and the cost of the sweater is $15 + $12 = $27.

C. TYPES OF MODELS

1. *Linear models* are used when a quantity in a given situation changes at a constant rate. For example, if an item costs a certain amount and the situation involves finding the total cost of *n* items, then the situation can be represented by a linear model.

2. *Polynomial models* are used when a quantity in a given situation changes at a rate that is nonlinear. For example, the height of a kicked football will increase, then decrease with time.

3. *Rational models* are used when a quantity is to be divided by an unknown number. For example, if a total cost is to be divided between an unknown number of people, then a rational model can be used.

4. *Exponential models* are used when a quantity in a given situation changes at an increasing rate or at a decreasing rate. For example, if a population doubles during each fixed time interval, then the population will grow at an increasing rate.

II. MODELING WITH EQUATIONS

A. MODELING WITH LINEAR EQUATIONS

1. Linear equations are used to model situations where the rate of change is constant. For example, if one bagel costs $2.25,

then the equation $c = 2.25b$ can be used to model the total cost c for b bagels.

> ▸ *In this situation, the variable b is said to be the independent variable and variable c is the dependent variable. The value of c depends on the value of b because the total cost will depend on how many bagels are bought.*

> ▸ *Rate of change is the rate of change of the dependent variable based on the per-unit change of the independent variable. In this situation, the unit change is buying one bagel, and the total cost increases by a constant amount of $2.25 each time. Since the rate of change is constant, the situation can be represented by a linear model.*

2. Sometimes you may have to manipulate linear equations to model a given situation. For example, if the relationship between the number of inches i and the number of centimeters c is modeled by the equation $c = 2.54i$ and the relationship between the number of yards y and the number of inches i is modeled by the equation $i = 36y$, then the relationship between the number of yards and the number of centimeters can be modeled by the equation $c = (2.54)(36y) = 91.44y$.

3. You can also use systems of linear equations to model real-world situations. For example, suppose pens cost $2, rulers cost $4, you want to buy a total of 8 items, and you want to spend $20. There are different ways to model the situation to determine the number of pens and the number of rulers you would buy.

> ▸ *One way to find the number of pens and rulers to purchase would be to graph the situation in the coordinate plane with the x- and y-axes representing the number of pens and rulers, respectively. One set of points would represent possible combinations of pens and rulers for a total of 8 items and a second set of points would represent possible combinations of pens and rulers for a total of $20, with the solution being represented by the coordinates of the point that is in both sets.*

> ▸ *Another approach is to write a system of equations to model the situation. Again, if x and y represent the number of pens and rulers, respectively, then the equations x + y = 8 and 2x + 4y = 20 model the*

situation. There is still a decision of how to solve the
system, such as using substitution, subtracting the
equations to eliminate a variable, or representing the
equations with matrices and using Cramer's rule. You
can graph the equations $x + y = 8$ and $2x + 4y = 20$
to find the point of intersection, which is the solution to
the system. The following graph shows the two equations
with the point of intersection at (6, 2).

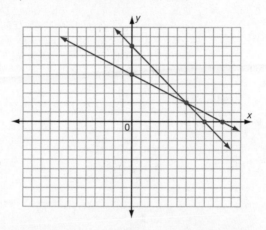

**Use Your Calculator to Find an Equation to Model Linear
Data** *Suppose you have collected the following data about
the number of math problems students completed on their
math homework and the total number of minutes required to
complete them.*

Number of Problems Completed	Minutes Required to Complete
10	41
8	35
11	44
6	24

*You observe that there appears to be a linear relationship be-
tween the number of problems and the time required. You can
use your calculator to find a linear equation that models that
relationship. First, press [STAT] and select EDIT. After clearing
previous data if necessary, enter the data for number of problems in L1 and for minutes to complete in L2.*

(continued)

(continued)

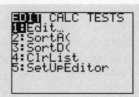

Now press [STAT] again and select CALC. Press 4 to select
LinReg(ax + B). Press [2ND] L1, [2ND] L2 and [ENTER]. The
calculator will give you the a and b coefficients for a linear
equation that models the data. Rounded to the nearest whole
number, the equation y = 4x + 2 will model the data reason-
ably well.

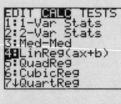
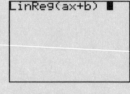
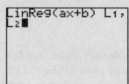
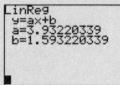

B. MODELING WITH POLYNOMIAL EQUATIONS

1. Polynomial equations can be used to model motion.
   For example, the equation $h = -16t^2 + vt + h_0$ gives the
   height h, after t seconds, of a projectile thrown straight up
   from an initial height of h_0 with an initial velocity of v feet
   per second.

2. Polynomial equations can also be used to model geometric
   shapes. For example, the formula for the volume of
   a rectangular prism is the product of its length, width,
   and height. If a rectangular prism has a length of x units,
   a width of $x - 2$ units, and a height of $x + 3$ units, then
   the volume V is given by $V = x(x - 2)(x + 3)$ or
   $V = x^3 + x^2 - 6x$.

C. MODELING WITH RATIONAL EQUATIONS

1. *Rational equations* can be used to model situations where some total quantity is shared by an unknown number of entities. For example, suppose a group of n students are sharing the cost of a limousine to go to a school dance. If the cost of the limousine is $250 and each dance ticket is $25, then the cost per student c can be modeled by the rational equation $c = \dfrac{250 + 25n}{n}$.

2. In situations involving direct, joint, and inverse variation, rational equations can also be used to model situations where inverse variation is involved.

   ▶ *A* direct variation *describes a situation where one variable increases as the other increases, or decreases as the other decreases. Direct variation is expressed by the equation y = kx, where k is the nonzero constant of variation. Direct variation can be modeled using a linear model.*

   ▶ *When one quantity varies directly as the product of two or more other quantities, the term* joint variation *is used. For example, the equation y = kxz represents the situation where y varies jointly as x and z for the nonzero constant of variation k.*

   ▶ *In an* inverse variation, *one quantity increases as the other decreases. Inverse variation is expressed by the equation xy = k or $y = \dfrac{k}{x}$, where x ≠ 0, y ≠ 0, and k is the nonzero constant of variation. Inverse variation can be modeled using rational functions.*

D. MODELING WITH EXPONENTIAL EQUATIONS

1. Situations involving bank accounts, loans, and interest rates are modeled with *exponential equations*. For example, the balance b in a savings account with an initial deposit of d dollars earning an annual interest rate r is given by the equation $b = d(1 + r)^n$, where n is the number of years the money remains untouched in the account. This means that the balance after n years for an initial deposit of $1,000 earning 2% annual interest can be modeled with the equation $b = 1000(1.02)^n$.

2. Exponential growth situations involve growth that occurs at an increasing rate. The general form of an equation for exponential growth is $y = ab^x$, where $a > 0$ and $b > 1$. For example, if an initial bacteria population of 300 bacteria doubles every hour, the number of bacteria will grow at an increasing rate. The equation $y = 300 \cdot 2^x$ models the number of bacteria after x hours.

3. *Exponential decay* situations involve decay that occurs at a decreasing rate. The general form of an equation for exponential decay is $y = ab^x$, where $a > 0$ and $0 < b < 1$. For example, if there are 50 grams of a toxic substance that has a half-life of 25 years, the amount of the substance will decrease at a decreasing rate. The equation $y = 50 \cdot \left(\dfrac{1}{2}\right)^x$ models the grams of the toxic substance after x intervals of 25 years each.

PROPERTIES
OF FUNCTIONS

KEY VOCABULARY

Asymptote A line that a graph approaches but never crosses.

Dependent variable The output from a function; for example, for the function $y = 2x$, the dependent variable is y.

Domain The set of all x-values in the ordered pairs of a relation.

End behavior The behavior of a graph as x approaches positive or negative infinity (∞ or $-\infty$).

Function A relation in which each element in the domain is paired with exactly one element in the range.

Function notation A special notation for writing functions. For example, the function $y = 2x$ written in function notation is $f(x) = 2x$.

Independent variable The input to a function; for example, in the function $y = 2x$, the independent variable is x.

Inverse functions Two functions are inverse functions if and only if both of their compositions are the identity function.

Linear function A function whose graph is a straight line.

One to one A function whose inverse is also a function.

Polynomial A term or the sum of terms that contain only numbers and variables raised to whole-number exponents.

Range The set of all y-values in the ordered pairs of a relation.

Rate of change The rate of change of the dependent variable based on the per-unit change of the independent variable.

Relation A set of ordered pairs.

Rise The vertical change of a line, calculated by $y_1 - y_2$.

Run The horizontal change of a line, calculated by $x_1 - x_2$.

Vertical line test The test that says if a vertical line crosses a graph at more than one point, then the graph does not represent a function.

x-intercept The x-coordinate of the point at which a graph crosses the x-axis.

y-intercept The y-coordinate of the point at which a graph crosses the y-axis.

I. FUNCTIONS

A. FUNCTION BASICS

1. A *relation* is a set of ordered pairs. The *domain* of the relation is the set of all first members of the ordered pairs. The *range* of the relation is the set of all second members of the ordered pairs.

2. A *function* is a special type of relation in which each element in the domain corresponds to exactly one element in the range. For example, the relation {(1, 2)(2, 4)(3, 6), (4, 8)} is a function, but the relation {(1, 2)(1, 4)(3, 6), (4, 8)} is not because 1 is paired with both 2 and 4.

3. Although a function can be represented as a set of ordered pairs, more commonly functions are represented as equations. For example, the equation $y = 2x$ represents a function because in the solution set of ordered pairs (x, y), each x-value corresponds to exactly one y-value.

4. Functions are often named by letters. For example, functions are often named f, g, or h.

5. *Function notation* is a special notation used to represent functions. For example, the equation $y = 2x$ is written as $f(x) = 2x$ in function notation. The name of the function is f, the input is x, and the output is $f(x)$. For example, $f(5) = 2(5) = 10$ means that the value of the function f at $x = 5$ is 10. This is called *evaluating the function* at a given value—in this case, 5.

6. The input to a function is often called the *independent variable*, while the output of a function is the *dependent variable*. The value of the dependent variable changes based on the value of the independent variable.

7. The *rate of change* of a function is the change in the value of the dependent variable per unit change of the independent variable.

8. Tables are another representation of functions. For example, the function $f(x) = 2x$ can be represented by the following table:

x	$f(x)$
-2	-4
-1	-2
0	0
3	6

9. Graphs are another representation of functions. For example, the function $f(x) = 2x$ can be represented by the following graph:

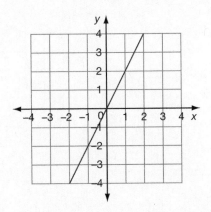

B. GRAPHS OF FUNCTIONS

1. The *graph of a function* is the graph of its ordered pairs.
2. The *vertical line test* says that if a vertical line can be drawn to intersect a graph at more than one point, then the graph does not represent a function. For example, see the following graph for the equation $x = y^2$.

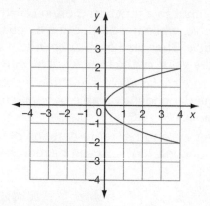

The graph does not represent a function because there are ways to draw a vertical line that intersects the graph at more than one point. For instance, a vertical line drawn at $x = 1$ intersects the graph at $y = 1$ and $y = -1$. Since the input value of 1 has two output values of 1 and -1, this means that $x = y^2$ is not a function. The dotted line is often used to show a vertical line test.

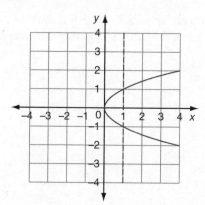

3. You can use the graph of a function to obtain the value of a function at any value.

4. You can determine the domain and range of a function by looking at its graph. For example, see the following graph for the function $y = x^2 - 2$.

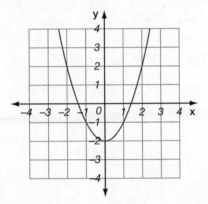

The domain, which is the set of inputs represented on the x-axis, will include all values of x when the graph is extended infinitely, so the domain of the function $y = x^2 - 2$ is the set of all real numbers or $\{x \mid x$ is a real number$\}$. However, the range, which is the set of outputs represented on the y-axis, will only include values of y greater than or equal to -2 no matter how far the graph is extended. Therefore, the range of the function $y = x^2 - 2$ is the set $\{y \mid y \geq -2\}$.

5. A function is said to be "increasing" if values of y increase or stay the same as values of x increase. A function is "strictly increasing" if the values of y only increase and the graph of the function is never flat. Likewise, a function is "decreasing" if the values of y decrease or stay the same as the values of x increase and "strictly decreasing" if the graph is never flat. A function can be increasing and decreasing for different intervals of x-values. A constant function is a horizontal line.

C. ADDING, SUBTRACTING, MULTIPLYING, AND DIVIDING FUNCTIONS

1. The sum of two functions f and g is given as $(f + g)(x) = f(x) + g(x)$, where the domain of $f + g$ is the set of all real numbers common to the domains of f and g. For example, if $f(x) = 2x$ and $g(x) = x + 3$, then $(f + g)(x) = 3x + 3$.

2. The difference of two functions f and g is given as $(f - g)(x) = f(x) - g(x)$, where the domain of $f - g$ is the set of all real numbers common to the domains of f and g. For example, if $f(x) = 2x$ and $g(x) = x + 3$, then $(f - g)(x) = x - 3$.

3. The product of two functions f and g is given as $(fg)(x) = f(x) \cdot g(x)$, where the domain of $f \cdot g$ is the set of all real numbers common to the domains of f and g. For example, if $f(x) = 2x$ and $g(x) = x + 3$, then $(fg)(x) = 2x^2 + 6x$.

4. The quotient of two functions f and g is given as $\left(\dfrac{f}{g}\right)(x) = \dfrac{f(x)}{g(x)}$, where the domain of $\dfrac{f}{g}$ is the set of all real numbers common to the domains of f and g and $g(x) \neq 0$. For example, if $f(x) = 2x$ and $g(x) = x + 3$, then $\left(\dfrac{f}{g}\right)(x) = \dfrac{2x}{x+3}$, $x \neq -3$.

D. COMPOSITION OF FUNCTIONS

1. The composite function $f \circ g$ is defined as $(f \circ g)(x) = f(g(x))$, where f and g are functions such that the range of g is a subset of the domain of f.

2. In the composition $f \circ g$, the output $g(x)$ is used as input to f.

E. INVERSE FUNCTIONS

1. An *inverse relation* is obtained by reversing the coordinates of each ordered pair in the relation.

2. Two functions can also be inverses. The inverse of a function f is symbolized as f^{-1}. If f and f^{-1} are inverse functions, then $f(a) = b$ if and only if $f^{-1}(b) = a$.

3. To find the inverse of a function, follow these steps:

    i. Replace $f(x)$ with y.

    ii. Interchange x and y.

    iii. Solve for y.

    iv. Replace y with $f^{-1}(x)$.

4. The identity function is defined as $I(x) = x$. If two functions f and g are inverses, then $(f \circ g)(x) = x$ and $(g \circ f)(x) = x$. This

means that two functions are inverse functions if and only if both of their compositions are the identity function.

5. When the inverse of a function is also a function, the function is said to be *one to one*.

II. LINEAR FUNCTIONS

A. LINEAR FUNCTION BASICS

1. *Linear functions* are functions whose graph is a straight line.

2. A linear function is said to be a function of the first degree, meaning it is a polynomial function of degree one. In a linear function, the greatest exponent of any variable is 1, and exponents of 1 are not written out. For example, if x is the input variable to a linear function, then x will have an exponent of 1 and be written as simply x, not x^1.

3. Graphs of linear functions can be described using intercepts and slope.

   i. The intercepts are the points where the graph crosses the x- and y-axes.

   ii. The slope represents the steepness of the line. The slope is the ratio of the vertical change of the line to its horizontal change.

B. INTERCEPTS

1. The *x-intercept* is the point where the graph crosses the x-axis. The y-coordinate of an x-intercept is always 0. The x-intercept is often given as a single value, which is the x-value of the ordered pair (x, y), where $y = 0$. A linear function has one x-intercept.

2. The *y-intercept* is the point where the graph crosses the y-axis. The x-coordinate of a y-intercept is always 0. The y-intercept is often given as a single value, which is the y-value of the ordered pair (x, y), where $x = 0$. A linear function has one y-intercept.

3. A linear function can be graphed given its x- and y-intercepts.

C. SLOPE

1. The *slope* of a line can be calculated given two different points on the line, (x_1, y_1) and (x_2, y_2).

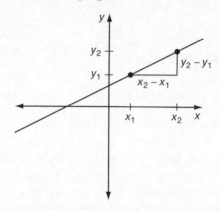

  i. The vertical change of the line is given by the change in y: $y_2 - y_1$. The vertical change of a line is called the *rise*.
  ii. The horizontal change of the line is given by the change in x: $x_2 - x_1$. The horizontal change of a line is called the *run*.
  iii. The slope of a line is given by the following:

$$\frac{\text{change in } y}{\text{change in } x} = \frac{\text{rise}}{\text{run}} = \frac{y_2 - y_1}{x_2 - x_1}, \text{ where } x_2 - x_1 \neq 0$$

2. The slope of a line can be positive, negative, zero, or undefined. A line with a positive slope rises from left to right, while a line with a negative slope falls from left to right. A horizontal line has a slope of zero, while the slope of a vertical line is undefined.
3. A linear function can be graphed given the slope and one point on the line.

D. EQUATIONS OF LINEAR FUNCTIONS

1. Slope-Intercept Form
    i. The slope-intercept form of the equation of a linear function is given by $y = mx + b$, where m is the slope of the line and b is the y-intercept.
    ii. Since a linear function can be graphed given the slope and one point on the line, the equation of a

linear function in slope-intercept form provides all the information necessary to easily graph a linear function.

a) Plot the point for the y-intercept.

b) Obtain a second point by writing the slope as a fraction in the form $\frac{rise}{run}$. Start at the y-intercept point and move vertically the number of units in the numerator, then horizontally the number of units in the denominator to plot the second point.

c) Draw a line through the two points.

iii. The rate of change of a linear function is given by its slope. The rate of change of a linear function is m when the function is in slope-intercept form $y = mx + b$.

2. Point-Slope Form

i. The point-slope form of the equation of a linear function is given by $y - y_1 = m(x - x_1)$, where m is the slope and (x_1, y_2) is a point on the line.

ii. A function with an equation given in point-slope form can be graphed by plotting the point (x_1, y_1) and then using the $\frac{rise}{run}$ form of the slope to plot a second point. The graph is the line through these two points.

iii. Since the slope is given by the variable m, the rate of change for a function whose equation is in point-slope form can be easily determined.

3. Standard Form

i. The standard form of the equation of a linear function is given by the equation $Ax + By = C$.

ii. A function with an equation given in standard form can be graphed by plotting the x-intercept and the y-intercept. The graph is the line through these two points.

iii. To find the rate of change for a function whose equation is in standard form, rewrite the equation in slope-intercept form. In slope-intercept form, the rate of change is given by the variable representing slope, m, the coefficient of the x-variable.

III. **POLYNOMIAL FUNCTIONS**

A. POLYNOMIAL FUNCTION BASICS

1. A *polynomial* is a term or the sum of terms that contain only numbers and variables raised to whole-number exponents.

2. A polynomial function is a function that is defined by a polynomial expression. The general form of a polynomial function is $a_n x^n + a_{n-1} x^{n-1} + \cdots + a_2 x^2 + a_1 x + a_0$, where the coefficients $a_n, a_{n-1}, \ldots a_2, a_1, a_0$ are real numbers, a_n is not zero, and n is a nonnegative integer. For example, $f(x) = x - 6$, $f(x) = x^2 + x - 6$, and $f(x) = x^3$ are all polynomial functions.

3. Graphs of polynomial functions can be described as continuous and smooth.

   i. "Continuous" means that you can draw the graph without taking your pencil off the paper.

   ii. "Smooth" means that the graphs have no corners.

B. GRAPHS OF POLYNOMIAL FUNCTIONS

1. End Behavior

   i. *End behavior* is what happens to the graph of a function as the graph moves to the far right or to the far left, as x approaches ∞ or $-\infty$.

   ii. Although graphs of polynomials may have many turns, at each end the graph will either increase without bound or decrease without bound.

   iii. The end behavior of the graph of a polynomial function can be determined by the degree of the polynomial and by its leading coefficient. The leading term is the term of the greatest degree, and the leading coefficient is the coefficient of that term.

      a) If the degree of the polynomial is odd and the leading coefficient is positive, then the end behavior is that the graph falls on the left and rises on the right. If the degree of the polynomial is odd and the leading coefficient is negative, then the end behavior is that the graph rises on the left and falls on the right.

b) If the degree of the polynomial is even and the leading coefficient is positive, then the end behavior is that the graph rises on both the left and the right. If the degree of the polynomial is even and the leading coefficient is negative, then the end behavior is that the graph falls on both the left and the right.

2. Real zeros of a polynomial function are the values of x at those points where a polynomial function crosses the x-axis. The number of real zeros of a polynomial function is never greater than the degree of the polynomial.

3. Graphing Quadratic Functions

   i. Graphs of quadratic functions are parabolas. Since quadratic functions are polynomial functions of degree two, the parabola opens upward if the leading coefficient is positive and downward if the leading coefficient is negative.

   ii. The equation of the parent graph for quadratic functions is $y = x^2$. This graph has its vertex at $(0, 0)$ and $x = 0$ as its axis of symmetry. See the following diagram for the graph of $y = x^2$.

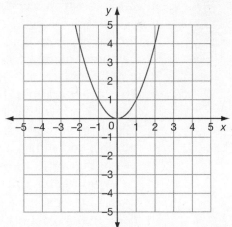

   iii. The graphs of other quadratic functions can be obtained by transforming the parent graph. For example, if the graph of $y = x^2$ is translated 3 units up, the new graph can be described by the equation

$y = x^2 + 3$. The graph shows $y = x^2$ and $y = x^2 + 3$ translated 3 units up.

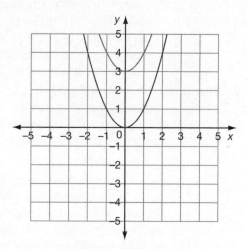

iv. The vertex form of a quadratic function is $y = a(x - h)^2 + k$, where (*h*, *k*) is the vertex of the parabola, $x = h$ is its axis of symmetry, and the value of *a* determines the shape of the parabola and the direction in which it opens.

v. If $a = 1$ in the vertex form, the shape and orientation of the parent graph does not change. The translation of the parent graph $y = x^2$ is given by the vertex form as follows:

a) The parent graph is shifted |*h*| units left if *h* is negative and |*h*| units right if *h* is positive.

b) The parent graph is shifted *k* units up if *k* is positive and *k* units down if *k* is negative.

vi. If $a \neq 1$ in the vertex form, the shape and orientation of the parent graph is described by the value of *a*.

a) If $a > 0$, the parabola opens upward.

b) If $a < 0$, the parabola opens downward.

c) If $|a| > 1$, the graph is stretched vertically and is narrower than the parent graph.

d) If $0 < |a| < 1$, the graph is compressed vertically and is wider than the parent graph.

vii. The graph of a quadratic function written in standard form $y = ax^2 + bx + c$ can be rewritten in vertex form by completing the square and then graphed.

viii. The graph of a quadratic function can intercept the x-axis at zero, one, or two points, meaning that the function has no real solutions, one real solution, or two real solutions, respectively.

Transform Graphs of Functions on Your Calculator *You can observe the effects of changing the values of a, h, and k in vertex form when graphing quadratic functions on your calculator. For example, here's how the parent graph $y = x^2$ is transformed for the equations $y = (x + 3)^2 - 1$ and $y = (x - 3)^2 + 1$. First, press [Y=] and enter the equations. Then press [GRAPH] to see the graphs.*

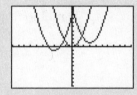

The three graphs appear but it is hard to distinguish which graph is which. Fortunately, you can change the style of the lines used to draw the graphs. Return to the Y= editor and select the Y_2 equation. Use the left arrow to move the cursor to the left of the Y, then press [ENTER] to cycle through the line drawing options. Change the options for the second and third equations as shown, then press [GRAPH] to see the effect.

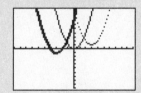

Now return to the Y= editor and enter the equations $y = 4x^2$, $y = 0.25x^2$, $y = -4x^2$, and $y = -0.25x^2$ to see the effects of changing the variable a. Press [GRAPH] to see the graphs.

Test Tip

(continued)

(*continued*)

> Wow, that's confusing! Fortunately, you can deactivate some of the graphs temporarily as you explore the transformations. Again, return to the Y= editor and select the Y_2 equation. Use the left arrow to move the cursor to the equal sign, then press [ENTER] to remove the highlight. Repeat the process for the Y_3, Y_6, and Y_7 equations. Change the line styles for the Y_4 and Y_5 equations. Then press [GRAPH] to see the effect.

 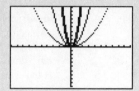

4. Graphing Polynomial Functions

    i. The basic shapes of the graphs of polynomial functions of degree greater than two are determined by whether the degree of the function is odd or even. The following graphs show $y = x^3 + 2x^2 - x - 1$ and $y = x^4 - 2x^3 - x^2 + x + 1$.

$$y = x^3 + 2x^2 - x - 1$$

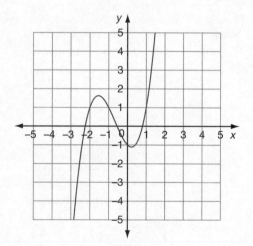

$$y = x^4 - 2x^3 - x^2 + x + 1$$

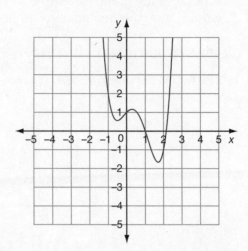

ii. Polynomial functions have relative maximums and relative minimums, which are also called *turning points*, where the function changes from increasing to decreasing or vice versa.

iii. A real zero of a polynomial function is the point at which the graph of the function intercepts the x-axis. If a and b are two numbers such that $f(a) < 0$ and $f(b) > 0$, then there is at least one real zero between a and b.

IV. RATIONAL FUNCTIONS

A. RATIONAL FUNCTION BASICS

1. A rational expression is a polynomial divided by a nonzero polynomial.

2. A rational function is a function that is defined by a rational expression. Since a function's domain cannot include real numbers that can cause division by zero, the domain of a rational function is the set of all real numbers except those that would make the denominator equal to zero.

3. Most graphs of rational functions are not continuous. This is because the graph has breaks at the excluded values that would cause the denominator to be equal to zero.

B. GRAPHS OF RATIONAL FUNCTIONS

1. The following graph shows $f(x) = \dfrac{1}{x}$.

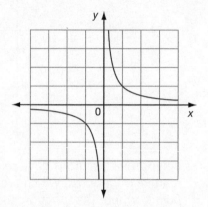

Note that there is a break in the graph at $x = 0$, because that value is excluded from the domain of the function because it would cause division by zero. The line $x = 0$ is called a *vertical asymptote* because the graph of the function approaches but never touches it.

2. A rational function can also have point discontinuity. The following graph shows the rational function $f(x) = \dfrac{x^2 + 3x + 2}{x + 1}$.

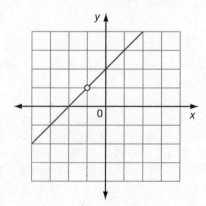

Note that the graph of this rational function is a line. This is because when the numerator is factored as $(x + 2)(x + 1)$, the rational expression $\dfrac{(x+2)(x+1)}{x+1}$ can be simplified as $x + 2$, and the graph of the function is the line $y = x + 2$ with one important difference: the value that would cause a denominator of zero is excluded from the domain. Since this value is $x = -1$, the graph of $f(x) = \dfrac{x^2 + 3x + 2}{x+1}$ has a hole at $x = -1$.

Test Tip

Check the Domains of Rational Functions When dealing with rational functions, you must constantly be vigilant for values that would make the denominator equal to zero and therefore that you must exclude from the domain. You must maintain this vigilance at every step. Although you may simplify a rational expression so that the variable is removed from the denominator, you MUST exclude any value that at any time made the denominator equal to zero from the domain. For example, even though you can simplify the rational expression

$\dfrac{(x+2)(x+1)}{x+1}$ as $x + 2$, you must nevertheless exclude the value

$x = -1$ from the domain of the function $f(x) = \dfrac{(x+2)(x+1)}{x+1}$.

V. EXPONENTIAL FUNCTIONS

A. EXPONENTIAL FUNCTION BASICS

1. In an exponential function, the base is a constant and the exponent is a variable.
2. The general form of an exponential function is $y = ab^x$, where $a \neq 0$, $b > 0$, and $b \neq 1$. An exponential function of the form $y = ab^x$ has the following characteristics:
   i. The function is continuous and one to one.
   ii. The domain is the set of real numbers.

   iii. If $a > 0$, then the range is the set of all positive numbers. If $a < 0$, then the range is the set of all negative numbers.

   iv. The graph has the *x*-axis as its horizontal asymptote.

   v. The *y*-intercept of $y = ab^x$, and the graph includes the point $(0, a)$.

   vi. The graphs of $y = ab^x$ and $y = a\left(\dfrac{1}{b}\right)^x$ are reflections across the *y*-axis.

B. GRAPHS OF EXPONENTIAL FUNCTIONS

1. The following graphs show $f(x) = 2^x$ and $f(x) = \left(\dfrac{1}{2}\right)^x$.

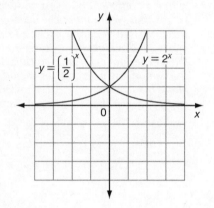

2. Graphs of exponential functions of the form $y = ab^x$ have the following characteristics:

   i. The graph has the *x*-axis as its horizontal asymptote.

   ii. The *y*-intercept of $y = ab^x$ is a, and the graph includes the point $(0, a)$.

   iii. The graphs of $y = ab^x$ and $y = a\left(\dfrac{1}{b}\right)^x$ are reflections across the *y*-axis.

3. An exponential function of the form $y = ab^x$ represents exponential growth if $a > 0$ and $b > 1$, and exponential decay if $a > 0$ and $0 < b < 1$.

LOGARITHMIC FUNCTIONS

KEY VOCABULARY

Change of base formula This formula lets you change a logarithmic expression with one base to an equivalent logarithmic expression with a different base. The change of base formula says that for $a > 0$, $b > 0$, $n > 0$, $a \neq 1$, and $b \neq 1$, $\log_a n = \dfrac{\log_b n}{\log_b a}$.

Common logarithm The base-10 log, usually written as $\log x$, not $\log_{10} x$.

Logarithm For $b > 0$, $b \neq 1$, and $x > 0$ $\log_b(x) = y$ if and only if $b^y = x$. The logarithm of x with base b is equal to the exponent that b must be raised to in order to equal x. A logarithm is an exponent.

Natural logarithm The base-e log, usually written as $\ln x$, not $\log_e x$.

 ## I. LOGARITHMS

A. LOGARITHM BASICS

1. *Logarithms* can be understood in terms of exponents. In fact, logarithms *are* exponents. For example, $2^5 = 32$. This can be rewritten as $\log_2(32) = 5$. This means that the exponent that the base 2 must be raised to in order to equal 32 is 5, and $\log_2(32)$ is an exponent.

2. Logarithms are defined in terms of exponents: $\log_b(x) = y$ if and only if $b^y = x$, where $b > 0$, $b \neq 1$, and $x > 0$. The logarithm of x with base b is equal to the exponent that b must be raised to in order to equal x.

3. Note that just as in an exponential expression, the base must be greater than zero but not equal to 1 in a logarithmic expression.

4. Equations in logarithmic form can be rewritten in exponential form, and vice versa. Here are some examples:

   i. $\log_2 (1024) = 10 \rightarrow 2^{10} = 1024$

   ii. $\log_2 \left(\dfrac{1}{4}\right) = -2 \rightarrow 2^{-2} = \dfrac{1}{4}$

   iii. $\log_3 (81) = 4 \rightarrow 3^4 = 81$

   iv. $\log_4 (1) = 0 \rightarrow 4^0 = 1$

B. LOGARITHM BASES

1. A logarithm can have any positive base. For example, $\log_2 x$ has a base of 2 and $\log_5 x$ has a base of 5.

2. Two bases are commonly used: the base-10 log, also called the *common log*, and the base-*e* log, also called the *natural log*.

   i. Common logarithms

      a) *Common logarithms* are usually written without the subscript 10: log x, not $\log_{10} x$.

      b) The [LOG] key on your calculator evaluates common logarithms.

      c) Common logs are used in measurements such as decibels, pH, and the Richter scale.

   ii. Natural logarithms

      a) *Natural logarithms* have as their base the number *e*, which is sometimes called the *natural base*. The number *e* is equal to approximately 2.72. The function $f(x) = e^x$ is called the *natural logarithmic function*.

      b) The [LN] key on your calculator evaluates natural logarithms.

      c) Natural logs are used to model situations involving exponential growth and decay.

3. If you have a logarithmic expression with one base and you want to write it as an equivalent logarithmic expression with a different base, you can use the *change of base formula*:

   $\log_a n = \dfrac{\log_b n}{\log_b a}$, where $a \neq 1$, $b \neq 1$, and a, b, and n are all positive. For example, if you want to write $\log_2 64$ as an equivalent logarithm with a base of 4, apply the change of base formula as follows: $\log_4 64 = \dfrac{\log_2 64}{\log_2 4} = \dfrac{6}{2} = 3$.

Use the Change of Base Formula on Your Calculator *Most calculators provide a [LOG] key for evaluating common logarithms and an [LN] key for evaluating natural logarithms. However, if you want to use logs with bases other than 10 or e, you will first have to convert the log to base 10 or e using the change of base formula. For example, suppose you want to*

enter the expression $\dfrac{15}{\log_2 32}$. *The change of base formula says*

that $\log_2 32 = \dfrac{\log_{10} 32}{\log_{10} 2}$, *so you can substitute* $\dfrac{\log_{10} 32}{\log_{10} 2}$ *for*

$\log_2 32$ *when you enter the expression into your calculator:*

Press 15/([LOG](32)/[LOG](2))

```
15/(log(32)/log(
2))
                3
■
```

Using the natural log in the formula gives the same result.

Press 15/([LN](32)/[LN](2))

```
15/(log(32)/log(
2))
                3
15/(ln(32)/ln(2)
)
                3
■
```

C. LOGARITHMIC EXPRESSIONS AND EQUATIONS

1. To find the value of a logarithmic expression, apply the definition of a logarithm. For example, to find the value of $\log_6 216$, ask "What exponent must 6 be raised to in order to equal 216?" You can use algebra to find the answer as follows:

   i. Set $\log_6 216$ equal to y: $y = \log_6 216$.

ii. Since the definition of a logarithm says that $\log_b (x) = y$ is equivalent to $b^y = x$, rewrite the equation as shown:

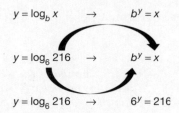

$$y = \log_b x \quad \rightarrow \quad b^y = x$$

$$y = \log_6 216 \quad \rightarrow \quad b^y = x$$

$$y = \log_6 216 \quad \rightarrow \quad 6^y = 216$$

iii. Now, you have an exponential equation that you can solve:

$6^y = 216$ Write the exponential equation.
$6^y = 6^3$ $216 = 6^3$
$y = 3$ Use the property of exponent equality.

iv. The value of $\log_6 216$ is 3.

2. A logarithmic equation contains one or more logarithms. You can solve a logarithmic equation by using the same approach you used to evaluate a logarithmic expression: apply the definition of a logarithm to rewrite logarithmic expressions as exponential expressions. Then you can apply properties of exponents to solve the equation. For example, here's how you could solve the logarithmic equation $\log_8 x = \dfrac{4}{3}$:

$$\log_8 x = \frac{4}{3}$$

$$x = 8^{\frac{4}{3}} \quad \text{Apply the definition of a logarithm.}$$

$$x = \left(2^3\right)^{\frac{4}{3}} \quad 8 = 2^3$$

$$x = 2^4 \quad \text{Use the power of a power property.}$$

$$x = 16 \quad \text{Simplify.}$$

3. Some logarithmic equations have logarithms with the same base on both sides. You can solve these logarithmically using the property of equality for logarithms: If $\log_b x = \log_b y$, then $x = y$. So, the logarithmic equation $\log_2 64 = \log_2 4x$ can be rewritten as $64 = 4x$, with the solution of $x = 16$.

4. There are other properties of logarithms you can use to solve logarithmic equations as well.

   i. The *product property of logarithms* says that the logarithm of a product is equal to the sum of the logarithms of its factors: $\log_b mn = \log_b m + \log_b n$. For example, $\log_2 32 = \log_2 (4 \bullet 8) = \log_2 4 + \log_2 8 = 2 + 3 = 5$.

   ii. The *quotient property of logarithms* says that the logarithm of a quotient is equal to the difference of the logarithms of its numerator and denominator: $\log_b \dfrac{m}{n} = \log_b m - \log_b n$. For example, $\log_2 8 = \log_2 \left(\dfrac{32}{4} \right) = \log_2 32 - \log_2 4 = 5 - 2 = 3$.

   iii. The *power property of logarithms* says that the logarithm of a power is the product of the logarithm and the exponent: $\log_b m^p = p\log_b m$. For example, $\log_2 64 = \log_2 8^2 = 2\log_2 8 = 6$.

   iv. For all bases b, $\log_b b = 1$ because $b^1 = b$.

   v. For all bases b, $\log_b 1 = 0$ because $b^0 = 1$.

   vi. For all bases b, $\log_b b^x = x$ because $b^x = b^x$.

5. You can use logarithms to solve exponential equations. If you cannot write both sides of an exponential equation as powers of the same base, you can solve the equation by taking the logarithm of each side of the equation instead. Here are some examples:

   i. The equation $2^x = 15$ cannot be solved by writing as a power of base 2. However, you can solve the equation by taking the log of each side:

$$2^x = 15$$
$$\log 2^x = \log 15 \quad \text{Take the common log of both sides.}$$
$$x \log 2 = \log 15 \quad \text{Use the power property of logarithms.}$$
$$x = \frac{\log 15}{\log 2} \quad \text{Divide both sides by log 2.}$$
$$x \approx 3.9069 \quad \text{Use a calculator.}$$

This answer is reasonable since $16 = 2^4$.

ii. Interest rate problems can often be solved by using logarithms. For example, the formula to find the amount A that a savings account will be worth after an initial investment P is compounded continuously at an annual rate r for t years is $A = Pe^{rt}$. To find how many years it will take an initial investment of $1,000 at a rate of 4% to be worth $2,000, you can solve the exponential equation $2,000 = 1,000e^{0.04t}$ as follows:

$$2,000 = 1,000e^{0.04t}$$

$2 = e^{0.04t}$	Divide both sides by 1,000.
$\ln 2 = \ln e^{0.04t}$	Take the natural log of both sides.
$\ln 2 = 0.04t \ln e$	Use the power property of logarithms.
$\dfrac{\ln 2}{0.04} = t$	Divide both sides by 0.04.
$t \approx 17.3$	Use a calculator.

It will take about 17 years for the investment to be worth $2,000.

II. LOGARITHMIC FUNCTIONS

A. GRAPHS OF LOGARITHMIC AND EXPONENTIAL FUNCTIONS

1. The graph of $f(x) = \log_2 x$ can be graphed in the coordinate plane. To graph the function, first make a table of values:

x	$\frac{1}{8}$	$\frac{1}{4}$	$\frac{1}{2}$	1	2	4	8
$f(x) = \log_2 x$	-3	-2	-1	0	1	2	3

See the following graph. The shape of the graph appears familiar.

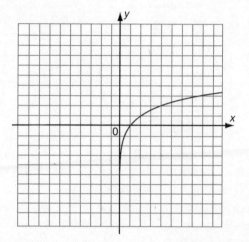

Now graph $g(x) = 2^x$ in the same coordinate plane.

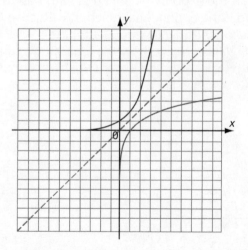

The graph of $f(x) = \log_2 x$ is the reflection of $g(x) = 2^x$ in the line $y = x$. You can see the relationship between the logarithmic and exponential functions when you compare the two tables of values.

x	$\dfrac{1}{8}$	$\dfrac{1}{4}$	$\dfrac{1}{2}$	1	2	4	8
$f(x) = \log_2 x$	-3	-2	-1	0	1	2	3

x	-3	-2	-1	0	1	2	3
$g(x) = 2^x$	$\dfrac{1}{8}$	$\dfrac{1}{4}$	$\dfrac{1}{2}$	1	2	4	8

Since you can obtain the inverse of a function by reversing x- and y-coordinates, you can see that $f(x) = \log_2 x$ and $g(x) = 2^x$ are inverse functions.

2. In general, the function $f(x) = \log_b x$ is called the *logarithmic function* with base b. The logarithmic function with base b is the inverse function of the exponential function with base b. Note that if the logarithmic function with base b is $f(x) = \log_b x$, then the exponential function with base b is $f^{-1}(x) = b^x$, and if the exponential function with base b is $f(x) = b^x$, then the logarithmic function with base b is $f^{-1}(x) = \log_b x$. The following graphs show the logarithmic function $f(x) = \log_b x$ with its inverse, the exponential function, $f^{-1}(x) = b^x$ for $b > 1$ and $0 < b < 1$.

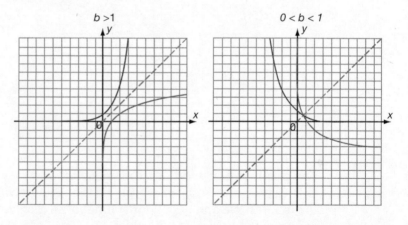

Notice that for both $b > 1$ and $0 < b < 1$, the graph of the exponential function has a horizontal asymptote of $y = 0$, while the graph of the logarithmic function has a vertical asymptote of $x = 0$.

3. A general form of the logarithmic function is $f(x) = a \log_e (bx - c) + d$. As values of a, b, c, and d change, the graph is transformed in the following ways:

    i. If $a > 0$, the graph will be stretched vertically, and if $0 < |a| < 1$, the graph will be compressed vertically. If a is negative, the graph will be reflected in the x-axis.

    ii. If $0 < |b| < 1$, the graph will be stretched horizontally, and if $|b| > 0$, the graph will be compressed horizontally. If b is negative, the graph will be reflected in the y-axis.

    iii. If $c > 0$, the graph is translated $|c|$ units to the right. If $c < 0$, the graph is translated $|c|$ units to the left.

    iv. If $d > 0$, the graph is translated $|d|$ units up. If $d < 0$, the graph is translated $|d|$ units down.

B. CHARACTERISTICS OF LOGARITHMIC FUNCTIONS

1. The domain of $f(x) = \log_b x$ is the set of all positive real numbers. The range of $f(x) = \log_b x$ is the set of all real numbers.

2. The x-intercept of all logarithmic functions is 1. Since $f(1) = \log_b 1 = 0$, this means that all graphs of logarithmic functions of the form $f(x) = \log_b x$ pass through $(1, 0)$.

3. Logarithmic functions of the form $f(x) = \log_b x$ have no y-intercept. This is because the graph of $f(x) = \log_b x$ has a vertical asymptote of $x = 0$.

4. If $b > 1$, then $f(x) = \log_b x$ is an increasing function, meaning it rises to the right.

5. If $0 < b < 1$, then $f(x) = \log_b x$ is a decreasing function, meaning it falls to the right.

6. The graph of $f(x) = \log_b x$ has a vertical asymptote of $x = 0$. This means the graph approaches but never touches the y-axis.

7. You can find the composition of logarithmic functions just as you would find the composition of other functions. For example, if $f(x) = 5 \ln (x) + 2$ and $g(x) = e^x$, then you can find $f(g(3))$. Since $g(3) = e^3$, this means $f(g(3)) = f(e^3)$. To find the value of $f(g(3))$, simplify the expression $5 \ln (e^3) + 2$ as follows:

$5 \ln (e^3) + 2 = 3 \bullet 5 \ln e + 2$ Use the power property of logarithms.

$\qquad = 15 \ln e + 2$ Simplify.

$\qquad = 15 + 2$ $\ln e = 1$

$\qquad = 17$ Simplify.

Test Tip

Domain of Logarithmic Functions *Since the domain of a logarithmic function only includes the positive real numbers, you may exclude some solutions when solving logarithmic equations. For example, you can solve the logarithmic equation* $\log_2 x + \log_2 (x + 3) = \log_2 10$ *as follows:*

$\log_2 x + \log_2 (x + 3) = \log_2 10$

$\log_2 (x \cdot (x + 3)) = \log_2 10$ *Use the product property of logarithms.*

$\log_2 (x^2 + 3x) = \log_2 10$ *Simplify.*

$x^2 + 3x = 10$ *Use the equality property of logarithms.*

$x^2 + 3x - 10 = 0$ *Subtract 10 from each side.*

$(x - 2)(x + 5) = 0$ *Factor.*

By solving both $x - 2 = 0$ *and* $x + 5 = 0$, *you find solutions of* $x = 2$ *or* $x = -5$. *Substituting* $x = 2$ *into the equation works, but substituting* $x = -5$ *does not because* $\log_2 (-5)$ *and* $\log_2 (-5 + 3)$ *are undefined. Therefore,* $x = -5$ *is an extraneous solution, and the correct solution is* $x = 2$.

TRIGONOMETRIC AND INVERSE TRIGONOMETRIC FUNCTIONS

$$\cot \theta = \tan\left(90° - \theta\right)$$

KEY VOCABULARY

Arccosine The inverse of the cosine function: if $y = \cos x$, then the inverse function is defined by $y = \cos^{-1} x$ or $y = \arccos x$.

Arcsine The inverse of the sine function: if $y = \sin x$, then the inverse function is defined by $y = \sin^{-1} x$ or $y = \arcsin x$.

Arctangent The inverse of the tangent function: if $y = \tan x$, then the inverse function is defined by $y = \tan^{-1} x$ or $y = \arctan x$.

Cofunctions Trigonometric functions and their reciprocals that are defined by a special relationship such that $\sin\theta = \cos(90° - \theta)$ and $\cos\theta = \sin(90° - \theta)$, $\tan\theta = \cot(90° - \theta)$ and $\cot\theta = \tan\left(90° - \theta\right)$, and $\sec\theta = \csc(90° - \theta)$ and $\csc\theta = \sec(90° - \theta)$.

Cosecant For an acute angle θ in a right triangle, cosecant θ is the reciprocal of sine θ: $\csc\theta = \dfrac{1}{\sin\theta}$ or $\dfrac{\text{hypotenuse}}{\text{opposite}}$.

Cosine For an acute angle θ in a right triangle, cosine θ is the ratio of the side adjacent θ and the hypotenuse: $\cos\theta = \dfrac{\text{adjacent}}{\text{hypotenuse}}$.

Cotangent For an acute angle θ in a right triangle, cotangent θ is the reciprocal of tangent θ: $\cot\theta = \dfrac{1}{\tan\theta}$ or $\dfrac{\text{adjacent}}{\text{opposite}}$.

Coterminal angles When an angle θ is in standard position in the coordinate plane, coterminal angles have the same terminal side.

Initial side When an angle θ is in standard position in the coordinate plane, the initial side is the fixed side.

Secant For an acute angle θ in a right triangle, secant θ is the reciprocal of cosine θ: $\sec\theta = \dfrac{1}{\cos\theta}$ or $\dfrac{\text{hypotenuse}}{\text{adjacent}}$.

Sine For an acute angle θ in a right triangle, sine θ is the ratio of the side opposite θ and the hypotenuse: $\sin\theta = \dfrac{\text{opposite}}{\text{hypotenuse}}$.

Tangent For an acute angle θ in a right triangle, tangent θ is the ratio of the side opposite θ and the side adjacent θ: $\tan\theta = \dfrac{\text{opposite}}{\text{adjacent}}$.

Terminal side When an angle θ is in standard position in the coordinate plane, the terminal side is rotated about the vertex at the origin.

Unit circle A circle with radius 1 whose center is at the origin of the coordinate plane.

Vertex When an angle θ is in standard position in the coordinate plane, the vertex is at the origin.

I. TRIGONOMETRIC RATIOS

A. TRIGONOMETRY AND RIGHT TRIANGLES

1. *Right triangles* contain an angle that measures 90° (a right angle). The other two angles are both acute angles (measures less than 90°) and complementary angles (the sum of their measures is 90°).

2. The *hypotenuse* of a right triangle is opposite the right angle and is the longest side of the triangle. The two other sides are called *legs*. When a leg is one side of one of the acute angles, that leg is said to be *adjacent* to that angle, and the other leg is said to be *opposite* that angle.

B. TRIGONOMETRIC RATIOS

1. The *trigonometric ratios* are the ratios of the sides of right triangles. The trigonometric ratios are defined in terms of

an acute angle in the right triangle that is represented by the Greek letter θ (theta) and that angle's relationship to its adjacent side, opposite side, and hypotenuse.

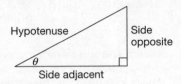

2. There are three trigonometric ratios: sine, cosine, and tangent.

   i. The *sine* is the ratio of the side opposite θ and the hypotenuse:

   $$\sin\theta = \frac{\text{opposite}}{\text{hypotenuse}}$$

   ii. The *cosine* is the ratio of the side adjacent θ and the hypotenuse:

   $$\cos\theta = \frac{\text{adjacent}}{\text{hypotenuse}}$$

   iii. The *tangent* is the ratio of the side opposite θ and the side adjacent to θ:

   $$\tan\theta = \frac{\text{opposite}}{\text{adjacent}}$$

3. The mnemonic SOH-CAH-TOA can be used to remember the trigonometric ratios.

   $$\sin\theta = \frac{\text{opposite}}{\text{hypotenuse}} \qquad \cos\theta = \frac{\text{adjacent}}{\text{hypotenuse}} \qquad \tan\theta = \frac{\text{opposite}}{\text{adjacent}}$$

4. Here's an example of how to find the trigonometric ratios for the following triangle:

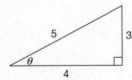

$$\sin\theta = \frac{\text{opposite}}{\text{hypotenuse}} = \frac{3}{5} \qquad \cos\theta = \frac{\text{adjacent}}{\text{hypotenuse}} = \frac{4}{5}$$

$$\tan\theta = \frac{\text{opposite}}{\text{adjacent}} = \frac{3}{4}$$

Test Tip **Similar Triangles and Trigonometric Ratios** *Since the corresponding sides of similar triangles are proportional, similar triangles have the same trigonometric ratios, as well.*

C. RECIPROCAL TRIGONOMETRIC RATIOS

1. The *reciprocal trigonometric ratios* are the reciprocals of the sine, cosine, and tangent ratios. The reciprocal trigonometric ratios are also defined in terms of an acute angle in the right triangle that is represented by the Greek letter θ (theta). There are three reciprocal trigonometric ratios: cosecant, secant, and cotangent.

   i. The *cosecant* is the reciprocal of the sine:

   $$\csc\theta = \frac{1}{\sin\theta} \text{ or } \frac{\text{hypotenuse}}{\text{opposite}}$$

   ii. The *secant* is the reciprocal of the cosine:

   $$\sec\theta = \frac{1}{\cos\theta} \text{ or } \frac{\text{hypotenuse}}{\text{adjacent}}$$

   iii. The *cotangent* is the reciprocal of the tangent:

   $$\cot\theta = \frac{1}{\tan\theta} = \frac{\text{adjacent}}{\text{opposite}}$$

2. Here's an example of how to find reciprocal trigonometric ratios:

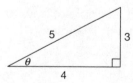

$$\csc\theta = \frac{\text{hypotenuse}}{\text{opposite}} = \frac{5}{3} \qquad \sec\theta = \frac{\text{hypotenuse}}{\text{adjacent}} = \frac{5}{4}$$

$$\cot\theta = \frac{\text{adjacent}}{\text{opposite}} = \frac{4}{3}$$

Cosecants, Secants, and Cotangents on Your Calculator

You may notice that there are no keys for cosecants, secants, and cotangents on your calculator. Since $\csc\theta$, $\sec\theta$, and

$\cot\theta$ are equal to $\dfrac{1}{\sin\theta}$, $\dfrac{1}{\cos\theta}$, and $\dfrac{1}{\tan\theta}$, respectively, you can calculate the reciprocal trigonometric ratios by using their reciprocals:

$$cosecant(x) = csc(x) = sin(x)\text{\^{}}-1$$
$$secant(x) = sec(x) = cos(x)\text{\^{}}-1$$
$$cotangent(x) = cot(x) = tan(x)\text{\^{}}-1$$

Test Tip

For example, to find the cosecant of 35°, first make sure your calculator is in degree mode by pressing the [MODE] key, moving the cursor to DEGREE and pressing [ENTER]. Then press [2nd] [MODE] to return to the home screen. Input sin(35), press the [x^ − 1] key to raise the entry to the (− 1) power, then press [ENTER] to complete the calculation.

D. TRIGONOMETRIC RATIOS IN SPECIAL TRIANGLES

1. *Special triangles* are 30°–60°–90° and 45°–45°–90° triangles with proportional relationships between the lengths of their sides. A 30°–60°–90° triangle has sides of x, $x\sqrt{3}$, and $2x$, and a 45°–45°–90° has sides of x, x, and $x\sqrt{2}$.

2. The trigonometric ratios for the acute angles in special triangles are shown in the following table:

Trigonometric Ratios for Acute Angles in Special Triangles

θ	$\sin \theta$	$\cos \theta$	$\tan \theta$	$\csc \theta$	$\sec \theta$	$\cot \theta$
30°	$\dfrac{1}{2}$	$\dfrac{\sqrt{3}}{2}$	$\dfrac{\sqrt{3}}{3}$	2	$\dfrac{2\sqrt{3}}{3}$	$\sqrt{3}$
45°	$\dfrac{\sqrt{2}}{2}$	$\dfrac{\sqrt{2}}{2}$	1	$\sqrt{2}$	$\sqrt{2}$	1
60°	$\dfrac{\sqrt{3}}{2}$	$\dfrac{1}{2}$	$\sqrt{3}$	$\dfrac{2\sqrt{3}}{3}$	2	$\dfrac{\sqrt{3}}{3}$

3. There are three sets of *cofunctions* in the relationships between the trigonometric and reciprocal trigonometric ratios:

   i. Sine and cosine: $\sin\theta = \cos(90° - \theta)$ and $\cos\theta = \sin(90° - \theta)$

   ii. Tangent and cotangent: $\tan\theta = \cot(90° - \theta)$ and $\cot\theta = \tan(90° - \theta)$

   iii. Secant and cosecant: $\sec\theta = \csc(90° - \theta)$ and $\csc\theta = \sec(90° - \theta)$

II. TRIGONOMETRIC FUNCTIONS

A. ANGLES IN THE COORDINATE PLANE

1. An *angle* is formed by two rays that have the same endpoint. That endpoint is called the *vertex*.

2. An angle can be described in terms of its vertex and the two rays that form it.

   i. The *initial side* of an angle is formed by one ray that is fixed.

   ii. The *terminal side* of an angle is formed by the other ray, which rotated about the vertex.

iii. The measure of an angle provides information about the amount of rotation required to move from the initial side of an angle to its terminal side.

iv. The measure of an angle also provides information about the direction of the rotation.

   a) If the rotation is counterclockwise, the angle measure is *positive.*

   b) If the rotation is clockwise, the angle measure is *negative.*

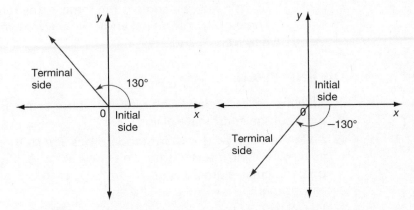

3. Quadrantal angles are angles in the standard position whose terminal sides coincide with either the *x*- or *y*-axis. Angles measuring 90°, 180°, 270°, and 360° are all quadrantal angles.

4. A measure of 360° represents one full rotation around a circle.

5. A measure greater than 360° represents multiple rotations around the circle.

6. *Coterminal angles* are angles in the standard position that have the same terminal angle. For example, if one angle in standard position measures 45° and another angle in standard position measures 405°, the two angles are coterminal because a full rotation of the terminal side of the 45° angle is 45° plus 360° or 405°.

7. The reference angle for any nonquadrantal angle θ in standard position is the acute angle formed by the *x*-axis and the terminal side of the angle.

i. If θ is in Quadrant I, then its reference angle θ' is defined as $\theta' = \theta$.

ii. If θ is in Quadrant II, then its reference angle θ' is defined as $\theta' = 180° - \theta$.

iii. If θ is in Quadrant III, then its reference angle θ' is defined as $\theta' = \theta - 180°$.

iv. If θ is in Quadrant IV, then its reference angle θ' is defined as $\theta' = 360° - \theta$.

v. If the measure of θ is greater than 360° or less than 0°, its reference angle is the same as the reference angle of its coterminal angle with a positive measure between 0° and 360°.

B. THE UNIT CIRCLE

1. The *unit circle* is a circle with radius 1 whose center is at the origin of the coordinate plane.

2. An angle θ can be drawn in standard position so that its terminal side intersects the unit circle at (x, y). If a perpendicular segment is drawn from (x, y) to the x-axis, a right triangle is formed as shown.

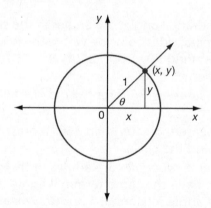

3. By the Pythagorean theorem, $x^2 + y^2 = 1$. This means that the hypotenuse has length 1, the side adjacent θ has length x, and the side opposite θ has length y. You can now define the trigonometric ratios in terms of x and y in the coordinate plane:

   i. $\sin\theta = \dfrac{\text{opposite}}{\text{hypotenuse}} = \dfrac{y}{1} = y$

ii. $\cos\theta = \dfrac{\text{adjacent}}{\text{hypotenuse}} = \dfrac{x}{1} = x$

iii. $\tan\theta = \dfrac{\text{opposite}}{\text{adjacent}} = \dfrac{y}{x}$

iv. $\csc\theta = \dfrac{\text{hypotenuse}}{\text{opposite}} = \dfrac{1}{y}$

v. $\sec\theta = \dfrac{\text{hypotenuse}}{\text{adjacent}} = \dfrac{1}{x}$

vi. $\cot\theta = \dfrac{\text{adjacent}}{\text{opposite}} = \dfrac{x}{y}$

4. For right triangles formed by angles of measure greater than 90°, reference angles are used.

C. TRIGONOMETRIC FUNCTION BASICS

1. For each trigonometric ratio, there is exactly one point (x, y) for any angle θ. This means that sine, cosine, tangent, cosecant, secant, and cotangent are all functions of the angle θ.

2. The domain and range for the trigonometric functions are defined as follows:

   i. Since sin θ and cos θ are defined for all measures of θ, the domain of the sine and cosine functions is the set of real numbers. Since $(\cos\theta, \sin\theta)$ are all points on the unit circle, the range of the sine and cosine functions is the set of real numbers between -1 and 1.

   ii. Since the other four trigonometric functions have variables in their denominators, certain angle measures will be excluded from the domains of these functions. For example, csc(180°) is undefined because the terminal side of a 180° angle in standard position is the negative x-axis, which intersects the unit circle at $(-1, 0)$. Since cosecant is defined as $\dfrac{1}{y}$, this means that csc(180°) would be $\dfrac{1}{y}$, which is undefined. So, csc(180°) is undefined.

   iii. Unlike the sine and cosine functions, the ranges of the other four trigonometric functions are not only between -1 and 1.

5. The signs of the trigonometric functions are determined by the signs of x and y in each quadrant:

   i. All the trigonometric functions are positive in Quadrant I. For example,

   $$\sin 45° = \frac{\sqrt{2}}{2}, \text{ while } \cos 45° = \frac{\sqrt{2}}{2} \text{ and } \tan 45° = 1.$$

   ii. Sine and cosecant functions are positive in Quadrant II. For example,

   $$\sin 135° = \frac{\sqrt{2}}{2}, \text{ while } \cos 135° = -\frac{\sqrt{2}}{2} \text{ and } \tan 135° = -1.$$

   iii. Tangent and cotangent functions are positive in Quadrant III. For example,

   $$\tan 225° = 1, \text{ while } \sin 225° = -\frac{\sqrt{2}}{2} \text{ and } \cos 225° = -\frac{\sqrt{2}}{2}.$$

   iv. Cosine and secant functions are positive in Quadrant IV. For example,

   $$\cos 315° = \frac{\sqrt{2}}{2}, \text{ while } \sin 315° = -\frac{\sqrt{2}}{2} \text{ and } \tan 315° = -1.$$

6. Since trigonometric ratios are the same for similar triangles, the functions can be defined for hypotenuses of lengths other than 1. For any angle in standard position with measure θ, a point (x, y) on its terminal side, and hypotenuse r such that $r = \sqrt{x^2 + y^2}$, the trigonometric functions of θ can be defined as follows:

   i. $\sin \theta = \dfrac{y}{r}$ and $\csc \theta = \dfrac{r}{y}$

   ii. $\cos \theta = \dfrac{x}{r}$ and $\sec \theta = \dfrac{r}{x}$

   iii. $\tan \theta = \dfrac{y}{x}$ and $\cot \theta = \dfrac{x}{y}$

II. INVERSE TRIGONOMETRIC FUNCTIONS

A. INVERSE TRIGONOMETRIC FUNCTION BASICS

1. When the trigonometric value of an angle is known, but the angle itself is unknown, the inverse trigonometric functions can be used to find the angle.
2. The inverse trigonometric functions are the following:

   i. The inverse of the sine function is the *arcsine* function.

   a) If $y = \sin x$, then the inverse function is defined by $y = \sin^{-1} x$ or $y = \arcsin x$.

   b) The domain of the arcsine function is the set of real numbers from -1 to 1.

   ii. The inverse of the cosine function is the *arccosine* function.

   a) If $y = \cos x$, then the inverse function is defined by $y = \cos^{-1} x$ or $y = \arccos x$.

   b) The domain of the arccosine function is also the set of real numbers from -1 to 1.

   iii. The inverse of the tangent function is the *arctangent* function.

   a) If $y = \tan x$, then the inverse function is defined by $y = \tan^{-1} x$ or $y = \arctan x$.

   b) The domain of the arctangent function is the set of all real numbers.

3. The following equations in each list are equivalent and can be used to rewrite trigonometric expressions:

   i. $y = \sin x$, $x = \sin^{-1} y$, and $x = \arcsin y$

   ii. $y = \cos x$, $x = \cos^{-1} y$, and $x = \arccos y$

   iii. $y = \tan x$, $x = \tan^{-1} y$, and $x = \arctan y$

B. USING INVERSE TRIGONOMETRIC FUNCTIONS

1. You can use inverse trigonometric functions to evaluate trigonometric expressions. For example, here's how you could evaluate the expression $\cos\left(\arcsin\dfrac{4}{5}\right)$ for an angle θ in

Quadrant I: If $\theta = \arcsin\left(\dfrac{4}{5}\right)$, then $\sin\theta = \dfrac{4}{5}$ by the definition of an inverse. Since $\sin\theta = \dfrac{\text{opposite}}{\text{hypotenuse}} = \dfrac{y}{r}$ and $\sin\theta = \dfrac{4}{5}$, you know that the right triangle formed with θ at the origin has a hypotenuse of length 5 and an adjacent leg of length 4. Therefore, the opposite leg must be of length 3 and since

$\cos\theta = \dfrac{\text{adjacent}}{\text{hypotenuse}} = \dfrac{x}{r}$, this means that $\cos\left(\arcsin\dfrac{4}{5}\right) = \dfrac{3}{5}$.

2. You can also use inverse trigonometric functions to solve equations. For example, here's how you could solve the equation $\cos x = \dfrac{1}{2}$: If $\cos x = \dfrac{1}{2}$, then x is an angle whose cosine is $\dfrac{1}{2}$. Therefore, $x = \arccos\dfrac{1}{2}$ and $x = 60°$ in Quadrant I and 300° in Quadrant IV.

Test Tip

Inverse Trigonometric Functions on Your Calculator To access the inverse trigonometric functions on your calculator, press [2ND][SIN] for SIN⁻¹(arcsin), [2ND][COS] for COS⁻¹ (arccos), and [2ND][TAN] for TAN⁻¹ (arctan).

PERIODIC AND PIECEWISE FUNCTIONS

KEY VOCABULARY

Amplitude The absolute value of half the difference between the maximum value and the minimum value of the graph of a periodic function.

Period The interval for which the values of a periodic function repeat.

Periodic function A function whose values repeat for some given interval of the domain.

Phase shift Horizontal translation of the graph of a trigonometric function.

Piecewise function A function that is defined by different equations that are used for different intervals of the domain.

Radians Units of angle measure based on the unit circle. A radian is the measure of an angle θ in standard position whose rays intercept an arc of length 1 on the unit circle. The radian measure of 360°, or one complete rotation about a circle, is 2π radians.

Step function A piecewise function whose graph looks like a set of stairs.

Vertical shift Vertical translation of the graph of a trigonometric function.

I. PERIODIC FUNCTIONS

A. PERIODIC FUNCTION BASICS

1. If the values of a function repeat for some given interval of the domain, the function is a *periodic function*.
2. In a periodic function, the interval for which the values of the function repeat is the period.
3. Some periodic functions are more easily analyzed when angles are measured in radians rather than degrees.

B. RADIAN MEASURE OF ANGLES

1. Angles can be measured using either degrees or radians.
2. *Radians* are based on the unit circle. A radian is the measure of an angle θ in standard position whose rays intercept an arc of length 1 on the unit circle. In the following diagram, the measure of angle θ is 1 radian.

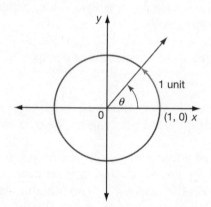

3. The radian measure of 360°, or one complete rotation about the circle, is 2π radians. Since the circumference of a circle is $2\pi r$ and the radius of the unit circle is 1, the distance of 1 complete rotation about the unit circle can be given as 2π.
4. To convert from degree to radian measure, multiply the number of degrees by $\dfrac{\pi \text{ radians}}{180°}$. For example, 90° is

$$90°\left(\frac{\pi \text{ radians}}{180°}\right) = \frac{90\pi}{180} \text{ radians} = \frac{\pi}{2} \text{ radians} .$$

5. To convert from radian to degree measure, multiply the number of radians by $\dfrac{180°}{\pi \text{ radians}}$. For example, $\dfrac{\pi}{3}$ radians is

$$\left(\dfrac{\pi}{3} \text{ radians}\right)\left(\dfrac{180°}{\pi \text{ radians}}\right) = \dfrac{180°}{3} = 60°.$$

6. The following table provides a quick reference for equivalent degree and radian measures of some special angles.

**Equivalent Degree and Radian Measures
of Select Special Angles**

Degrees	30°	45°	60°	90°	120°	135°	150°	180°
Radians	$\dfrac{\pi}{6}$	$\dfrac{\pi}{4}$	$\dfrac{\pi}{3}$	$\dfrac{\pi}{2}$	$\dfrac{2\pi}{3}$	$\dfrac{3\pi}{4}$	$\dfrac{5\pi}{6}$	π

Degrees	210°	225°	240°	270°	300°	315°	330°	360°
Radians	$\dfrac{7\pi}{6}$	$\dfrac{5\pi}{4}$	$\dfrac{4\pi}{3}$	$\dfrac{3\pi}{2}$	$\dfrac{5\pi}{3}$	$\dfrac{7\pi}{4}$	$\dfrac{11\pi}{6}$	2π

Test Tip

Degree Mode or Radian Mode? *Make sure that your calculator is set to degree mode when you are working with degrees and radians when you are working with radians. To check, press [MODE]. If RADIAN is not highlighted, press the [↓][↓][←] and [ENTER] to change to radian mode.*

Degree Mode

```
NORMAL  SCI   ENG
FLOAT  0123456789
RADIAN DEGREE
FUNC  PAR   POL   SEQ
CONNECTED  DOT
SEQUENTIAL  SIMUL
REAL  a+bi  re^θi
FULL  HORIZ  G-T
SET CLOCK 01/06/01 11:43
```

Radian Mode

```
NORMAL  SCI   ENG
FLOAT  0123456789
RADIAN DEGREE
FUNC  PAR   POL   SEQ
CONNECTED  DOT
SEQUENTIAL  SIMUL
REAL  a+bi  re^θi
FULL  HORIZ  G-T
SET CLOCK 01/07/01 09:34
```

When deciding whether to use degrees or radians when solving a test problem, look at the answers. If they are given in degrees, using degree mode will probably work best. If they are given in radians, using radian mode is the most likely one to use.

C. THE SINE AND COSINE FUNCTIONS

1. The Sine Function

    i. Following is a graph showing $y = \sin x$. You can see from the graph that the values of the function repeat for a given interval of the domain. Therefore, the *sine function* is a periodic function.

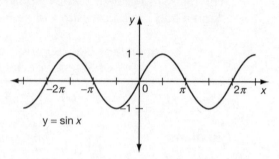

$y = \sin x$

    ii. The sine function repeats the values for the interval $-2\pi < x < 0$. The graph shows that these same x-values are repeated in the interval $0 < x < 2\pi$. The length of each interval is 2π. Therefore, the period for the sine function is 2π.

    iii. The *domain* of the sine function is the set of all real numbers.

    iv. The *range* of the sine function is the set of all real numbers between 1 and –1, inclusive.

    v. The x-intercepts of $y = \sin x$ are given by πn, where n is an integer.

    vi. The y-intercept of $y = \sin x$ is 0.

    vii. The maximum value for $y = \sin x$ is $y = 1$. The maximum values occur at $x = \dfrac{\pi}{2} + 2\pi n$, where n is an integer.

    viii. The minimum value for $y = \sin x$ is $y = -1$. The minimum values occur at $x = \dfrac{3\pi}{2} + 2\pi n$, where n is an integer.

2. The Cosine Function

    i. Following is the graph of $y = \cos x$. You can see from the graph that the values of the function repeat for a given interval of the domain. Therefore, the *cosine function* is also a periodic function.

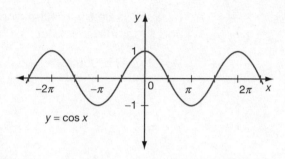

$y = \cos x$

ii. The cosine function repeats the values for the interval $-2\pi < x < 0$. The graph shows that these same x-values are repeated in the interval $0 < x < 2\pi$. The length of each interval is 2π. Therefore, the period for the cosine function is 2π.

iii. The domain of the cosine function is the set of all real numbers.

iv. The range of the cosine function is the set of all real numbers between –1 and 1, inclusive.

v. The x-intercepts of $y = \cos x$ are $\dfrac{\pi}{2} + \pi n$, where n is an integer.

vi. The y-intercept of $y = \cos x$ is 1.

vii. The maximum value for $y = \cos x$ is $y = 1$. The maximum values occur at $x = \pi n$, where n is an even integer.

viii. The minimum value for $y = \cos x$ is $y = -1$. The minimum values occur at $x = \pi n$, where n is an odd integer.

3. Amplitude

i. The *amplitude* of the graph of a periodic function is the absolute value of half the difference between its maximum value and its minimum value.

ii. Since both the sine function and the cosine function have a maximum value of 1 and a minimum value of –1, the amplitude of both their graphs is $\left| \dfrac{1-(-1)}{2} \right| = 1.$

iii. Following are graphs of the functions $y = \sin x$ and $y = 2 \sin x$. Although the period of $y = 2 \sin x$ is the same as the period of $y = \sin x$, the amplitude is greater. Since the maximum value of $y = 2 \sin x$ is 2 and the minimum value is -2, the amplitude of

$y = 2 \sin x$ is $\left| \dfrac{2 - (-2)}{2} \right| = 2$.

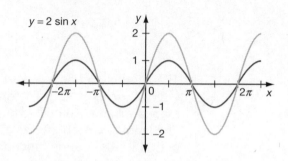

$y = 2 \sin x$

iv. In general, the amplitude of the functions $y = a \sin x$ and $y = a \cos x$ is $|a|$.

4. Translating the Sine and Cosine Functions

   i. A horizontal translation of a trigonometric function is called a *phase shift*.

   ii. The phase shift of $y = a \sin b (x - h)$ and $y = a \cos b (x - h)$ is h, where $b > 0$. If $h > 0$, then the shift is to the right. If $h < 0$, then the shift is to the left.

   iii. A vertical translation of a trigonometric function is called a *vertical shift*.

   iv. The vertical shift of $y = a \sin b (x - h) + k$ and $y = a \cos b (x - h) + k$ is k. If $k > 0$, then the shift is up. If $k < 0$, then the shift is down.

D. OTHER PERIODIC FUNCTIONS

1. The Tangent Function

   i. Following is the graph of $y = \tan x$. You can see from the graph that the values of the function repeat for a given interval of the domain. Therefore, the *tangent function* is a periodic function.

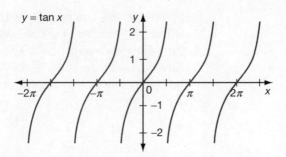

$y = \tan x$

ii. The tangent function is not defined for values

of $\dfrac{\pi}{2}$, $\dfrac{3\pi}{2}$, . . ., $\dfrac{\pi}{2} + k \bullet 2\pi$ or, in degrees,

90°, 270°, . . ., 90° + $k \bullet$ 180°. The graph has vertical asymptotes at each x-intercept where the tangent function is undefined.

iii. The *period* of the tangent function is π radians.

iv. Since the tangent function has no minimum or maximum, it has no amplitude.

v. The phase shift of $y = a \tan b (x - h)$ is h, where $b > 0$. If $h > 0$, then the shift is to the right. If $h < 0$, then the shift is to the left.

vi. The vertical shift of $y = a \tan b (x - h) + k$ is k. If $k > 0$, then the shift is up. If $k < 0$, then the shift is down.

2. The Secant, Cosecant, and Cotangent Functions

i. Following are the graphs of the secant and cosine functions. As you can see, the secant and cosine functions are reciprocals. The period of the secant function is 2π radians. Since the secant function has no minimum or maximum, the graph has no amplitude.

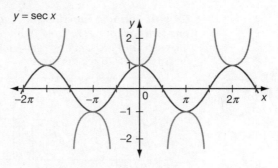

$y = \sec x$

ii. Following are the graphs of the cosecant and sine functions. As you can see, the cosecant and sine functions are reciprocals. The period of the cosecant function is 2π radians. Since the cosecant function has no minimum or maximum, the graph has no amplitude.

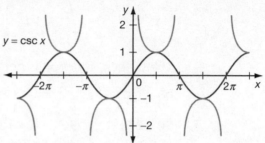

iii. Following are the graphs of the cotangent and tangent functions. As you can see, the cotangent and tangent functions are reciprocals. The period of the cotangent function is π radians. Since the cotangent function has no minimum or maximum, the graph has no amplitude.

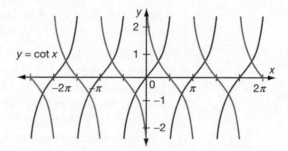

Graphic Periodic Functions on Your Calculator To graph the sine function, press [Y=] and input [SIN][x][ENTER]. To graph the cosecant function, press [Y=] and input 1/[SIN][x][ENTER]. Press [GRAPH] to see the graphs.

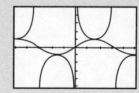

II. PIECEWISE FUNCTIONS

A. PIECEWISE FUNCTION BASICS

1. A *piecewise function* is defined by different equations that are used for different intervals of the domain. Following are two piecewise functions and their graphs:

$$f(x)\begin{cases} -2 \text{ if } x \le -6 \\ \dfrac{1}{2}x + 1 \text{ if } -6 < x < 2 \\ -x + 4 \text{ if } x \ge 2 \end{cases} \qquad g(x)\begin{cases} -2 \text{ if } x \le -6 \\ \dfrac{1}{2}x + 5 \text{ if } -6 < x < 2 \\ -x + 6 \text{ if } x \ge 2 \end{cases}$$

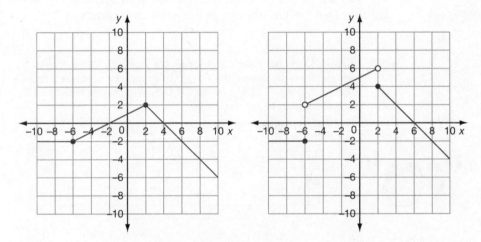

2. The pieces of a piecewise graph do not necessarily connect over the different intervals, as shown in the graph of function *g*.

B. STEP FUNCTIONS

1. A *step function* is a piecewise function whose graph looks like a set of stairs.

2. An example of a stepwise function is the greatest integer function, which is written as $f(x) = [\![x]\!]$. The symbol $[\![x]\!]$ means the greatest integer that is not greater *x*. For example, if $x = 5.9$, then $f(x) = 5$ since 5 is the greatest integer that is not greater than 5.9. Following is the graph of the greatest integer function.

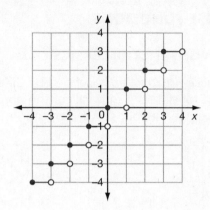

3. The domain of the greatest integer function is the set of all real numbers, while the range is the set of integers.

Graph Steps on Your Calculator *On your calculator, the greatest integer function is int(x). To graph the greatest integer function, press [Y=], then press [MATH] and choose NUM and 5. Press [GRAPH] to see the graph.*

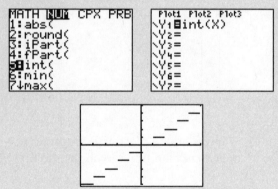

C. ABSOLUTE VALUE FUNCTIONS

1. The *parent absolute value function* $f(x) = |x|$ is another example of a piecewise function. The function is represented by the following table.

Absolute Value Function

x	−3	−2	−1	0	1	2	3
$f(x) = |x|$	3	2	1	0	1	2	3

2. Following is the graph of the absolute value function.

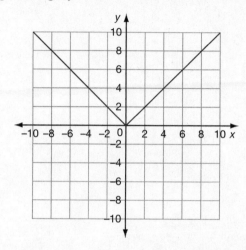

Note that for the domain interval where $x \geq 0$, the value of $f(x)$ is x. However, for the domain interval where $x < 0$, the value of $f(x)$ is $-x$. This means that the absolute value function can be written as a piecewise function: $f(x) \begin{cases} -x \text{ if } x < 0 \\ x \text{ if } x \geq 0 \end{cases}$.

RECURSIVE FUNCTIONS

Chapter

19

KEY VOCABULARY

Recursive function A function that is defined in terms of itself.

 I. RECURSION

A. RECURSION BASICS

1. *Recursion* is the process of repeating something in a self-referential way. For example, reflecting the image from a reflecting mirror in another reflecting mirror produces a seemingly endless sequence of images, with each one being a reflection of the previous one, which is a reflection of the previous one, which is a reflection of the previous one, and so on.
2. Recursion is a common application in mathematics. For example, you use recursion when you define arithmetic and geometric sequences and series recursively.

B. RECURSION IN MATHEMATICS

1. Mathematical definitions involving recursion usually involve a base case or cases followed by a rule that relates each successive case to the previous one.
2. The set of natural numbers can be defined recursively. Starting with the declaration that 1 is a natural number, the recursive definition of natural numbers is that if n is a natural number, then the successor $n + 1$ is a natural number.
3. Finding the factorial is also a recursive process. Starting with the declaration that $0! = 1$, the recursive process of finding a factorial of some number n is to find the product of n and $(n - 1)!$.

4. The Fibonacci sequence can be defined recursively. Starting with the declaration that the first number in the Fibonacci sequence is 0 and the second number in the Fibonacci sequence is 1, the recursive process of finding term n in the Fibonacci sequence is recursively defined as the sum of the term $n - 1$ and term $n - 2$. The Fibonacci sequence: 0, 1, 1, 2, 3, 5, 8, 13, 21, 34, . . . The rule for the Fibonacci sequence is $x_n = x_{n-1} + x_{n-2}$, where x_n is the nth term in the sequence, x_{n-1} is the previous term, the $n-1$ term of the sequence, and x_{n-2} is the $n - 2$ term of the sequence.

II. RECURSIVE FUNCTIONS

A. DEFINING RECURSIVE FUNCTIONS

1. Definitions of *recursive functions* generally include a recursive definition that leads to values that are nonrecursively defined.

2. An example of a function that can be defined recursively is a function F for term n of the Fibonacci number sequence: $F(n) = F(n-1) + F(n-2)$. The definition must also include the nonrecursively defined values $F(0) = 0$ and $F(1) = 1$.

> **Generating Recursive Functions on Your Calculator** *You can generate the values of recursive functions on your graphing calculator. Here's how you could generate the value of the Fibonacci sequence. Note that you could generate other recursive functions using this process as a model.*
>
> *Before you start, press [MODE], choose Seq in the fourth line, and press [ENTER] to select it.*

> *Now press [Y=]. You will notice a difference in the screen.*

(continued)

(continued)

To define the Fibonacci sequence, you must specify nMin, which is where you will start counting; u(n), which is the rule for the pattern; and u(nMin), which is the first number in the sequence.

```
Plot1 Plot2 Plot3
nMin=0
·u(n)█(n-1)+u(n
-2)
 u(nMin)█(1,0)
\v(n)=
 v(nMin)=
\w(n)=
```

Note that you can input the u as the lowercase u by pressing [2ND]7. Pressing the [X,T,θ,n] key in Seq mode will give you the variable n.

The results will be sent to the table. In order for the results to display correctly, press [2ND][WINDOW] for TBLSET and set the values as shown:

```
TABLE SETUP
 TblStart=0
 ΔTbl=1
Indpnt: Auto Ask
Depend: Auto Ask
```

Finally, press [2ND][GRAPH] to see the table and the Fibonacci sequence.

```
 n    │ u(n)
 0    │ 0
 1    │ 1
 2    │ 1
 3    │ 2
 4    │ 3
 5    │ 5
 6    │ 8
u(n)=0
```

B. EVALUATING RECURSIVE FUNCTIONS

1. To evaluate a recursive function at a certain value, you also have to evaluate it recursively at values that precede it.

2. To find the seventh term of the Fibonacci sequence, you can evaluate $F(6)$. Note that since the function definition starts at $n = 0$, the input to the function is one less than the ordinal value.

$$F(6) = F(6-1) + F(6-2) = F(5) + F(4)$$

It turns out that to evaluate $F(6)$, you must also evaluate $F(4)$ and $F(5)$:

$$F(4) = F(4-1) + F(4-2) = F(3) + F(2)$$
$$F(5) = F(5-1) + F(5-2) = F(4) + F(3)$$

The recursion continues to the nonrecursive definitions $F(0) = 0$ and $F(1) = 1$, then the succeeding function definitions reference previous ones to evaluate $F(6)$ as follows:

$$F(0) = 0$$
$$F(1) = 1$$
$$F(2) = F(1) + F(0) = 1 + 0 = 1$$
$$F(3) = F(2) + F(1) = 1 + 1 = 2$$
$$F(4) = F(3) + F(2) = 2 + 1 = 3$$
$$F(5) = F(4) + F(3) = 3 + 2 = 5$$
$$F(6) = F(5) + F(4) = 5 + 3 = 8$$

So, the seventh term of the Fibonacci sequence is 8.

Test Tip

Evaluating Recursive Functions with Pencil and Paper If you have to solve a problem involving recursive functions on the test, you may only need to evaluate a recursive function for a very low value or values. In this case, working through the recursion by hand with pencil and paper may be the best approach.

PARAMETRIC FUNCTIONS

KEY VOCABULARY

Parameter The third variable in a set of parametric equations. The parameter is usually denoted by t and represents time.

Parametric equations Parametric equations express a relationship between x and y in terms of a third variable.

 PARAMETRIC EQUATIONS

A. **PARAMETRIC EQUATION BASICS**

1. *Parametric equations* express a relationship between x and y in terms of a third variable.
2. The third variable, usually denoted by t, is called a *parameter*.

B. **MODELING WITH PARAMETRIC EQUATIONS**

1. Parametric equations are usually used to model motion, with the parameter t representing time.
2. Parametric equations of the form $x = x(t)$ and $y = y(t)$ can be used to represent the location of an object on the coordinate plane at time t.
3. To find the location of the object at time t, substitute the same value for t into each parametric equation.

II. GRAPHING PARAMETRIC EQUATIONS

A. PARAMETRIC EQUATIONS OF A LINE

1. For a line that has parametric equations of $x = 2 + t$ and $y = 6 + t$, substituting $t = 0$ gives the point (2, 6) on the line; substituting $t = 1$ gives the point (3, 7); substituting $t = 2$ gives the point (4, 8); and so on.

2. To find the slope of the line with the parametric equations $x = 2 + t$ and $y = 6 + t$, different approaches can be used:

   i. Find the points for $t = 0$ and $t = 1$: (2, 6) and (3, 7). Use these two points in the slope formula: $\frac{7-6}{3-2} = \frac{1}{1} = 1$. The slope of the line is 1.

   ii. Express y in terms of x: Rewrite the equation $x = 2 + t$ as $t = x - 2$ and substitute $x - 2$ for t in the equation $y = 6 + t$. You can simplify the resulting equation, $y = 6 + (x - 2)$ as $y = x + 4$. Since the line is in slope-intercept form $y = mx + b$, where m is slope, the slope of the line is 1.

B. PLOTTING POINTS FOR THE GRAPH OF PARAMETRIC EQUATIONS

1. You can use the following table to identify the points to plot in order to graph the parametric equations $x = 2 + t$ and $y = 6 + t$. For each point, the two equations are both evaluated for the given value of t.

t	0	1	2	3	4
x	2	3	4	5	6
y	6	7	8	9	10

2. You can then graph the equations by plotting any two points and drawing a line through them.

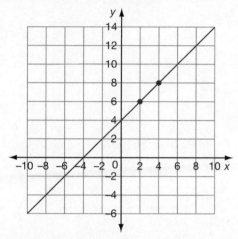

Note that the slope of the line is 1 and the *y*-intercept is 4, confirming the equation of the line as $y = x + 4$.

Graphing Parametric Equations on Your Calculator *Here's how to use your graphing calculator to graph the parametric equations $x = 2 + t^2$ and $y = 6 + t$.*

Start by putting your calculator into parametric mode: Press [MODE] PAR. In parametric mode, the standard window still has the usual x and y axes, but uses a minimum of 0 for T and a maximum of 6.28 for T for the graph. The interpretation is that T represents time and is therefore not negative. Also, the [X, T, θ, n] key displays T in parametric mode.

Next, press [Y=] and input $x = 2 + t^2$ into $X1_T$ and $y = 6 + t$ into $Y1_T$.

```
Plot1 Plot2 Plot3
\X1T=2+T²
 Y1T=6+T
\X2T=
 Y2T=
\X3T=
 Y3T=
\X4T=
```

(continued)

(continued)

Press [GRAPH] to see the graph.

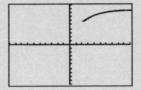

Note that if you press [TRACE], you can use the right arrow key to move along the graph and see the corresponding values.

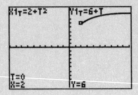

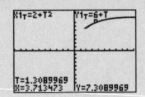

LIMITS

KEY VOCABULARY

Limit A value that a function approaches as its independent variable approaches a given value.

I. UNDERSTANDING LIMITS

A. LIMIT BASICS

1. A *limit* is a value that a function approaches as its independent variable approaches a given value.

2. The definition of a limit can be written as $L = \lim_{x \to a} f(x)$. This means that L is the limit of $f(x)$ as x gets closer to a number a.

B. LIMIT EXAMPLES

1. Limits can be found for continuous functions. For example, if $f(x) = 3x + 2$, the following questions might be asked:
   - i. What is the limit of $f(x)$ as x approaches 3?
   - ii. What is the limit of $3x + 2$ as x approaches 3?
   - iii. What is $\lim_{x \to 3} 3x + 2$?

2. Limits can also be found for discontinuous functions. For example, if $f(x) = \dfrac{3x^2 - 7x - 6}{x - 3}$, the following questions might be asked:
   - i. What is the limit of $f(x)$ as x approaches 3?
   - ii. What is the limit of $\dfrac{3x^2 - 7x - 6}{x - 3}$ as x approaches 3?
   - iii. What is $\lim_{x \to 3} \dfrac{3x^2 - 7x - 6}{x - 3}$?

The Pencil Test *Recall that continuous functions are functions whose graphs have no holes and no discontinuities, while discontinuous functions are functions whose graphs have holes or discontinuities. An easy way to distinguish between continuous and discontinuous functions is the pencil test: the graph of a continuous function can be drawn without taking your pencil off the paper, but the graph of a discontinuous function cannot be drawn without taking your pencil off the paper.*

II. EVALUATING LIMITS

A. LIMITS OF CONTINUOUS FUNCTIONS

1. Continuous functions include linear functions, polynomial functions, the sine and cosine functions, exponential functions, and logarithmic functions of the form $f(x) = \log_a x$ if $x > 0$.

2. For a continuous function, the limit of $f(x)$ as x approaches a is equal to $f(a)$. In notation, this is expressed as $\lim_{x \to a} f(x) = f(a)$. For example, to evaluate $\lim_{x \to 3} 3x + 2$, simply substitute 3 for x and evaluate: $3(3) + 2 = 11$. So, $\lim_{x \to 3} 3x + 2 = 11$.

B. LIMITS OF DISCONTINUOUS FUNCTIONS

1. The most common type of discontinuous functions are rational functions.

2. The process of evaluating the limit of a discontinuous function is more complicated than evaluating the limit of a continuous function. For example, consider the rational function $f(x) = \dfrac{3x^2 - 7x - 6}{x - 3}$.

   i. When evaluating $\lim_{x \to 3} \dfrac{3x^2 - 7x - 6}{x - 3}$, you cannot simply substitute 3 for x because this would result in division by zero.

ii. An approach to solving the problem is to factor the numerator to see if the denominator can be canceled out.

$$\frac{3x^2 - 7x - 6}{x - 3} = \frac{(3x + 2)(x - 3)}{x - 3}$$

$$= 3x + 2, \; x \neq 3$$

iii. Now you can evaluate $\lim\limits_{x \to 3} 3x + 2$ by simply substituting 3 for x. Note that this problem may look familiar since you have already evaluated $\lim\limits_{x \to 3} 3x + 2$. Again, $\lim\limits_{x \to 3} 3x + 2 = 11$.

iv. The limit can be visualized in the following graph of $f(x) = \dfrac{3x^2 - 7x - 6}{x - 3}$.

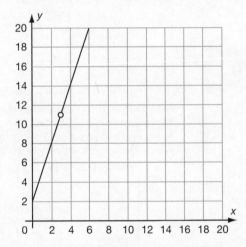

It can be seen that $f(x)$ approaches 11 as x approaches 3. Note that there is a hole at $x = 3$, where division by zero is undefined. This is not a problem with the limit, however, since $\lim\limits_{x \to 3} \dfrac{3x^2 - 7x - 6}{x - 3}$ means x approaches but never actually reaches 3.

Find Limits with Your Graphing Calculator *You can use your graphing calculator to find limits. For example, here's how you could find* $\lim\limits_{x \to 3} \dfrac{3x^2 - 7x - 6}{x - 3}$ *with your calculator.*

First, press [Y=] and input $y = \dfrac{3x^2 - 7x - 6}{x - 3}$. *Then press*

[GRAPH] to display the graph. Since you are interested in the area of the graph in the vicinity of x = 3, be sure to set the window so that part of the graph is displayed. Following are the settings for the display.

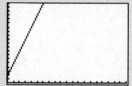

Next, press [TRACE], then input 3 and press ENTER. This will give you the y-value at x = 3. Note, however, that there is no y-value when x = 3. This is because the function is undefined for x = 3.

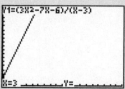

Now explore the y-values as x approaches 3. One way to do this is to press [TRACE] and then use the left and right arrows to move the cursor along the graph. Note that you can use [ZOOM] to get closer to x = 3.

 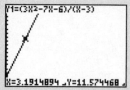

Another way to explore the y-values as x approaches 3 is to press [TRACE] and enter values that are very close to 3.

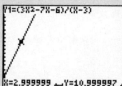 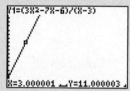

Note that the limit you find on a graphing calculator should be the same as the limit you find algebraically.

PART IV:
GEOMETRY AND MEASUREMENT

Chapter 7

COORDINATE GEOMETRY

KEY VOCABULARY

Circle The set of all points in a plane that are equidistant from a given point.

Dilation Transforming a figure by enlarging or reducing it.

Ellipse The set of all points in the plane for which the *sum* of their distances from two fixed points in the plane is constant.

Hyperbola The set of all points in the plane for which the *difference* of their distances from two fixed points in the plane is constant.

Line A set of collinear points.

Midpoint The point that divides a line segment into two congruent segments.

Parabola The set of all points in the plane that are the same distance from a point called the *focus* and a line called the *directrix*.

Parallel lines Two lines that do not intersect. Two lines are parallel if they have the same slope.

Perpendicular lines Two lines that intersect at right angles. Two lines are perpendicular if the product of their slopes is -1.

Plane A flat surface comprised of points.

Point A single location with neither shape nor size.

Polar coordinate system A system for giving locations of points using distance and angles.

Reflection Transforming a figure by flipping it.

Rotation Transforming a figure by turning it about a given point at a given angle.

Segment bisector Any segment, line, or plane that intersects a line segment at its midpoint.

Slope The steepness of a line, given by the ratio of rise (change in y) over run (change in x).

Translation Transforming a figure by shifting it up, down, left, or right.

 I. COORDINATE GEOMETRY BASICS

A. POINTS, LINES, AND PLANES

1. *Point, line,* and *plane* are the three undefined terms of geometry. The terms are not based on other concepts. The terms are explained using descriptions and examples instead of formal definitions.

    i. Points
       a) A point is a single location.
       b) Points are named by a capital letter. For example, one point could be called point P and another point could be called point Q.
       c) Points are drawn as a dot.
       d) Points do not have shape or size.

    ii. Lines
       a) A line is a set of points.
       b) Points on the same line are collinear.
       c) Lines can be named in the following two ways:
          ▸ *Lines can be named by the letters representing two points on the line. For example, if P and Q are points on the line, then the line can be named as line PQ or $\overleftrightarrow{PQ}$. Note that the same line can also be named QP or $\overleftrightarrow{QP}$.*
          ▸ *Lines can also be named by a lowercase script letter, such as line ℓ.*

      d) Lines are drawn with an arrowhead on each end.

      e) Lines do not have thickness or width.

      f) There is exactly one line through any two points.

   iii. Planes

      a) A plane is a flat, two-dimensional surface comprised of points.

      b) Points on the same plane are coplanar.

      c) Planes can be named in the following two ways:

         ▸ *Planes can be named by the letters representing three noncollinear points on the plane. For example, if P, Q, and R are noncollinear points on a plane, then the plane can be named as plane PQR, plane PRQ, plane QPR, plane QRP, plane RPQ, or plane RQP.*

         ▸ *Planes can also be named by an uppercase script letter, such as plane M .*

      d) Planes are often drawn as parallelograms.

      e) Planes have no depth.

      f) Planes extend infinitely in all directions.

      g) There is exactly one plane through any three noncollinear points.

  2. Two lines intersect in a point.

  3. Lines can intersect planes.

  4. Planes can intersect each other.

B. LINE SEGMENTS

1. A line segment has two endpoints and can be named by the endpoints. For example, a line segment with endpoints P and Q can be named $\overline{PQ}$ or $\overline{QP}$.

2. Since a line segment has two endpoints, it can be measured. The measure of a line segment is also represented by the names of the endpoints, but is given without the bar above. For example, the measure of a line segment with endpoints P and Q can be represented as PQ or QP.

C. RAYS

1. A ray is a part of a line that has one endpoint and extends infinitely in the other direction. A ray is named with the endpoint first followed by any other point on the ray. Rays

are indicated by an arrow or harpoon pointing right over the letters. For example, a ray with endpoint P and having points Q and R on the ray can be named $\overrightarrow{PQ}$ or $\overrightarrow{PR}$. Note that the ray cannot be named $\overrightarrow{QP}$ or $\overrightarrow{RP}$ since Q and R are not endpoints.

2. A point on a line divides the line into two opposite rays, with that point as the endpoint of both rays. For example, if point Q is between points P and R on a line, then the line can be separated into the opposite rays $\overrightarrow{QP}$ and $\overrightarrow{QR}$. Rays $\overrightarrow{QP}$ and $\overrightarrow{QR}$ are said to be *collinear*.

3. Two noncollinear rays that have a common endpoint form an angle. The common endpoint is the vertex of the angle, and the rays form the sides of the angle. An angle with vertex Q and sides $\overrightarrow{QP}$ and $\overrightarrow{QR}$ can be named $\angle PQR$, $\angle RQP$, or $\angle Q$.

D. THE COORDINATE PLANE

1. On the coordinate plane, there is a horizontal number line called the *x*-axis and a vertical number line called the *y*-axis that intersects at zero.

2. Points on the coordinate plane are named using ordered pairs that represent their horizontal and vertical coordinates. For example, the point $(-3, 5)$ is at the intersection of -3 on the *x*-axis and 5 on the *y*-axis.

 II. LINES

A. LINE SEGMENTS IN THE COORDINATE PLANE

1. The length of a line segment can be found by finding the distance between its two endpoints. In the coordinate plane, the distance d between two points (x_1, y_1) and (x_2, y_2) is given by the formula $d = \sqrt{(x_2 - x_1)^2 + (y_2 - y_1)^2}$. For example, in the following coordinate plane, the distance between points P and Q can be found as follows:

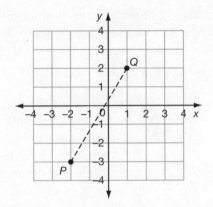

i. Identify the coordinates of *P* and *Q*: $P(-2, -3)$ and $Q(1, 2)$.

ii. Substitute the coordinates into the formula:

$$d = \sqrt{\left(1-(-2)\right)^2 + \left(2-(-3)\right)^2}$$
$$d = \sqrt{3^2 + 5^2}$$
$$d = \sqrt{9 + 25}$$
$$d = \sqrt{34}$$

So, $PQ = \sqrt{34}$.

Use the Correct Signs in the Distance Formula *A common error is to subtract the quantities $(x_2 - x_1)^2$ and $(y_2 - y_1)^2$ in the distance formula before taking the square root, instead of adding them. This may be because the x- and y-coordinates are subtracted within the parentheses.*

2. The *midpoint* of a line segment is the point that divides the line segment into two congruent segments.

3. If the endpoints of a line segment have coordinates (x_1, y_1) and (x_2, y_2), then the coordinates of the midpoint of the segment are $\left(\dfrac{x_1 + x_2}{2}, \dfrac{y_1 + y_2}{2}\right)$. For example, for points $P(-2, -3)$ and $Q(1, 2)$ in the preceding coordinate plane, the midpoint is $\left(\dfrac{-2+1}{2}, \dfrac{-3+2}{2}\right)$ or $\left(-\dfrac{1}{2}, -\dfrac{1}{2}\right)$.

4. A *segment bisector* is any segment, line, or plane that intersects a line segment at its midpoint.

B. EQUATIONS OF LINES

1. The slope-intercept form of the equation of a line is given by $y = mx + b$, where m is the slope and b is the y-intercept.

   i. Since a horizontal line has zero slope, the equation of a horizontal line is of the form $y = b$. For example, the equation of the following line is $y = 4$.

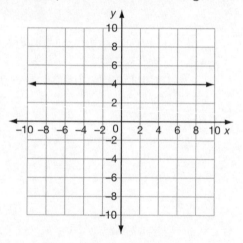

   ii. The slope of a vertical line is undefined.

2. The point-slope form of the equation of a line is given by $y - y_1 = m(x - x_1)$, where m is the slope and (x_1, y_1) is a point on the line.

3. The standard form of the equation of a linear function is given by $Ax + By = C$ with A and B not both zero.

C. PARALLEL AND PERPENDICULAR LINES

1. In the coordinate plane, the *slope* of a line is the ratio of its vertical rise to its horizontal run. The slope m of a line containing points (x_1, y_1) and (x_2, y_2) can be found using the formula $m = \dfrac{y_2 - y_1}{x_2 - x_1}$, where $x_1 \neq x_2$. For example, you can use the coordinates of points P and Q on the following line to find the slope m of the line.

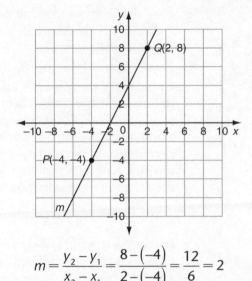

$$m = \frac{y_2 - y_1}{x_2 - x_1} = \frac{8 - (-4)}{2 - (-4)} = \frac{12}{6} = 2$$

So, the slope of line m is 2. Note that since the y-intercept is 4, the equation of the line in slope-intercept form is $y = 2x + 4$.

2. In the coordinate plane, two nonvertical lines are *parallel* if and only if they have the same slope.
   i. If you know that two lines are parallel, then you also know that they have the same slope.
   ii. Also, if you know that two lines have the same slope, then you also know that they are parallel.
   iii. Since parallel lines are lines that do not intersect, two lines that have the same slope do not intersect.
   iv. To determine if two lines are parallel, determine if they have the same slope. If the equations of both lines are in slope-intercept form $y = mx + b$, then the lines are parallel if the value of m is the same in both equations. For example, the lines with the equations $y = 2x + 4$ and $y = 2x - 7$ are parallel. If lines are not already in slope-intercept, rewrite them in that form in order to determine if they are parallel.

3. In the coordinate plane, two nonvertical lines are *perpendicular* if and only if the product of their slopes is -1. This means that two lines are perpendicular if the slope of one line is the negative reciprocal of the slope of the other line.
   i. If you know that two lines are perpendicular, then you also know that the product of their slopes is -1.

ii. Also, if you know that the product of the slopes of two lines is −1, then you also know that the lines are perpendicular.

iii. Perpendicular lines intersect at 90° angles.

iv. To determine if two lines are perpendicular, determine if the products of their slopes have a product of −1. If the equations of both lines are in slope-intercept form $y = mx + b$, then the lines are perpendicular if m in one equation is the negative reciprocal of m in the other equation. For example, the lines with the equations $y = 2x + 4$ and $y = -\dfrac{1}{2}x - 7$ are perpendicular since $2\left(-\dfrac{1}{2}\right) = -1$.

v. Given the graphs of two lines in the coordinate plane, you can use what you know about slopes and y-intercepts to write the equations of both lines in slope-intercept form. Then you can determine if the lines are perpendicular. For example, you can use what you know about slopes and y-intercepts to determine if lines m and n in the following coordinate plane are perpendicular.

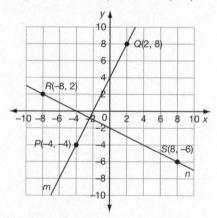

The slope of line m is 2 and the y-intercept is 4, so the equation of line m in slope-intercept form is $y = 2x + 4$. The slope of line n is $-\dfrac{1}{2}$ and the y-intercept is −2, so the equation of line n in slope-intercept form is $y = -\dfrac{1}{2}x - 2$. Since the product of the slopes $2\left(-\dfrac{1}{2}\right) = -1$, lines m and n are perpendicular.

Remember, It's the <u>Negative</u> Reciprocal *Two lines are perpendicular if the slopes of the two lines are negative reciprocals of each other. A common error is to forget the negative part of the slopes when determining if two lines are perpendicular. For example, the lines with the equations $y = 2x + 4$ and $y = -\frac{1}{2}x - 7$ are perpendicular, but the lines with the equations $y = 2x + 4$ and $y = \frac{1}{2}x - 7$ are not perpendicular.*

D. PERPENDICULARS AND DISTANCE

1. The shortest distance from a line to a point not on the line is the length of the perpendicular line segment from the line to the point.

2. Parallel lines are always equidistant. That means the length of a perpendicular segment with an endpoint on each line is always the same.

3. Each point on the perpendicular bisector of the line segment with endpoints P and Q is equidistant from point P and point Q. For example, if you wanted to find an equation whose graph is the set of points equidistant from $P(2, 2)$ and $Q(6, 6)$, you could graph the line segment with those endpoints and find its perpendicular bisector. The equation of the line that is the perpendicular bisector is the equation whose graph is the set of points equidistant from $P(2, 2)$ and $Q(6, 6)$, as shown in the following graph.

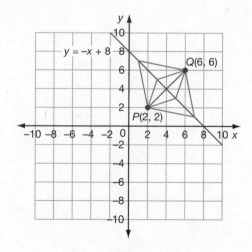

The midpoint of the line segment between $P(2, 2)$ and $Q(6, 6)$ can be found using the midpoint formula:

$\left(\dfrac{x_1+x_2}{2}, \dfrac{y_1+y_2}{2}\right) = \left(\dfrac{2+6}{2}, \dfrac{2+6}{2}\right) = (4,4)$. Since the slope of the line containing $P(2, 2)$ and $Q(6, 6)$ is 1, the slope of the line perpendicular to that line is -1. You can use the point-slope formula $y - y_1 = m(x - x_1)$ to determine the equation of the line where m is the slope and (x_1, y_1) is a point on the line. Substitute -1 for m and $(4, 4)$ for (x_1, y_1) as shown in the following equation:

$$y - 4 = -1(x - 4)$$
$$y - 4 = -x + 4$$
$$y = -x + 8$$

The equation whose graph is the set of points equidistant from $P(2, 2)$ and $Q(6, 6)$ is $y = -x + 8$.

E. POLYGONS IN THE COORDINATE PLANE

1. Polygons are many-sided figures with sides that are line segments.

2. In the coordinate plane, polygons can be represented by the coordinates of their vertices. For example, in the following coordinate plane, rectangle $ABCD$ has vertices $A(-6, 6)$, $B(4, 6)$, $C(4, -2)$, and $D(-6, -2)$.

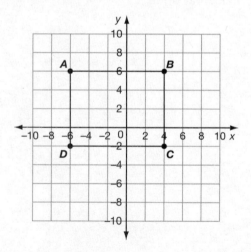

You can solve geometric problems about the figure by using coordinates. For example, since $AB = 10$ units and $BC = 8$ units, the perimeter of rectangle *ABCD* is 36 units and its area is 80 square units.

3. In the coordinate plane, slope and distance can provide information about polygons. For example, slope and distance can be used to determine if the figure *EFGH* in the following coordinate plane is a parallelogram.

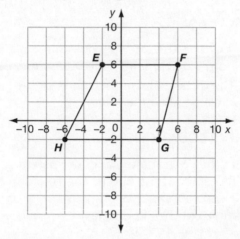

One way to prove that a figure is a parallelogram is to show that both pairs of opposite sides are parallel. So, if $\overline{EF} \parallel \overline{GH}$ and $\overline{EH} \parallel \overline{FG}$, then *EFGH* is a parallelogram. Since lines in the coordinate plane are parallel if their slopes are the same, you can solve this problem by finding slopes.

The coordinates of the vertices are $E(-2, 6)$, $F(6, 6)$, $G(4, -2)$, and $H(-6, -2)$. Now, calculate the slope for each line segment:

$$\text{slope of } \overline{EF} = \frac{6-6}{6-(-2)} = \frac{0}{8} = 0$$

$$\text{slope of } \overline{FG} = \frac{-2-6}{4-6} = \frac{-8}{-2} = 4$$

$$\text{slope of } \overline{GH} = \frac{-2-(-2)}{-6-4} = \frac{0}{-10} = 0$$

$$\text{slope of } \overline{EH} = \frac{-2-6}{-6-(-2)} = \frac{-8}{-4} = 2$$

The slope of $\overline{FG}$ is 4 and the slope of $\overline{EH}$ is 2. Since the slopes are not equal, $\overline{FG}$ and $\overline{EH}$ are not parallel. Since $\overline{FG}$ and $\overline{EH}$ are not parallel, $EFGH$ is not a parallelogram.

III. CIRCLES

A. CIRCLE BASICS

1. A *circle* is the set of all points in a plane that are equidistant from a given point called the *center* of the circle.
2. The distance from the center of the circle to any point on the circle is called the *radius*.

B. CIRCLE EQUATIONS

1. In the coordinate plane, the parent graph of the circle has its center at the origin. The equation of a circle with radius r and center at the origin is $x^2 + y^2 = r^2$. For example, the radius of the circle below is 4, so its equation is $x^2 + y^2 = 4^2 = 16$.

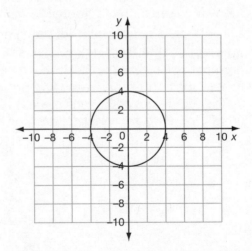

   i. The standard form of the equation of a circle with radius r and center at (h, k) is $(x - h)^2 + (y - k)^2 = r^2$. For example, the following circle has a center

of (6, −4) and a radius of 4, so its equation is
$(x-6)^2 + (y-(-4))^2 = 4^2$ or $(x-6)^2 + (y+4)^2 = 16.$

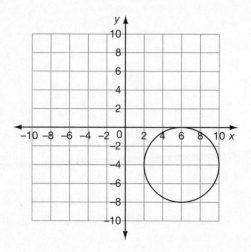

IV. ELLIPSES

A. ELLIPSE BASICS

1. An *ellipse* is the set of all points in the plane for which the sum of their distances from two fixed points in the plane is constant.
2. The two fixed points are called *foci*.
3. The midpoint of the line segment joining the two foci is the center of the ellipse.
4. An ellipse has two axes of symmetry:
    i. The major axis is that longer line segment that contains the foci.
    ii. The minor axis is the shorter line segment.
    iii. The endpoints of each axis are the vertices of the ellipse.

B. ELLIPSE EQUATIONS

1. In the coordinate plane, the parent graph of the ellipse has its center at the origin, with its axes along the *x*- and *y*-axes. The vertices of the major axis are (*a*, 0) and (−*a*, 0). The

vertices of the minor axis are (0, *b*) and (0, −*b*). The foci are (*c*, 0) and (−*c*, 0).

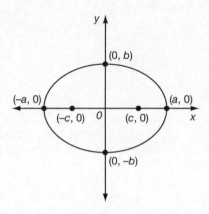

2. An ellipse can be oriented so that its foci are on the *x*-axis or the *y*-axis.

   i. Foci on the *x*-axis

     a) The equation of an ellipse with foci on the *x*-axis and center at the origin is $\dfrac{x^2}{a^2}+\dfrac{y^2}{b^2}=1$, where *a* > b > 0. In this equation, the major axis vertices are (*a*, 0) and (−*a*, 0), and the minor axis vertices are (0, *b*) and (0, −*b*).

     b) The equation of an ellipse with major axis parallel to the *x*-axis and center at (*h*, *k*) is $\dfrac{(x-h)^2}{a^2}+\dfrac{(y-k)^2}{b^2}=1$, where $c^2 = a^2 - b^2$. For an ellipse with this equation, the major axis is *y* = *k* and the minor axis is *x* = *h*. The foci are (*h* ± *c*, *k*), the major axis vertices are (*h* ± *a*, *k*), and the minor axis vertices are (*h*, *k* ± *b*).

   ii. Foci on the *y*-axis

     a) The equation of an ellipse with foci on the *y*-axis and center at the origin is $\dfrac{y^2}{a^2}+\dfrac{x^2}{b^2}=1$, where *a* > b > 0. In this equation, the major axis vertices are (0, *b*) and (0, −*b*), and the minor axis vertices are (*a*, 0) and (−*a*, 0).

b) The equation of an ellipse with major axis parallel to the y-axis and center at (h, k) is

$$\frac{(y-k)^2}{a^2} + \frac{(x-h)^2}{b^2} = 1,$$ where $c^2 = a^2 - b^2$. For an ellipse with this equation, the major axis is $x = h$ and the minor axis is $y = k$. The foci are $(h, k \pm c)$, the major axis vertices are $(h, k \pm a)$, and the minor axis vertices are $(h \pm b, k)$.

3. You can determine the orientation of an ellipse from its equation. If a^2 is the denominator of the x^2 term, then the major axis is parallel to the x-axis. If a^2 is the denominator of the y^2 term, then the major axis is parallel to the y-axis.

V. HYPERBOLAS

A. HYPERBOLA BASICS

1. A *hyperbola* is the set of all points in the plane for which the difference of their distances from two fixed points in the plane is constant.
2. The two fixed points are called *foci*.
3. The midpoint of the line segment joining the two foci is the center of the hyperbola.
4. The point on each branch of the hyperbola nearest the center is called a *vertex*.
5. The lines that the curves of the hyperbola approach as it moves away from the center are the asymptotes of the hyperbola.
6. A hyperbola has two axes of symmetry:
    i. The transverse axis is the line segment that connects the vertices.
    ii. The conjugate axis is the line segment through the center of the hyperbola and perpendicular to the transverse axis.
7. A rectangle is formed by the transverse and conjugate axes of the hyperbola that contains the asymptotes of the hyperbola as its diagonal. This rectangle can be used as a guide for graphing the asymptotes.

B. HYPERBOLA EQUATIONS

1. In the coordinate plane, the parent graph of the hyperbola has its center at the origin, with its axes along the *x*- and *y*-axes. In this equation, the vertices are $(a, 0)$ and $(-a, 0)$, and the foci are $(c, 0)$ and $(-c, 0)$. The length *b* is related to *a* and *c* by the equation $c^2 = a^2 + b^2$ in the rectangle whose diagonals are the asymptotes of the hyperbola. The distance from the center of the hyperbola to each vertex along the transverse axis is *a*, and the distance from the center of the hyperbola to the rectangular guide along the conjugate axis is *b*. The foci are $(c, 0)$ and $(-c, 0)$.

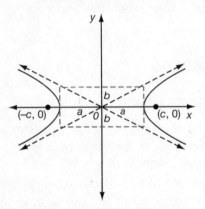

2. A hyperbola can be oriented so that its foci are on the *x*-axis or the *y*-axis.

   i. Foci on the *x*-axis

      a) The equation of a hyperbola with foci on the *x*-axis and center at the origin is $\dfrac{x^2}{a^2} - \dfrac{y^2}{b^2} = 1$. In this equation, the vertices are $(a, 0)$ and $(-a, 0)$, and the foci are $(c, 0)$ and $(-c, 0)$. The length *b* is related to *a* and *c* by the equation $b^2 = c^2 - a^2$ in the rectangle whose diagonals are the asymptotes of the hyperbola.

      b) The equation of a hyperbola with transverse axis parallel to the *x*-axis and center at (h, k) is $\dfrac{(x - h)^2}{a^2} - \dfrac{(y - k)^2}{b^2} = 1$, where $b^2 = c^2 - a^2$. For a hyperbola with this equation, the transverse axis is $y = k$ and the conjugate axis is $x = h$. The foci are $(h \pm c, k)$, and the vertices are $(h \pm a, k)$.

  ii. Foci on the *y*-axis

    a) The equation of a hyperbola with foci on the *y*-axis and center at the origin is $\dfrac{y^2}{a^2} - \dfrac{x^2}{b^2} = 1$. In this equation, the vertices are $(0, a)$ and $(0, -a)$. The length b is related to a and c by the equation $b^2 = c^2 - a^2$ in the rectangle whose diagonals are the asymptotes of the hyperbola.

    b) The equation of a hyperbola with transverse axis parallel to the *y*-axis and center at (h, k) is $\dfrac{(y-k)^2}{a^2} - \dfrac{(x-h)^2}{b^2} = 1$, where $b^2 = c^2 - a^2$. For a hyperbola with this equation, the transverse axis is $x = h$ and the conjugate axis is $y = k$. The foci are $(h, k \pm c)$, and the vertices are $(h, k \pm a)$.

3. You can determine the orientation of a hyperbola from its equation. If a^2 is the denominator of the x^2 term, then the transverse axis is parallel to the *x*-axis. If a^2 is the denominator of the y^2 term, then the transverse axis is parallel to the *y*-axis.

4. A rectangle that contains the asymptotes of the hyperbola as its diagonals is formed by the transverse and conjugate axes of the hyperbola. This rectangle can be used as a guide for graphing and writing the equations of the asymptotes.

  i. Foci on the *x*-axis

    a) For a hyperbola with transverse axis parallel to the *x*-axis and center at the origin, it can be determined from the vertices of the rectangle that the asymptotes have slopes equal to $\pm \dfrac{b}{a}$. Since the asymptotes have a *y*-intercept of 0, the equations for the asymptotes are $y = \pm \dfrac{b}{a} x$.

    b) For a hyperbola with transverse axis parallel to the *x*-axis and center at (h, k), that is a hyperbola with standard form $\dfrac{(x-h)^2}{a^2} - \dfrac{(y-k)^2}{b^2} = 1$, the

equations of the asymptotes are $y = \pm\dfrac{b}{a}(x-h)+k$.

    ii. Foci on the *y*-axis

        a) For a hyperbola with transverse axis parallel to the *y*-axis and its center at the origin, it can be determined from the vertices of the rectangle that the asymptotes have slopes equal to $\pm\dfrac{a}{b}$.

Since the asymptotes have a *y*-intercept of 0, the equations for the asymptotes are $y = \pm\dfrac{a}{b}x$.

        b) For a hyperbola with transverse axis parallel to the *y*-axis and center at (*h*, *k*), that is a hyperbola

with standard form $\dfrac{(y-k)^2}{a^2} - \dfrac{(x-h)^2}{b^2} = 1$, the

equations of the asymptotes are $y = \pm\dfrac{a}{b}(x-h)+k$.

VI. PARABOLAS

A. PARABOLA BASICS

1. A *parabola* is the set of all points in the plane that are the same distance from a point called the *focus* and a line called the *directrix*.
2. The axis of a parabola is the axis of symmetry of the parabola that passes through the focus. The axis of the parabola is perpendicular to the directrix.
3. The vertex of the parabola is the point at which the axis intersects the parabola.

B. PARABOLA EQUATIONS

1. In the coordinate plane, all points on the graph of a parabola are equidistant from the focus, labeled *F*, and the line known as the *directrix*. The distance from the focus to the vertex is equal to the distance from the intersection of the axis of symmetry and the directrix to the vertex, and is represented by the variable *p*.

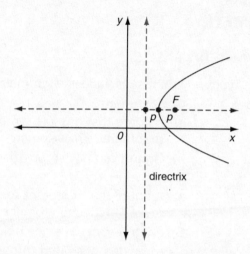

2. A parabola can be oriented so that its axis is parallel to the *x*-axis or the *y*-axis.

    i. Axis parallel to the *x*-axis

      a) For a parabola with axis parallel to the *x*-axis, if the vertex of a parabola has coordinates (h, k) and the distance from the vertex to the focus is represented by the letter *p*, the standard form of the equation of a parabola is $(y - k)^2 = 4p(x - h)$.

      b) The coordinates of the focus are $(h + p, k)$, the axis of symmetry is $y = k$, and the equation of the directrix is $x = h - p$.

      c) If $p > 0$, the parabola opens to the right. If $p < 0$, the parabola opens to the left.

    ii. Axis parallel to the *y*-axis

      a) For a parabola with axis parallel to the *y*-axis, if the vertex of a parabola has coordinates (h, k) and the distance from the vertex to the focus is represented by the letter *p*, the standard form of the equation of a parabola is $(x - h)^2 = 4p(y - k)$.

      b) The coordinates of the focus are $(h, k + p)$, the axis of symmetry is $x = h$, and the equation of the directrix is $y = k - p$.

      c) If $p > 0$, the parabola opens upward. If $p < 0$, the parabola opens downward.

VII. SYMMETRY

A. SYMMETRY BASICS

1. Types of symmetry include line symmetry and point symmetry.
    i. Line Symmetry
        a) A figure that has line symmetry can be folded so that the two halves match exactly.
        b) Figures can have more than one line of symmetry
    ii. Point Symmetry
        a) A figure that has point symmetry has a common point of reflection for all points on the figure.
        b) A figure can have one point of symmetry.
2. Symmetry can be demonstrated through a set of formal geometric rules.

B. SYMMETRY IN THE COORDINATE PLANE

1. In the coordinate plane, symmetry can be determined by using coordinates of points associated with a figure.
2. The line of symmetry of a figure in the coordinate plane can be given by the equation of the line. For example, if the *x*-axis is the line of symmetry, then the line of symmetry is $y = 0$.
3. The distance formula can be used to determine if a figure in the coordinate plane has point symmetry. For example, in the following square, the distance formula can be used to determine that *P* is the point of symmetry because $AP = CP$, $BP = DP$, $EP = FP$, and so on.

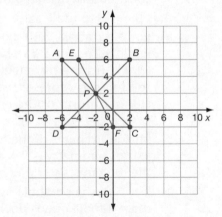

The coordinates of the point of symmetry are $P(-2, 2)$. The coordinates of the vertices are $A(-6, 6)$, $B(2, 6)$, $C(2, -2)$, and $D(-6, -2)$. The coordinates of additional points on the square are $E(-4, 6)$ and $F(0, -2)$. Now, use the distance formula to calculate the distance between P and the other points.

$$AP = \sqrt{(2-6)^2 + (-2-(-6))^2} = \sqrt{(-4)^2 + 4^2} = \sqrt{16+16} = \sqrt{32} = 4\sqrt{2}$$

$$BP = \sqrt{(2-6)^2 + (-2-2)^2} = \sqrt{(-4)^2 + (-4)^2} = \sqrt{16+16} = \sqrt{32} = 4\sqrt{2}$$

$$CP = \sqrt{(2-(-2))^2 + (-2-2)^2} = \sqrt{4^2 + (-4)^2} = \sqrt{16+16} = \sqrt{32} = 4\sqrt{2}$$

$$DP = \sqrt{(2-(-2))^2 + (-2-(-6))^2} = \sqrt{4^2 + 4^2} = \sqrt{16+16} = \sqrt{32} = 4\sqrt{2}$$

$$EP = \sqrt{(2-6)^2 + (-2-(-4))^2} = \sqrt{(-4)^2 + 2^2} = \sqrt{16+4} = \sqrt{20} = 2\sqrt{5}$$

$$FP = \sqrt{(2-(-2))^2 + (-2-0)^2} = \sqrt{4^2 + (-2)^2} = \sqrt{16+4} = \sqrt{20} = 2\sqrt{5}$$

So, $AP = CP$, $BP = DP$, $EP = FP$.

VIII. TRANSFORMATIONS

A. TRANSFORMATION BASICS

1. A transformation maps one figure called a *pre-image* onto another figure called an *image*.
2. There are different types of transformations, including the following:
    i. A *translation* is the slide of a figure.
    ii. A *reflection* is the flip of a figure.
    iii. A *rotation* is a turn of a figure about a point.
    iv. A *dilation* is an enlargement or reduction of a figure.

3. Transformations can be either congruence transformations or similarity transformations.
   i. Congruence transformations
      a) In a congruence transformation, the image is congruent to the pre-image.
      b) A congruence transformation is also called an *isometry* or a *rigid motion*.
      c) The size and shape of the pre-image and image are the same in a congruence transformation.
      d) A congruence transformation preserves distance, angle measure, collinearity, and betweenness of points.
   ii. Similarity transformations
      a) In a similarity transformation, the image is congruent to the pre-image.
      b) The shape of the pre-image and image are the same in a similarity transformation, but the size is not.
      c) A similarity transformation preserves angle measure, collinearity, and betweenness of points, but not distance.

B. TRANSFORMATIONS IN THE COORDINATE PLANE

1. In the coordinate plane, transformations are described by rules based on the coordinates of the figure.
2. To describe mappings from pre-images to images in the coordinate plane, certain naming conventions and notations are used.
   i. Prime marks are used to distinguish points on a pre-image from points on an image. For example, if P is a point on the pre-image, then P' is the corresponding point on the image.
   ii. If more than one transformation takes place, additional prime marks are added. For example, if P is a point on the pre-image, then P' is the corresponding point after the first transformation, P'' is the corresponding point after the second transformation, P''' is the corresponding point after the third transformation, and so on.

iii. For a point P, notation such as $P(x, y) \rightarrow P'(-x, y)$ describes the mapping of point P in the pre-image to point P' in the image. Expressions can be written in this notation to describe different mappings. For the mapping $P(x, y) \rightarrow P'(-x, y)$, point P in the image and point P' in the image are equidistant from the y-axis.

C. TRANSLATIONS IN THE COORDINATE PLANE

1. Translations in the coordinate plane move all points in a figure the same distance in the same direction.

2. If a and b are fixed values, then a translation of a figure in the coordinate plane moves every point $P(x, y)$ in the figure to an image $P'(x + a, y + b)$. This mapping can be described using the notation $P(x, y) \rightarrow P'(x + a, y + b)$.

3. In the following coordinate plane, the pre-image trapezoid has coordinates $A(2, 2)$, $B(2, 6)$, $C(8, 7)$, and $D(8, 2)$. After a translation 10 units to the left and 9 units down, the image has coordinates $A'(-8, -7)$, $B'(-8, -3)$, $C'(-2, -2)$, and $D'(-2, -7)$. This translation can be described by the rule $P(x, y) \rightarrow P'(x - 10, y - 9)$.

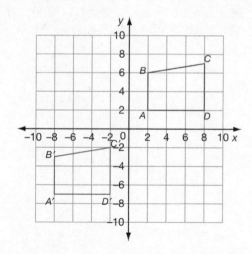

4. Translations are also called *slides*, *shifts*, and *glides*.

5. Translations are congruence transformations because they preserve both shape and size.

D. REFLECTIONS IN THE COORDINATE PLANE

1. Reflections in the coordinate plane reflect all points in a figure in a given line.
2. If *a* and *b* are fixed values, then a reflection of a figure in the coordinate plane can be described based on the line of reflection.

   i. If the *x*-axis is the line of reflection, then a reflection maps every point $P(x, y)$ in the figure to an image $P'(x, -y)$. This mapping can be described using the notation $P(x, y) \rightarrow P'(x, -y)$.

   ii. If the *y*-axis is the line of reflection, then a reflection maps every point $P(x, y)$ in the figure to an image $P'(-x, y)$. This mapping can be described using the notation $P(x, y) \rightarrow P'(-x, y)$.

   iii. If the line $y = x$ is the line of reflection, then a reflection maps every point $P(x, y)$ in the figure to an image $P'(y, x)$. This mapping can be described using the notation $P(x, y) \rightarrow P'(y, x)$.

3. In the following coordinate plane, the pre-image trapezoid has coordinates $A(2, 2)$, $B(2, 6)$, $C(8, 7)$, and $D(8, 2)$. After a reflection in the *y*-axis, the image has coordinates $A'(-2, 2)$, $B'(-2, 6)$, $C'(-8, 7)$, and $D'(-8, 2)$. This translation can be described by the rule $P(x, y) \rightarrow P'(-x, y)$.

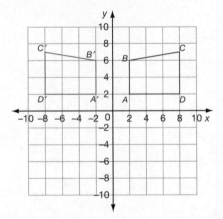

4. Reflections are also called *flips*.
5. Reflections are congruence transformations because they preserve both shape and size.

E. ROTATIONS IN THE COORDINATE PLANE

1. Rotations in the coordinate plane turn all points in a figure a given angle and direction about a fixed point.

2. The fixed point is called the *center of rotation*.

3. The angle of rotation is the angle formed by the pre-image and image with the center of rotation as its vertex. The angle of rotation is usually given with a degree measurement and direction, such as a 120° counterclockwise rotation or a 270° clockwise rotation.

4. If the origin is the center of rotation, then a rotation of a figure in the coordinate plane can be described based on the angle of rotation.

   i. For a counterclockwise rotation of 90° about the origin, every point $P(x, y)$ in the figure is mapped to an image $P'(-y, x)$. This mapping can be described using the notation $P(x, y) \rightarrow P'(-y, x)$.

   ii. For a counterclockwise rotation of 180° about the origin, every point $P(x, y)$ in the figure is mapped to an image $P'(-x, -y)$. This mapping can be described using the notation $P(x, y) \rightarrow P'(-x, -y)$.

   iii. For a counterclockwise rotation of 270° about the origin, every point $P(x, y)$ in the figure is mapped to an image $P'(y, -x)$. This mapping can be described using the notation $P(x, y) \rightarrow P'(y, -x)$.

   iv. In the following diagram, the pre-image trapezoid has coordinates $A(2, 2)$, $B(2, 6)$, $C(8, 7)$, and $D(8, 2)$. After a 90° counterclockwise rotation about the origin, the image has coordinates $A'(-2, 2)$, $B'(-6, 2)$, $C'(-7, 8)$, and $D'(-2, 8)$. This rotation can be described by the rule $P(x, y) \rightarrow P'(-y, x)$.

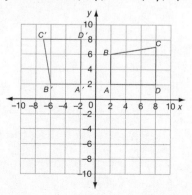

v. Rotations are also called *turns*.

vi. Rotations are congruence transformations because they preserve both shape and size.

F. DILATIONS IN THE COORDINATE PLANE

1. Dilations in the coordinate plane reduce or enlarge a figure based on a given scale factor and a center of dilation.

2. The scale factor of a dilation is usually represented by the variable *r*.

3. If $P(x, y)$ is the pre-image of a dilation with the center of dilation at the origin and the scale factor is *r*, then the image is $P'(rx, ry)$.

4. In the following diagram, the pre-image trapezoid has coordinates $A(2, 2)$, $B(2, 6)$, $C(8, 7)$, and $D(8, 2)$. After a dilation by a scale factor of $\dfrac{1}{2}$ with the origin of the center of dilation, the image has coordinates $A'(1, 1)$, $B'(1, 3)$, $C'\left(4, \dfrac{7}{2}\right)$, and $D'(4, 1)$. This dilation, which is a reduction, can be described by the rule $P(x,y) \rightarrow P'\left(\dfrac{1}{2}x, \dfrac{1}{2}y\right)$.

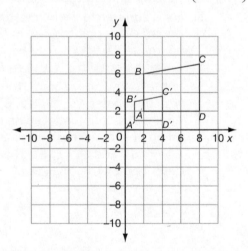

5. The type of dilation can be determined by the value of *r*:

   a) If $|r| > 1$, then the dilation is an enlargement.

   b) If $0 < |r| < 1$, then the dilation is a reduction.

   c) If $|r| = 1$, then the image is congruent to the pre-image.

6. Dilations are similarity transformations because they preserve shape, but not size.

G. COMPOSITION OF TRANSFORMATIONS IN THE COORDINATE PLANE

1. A composition is a transformation comprised of successive transformations.

2. For each successive transformation, an additional prime mark is added in the notation.

3. The same transformation can be made by various compositions. For example, in the following diagram, the pre-image trapezoid has coordinates $A(2, 2)$, $B(2, 6)$, $C(8, 7)$, and $D(8, 2)$. The image has coordinates $A'(-2, -2)$, $B'(-2, -6)$, $C'(-8, -7)$, and $D'(-8, -2)$. This transformation can be described as a 180° counterclockwise rotation about the origin, or as a reflection in the x-axis followed by a reflection in the y-axis. The rotation can be described by the rule $P(x, y) \rightarrow P'(-x, -y)$. Alternately, the reflection in the x-axis can be described by the rule $P(x, y) \rightarrow P'(x, -y)$ and the reflection in the y-axis can be described by the rule $P(x, y) \rightarrow P'(-x, y)$, so that the result of the composition is the same as the rotation: $P(x, y) \rightarrow P'(-x, -y)$.

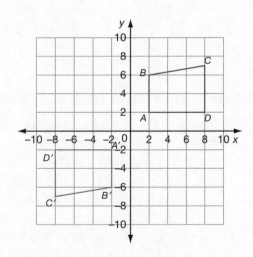

IX. POLAR COORDINATES

A. POLAR COORDINATE BASICS

1. A *polar coordinate system* gives the position of a point based on a fixed point and an angle made with a fixed ray from that point.
2. Polar coordinates give locations of points using distance and angles.
3. The fixed point *O* is called the *pole* or the *origin*.
4. The horizontal ray toward the right from the pole is the *polar axis*.

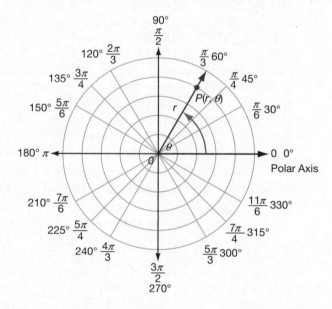

B. REPRESENTING POINTS WITH POLAR COORDINATES

1. The location of a point *P* in the polar coordinate system is given by the polar coordinates $P(r, \theta)$.
   - i. The coordinate *r* is the distance from the origin to *P*.
   - ii. The coordinate θ is the angle formed by the polar axis and $\overrightarrow{OP}$. The angle can be measured in degrees or radians.
   - iii. If each concentric circle represents one unit, the point *P* in the preceding graph can be represented as either $P\left(4, \dfrac{\pi}{3}\right)$ or $P(4, 60°)$.

2. If r is positive in $P(r, \theta)$, then θ is the measure of an angle in standard position with $\overrightarrow{OP}$ as its terminal side. If r is negative in $P(r, \theta)$, then θ is the measure of an angle that has the ray opposite $\overrightarrow{OP}$ as its terminal side.

3. If θ is positive, then θ is measured counterclockwise from the polar axis. If θ is negative, then θ is measured clockwise from the polar axis.

4. If a point P has polar coordinates (r, θ), then it also has polar coordinates $(r, \theta + 2\pi)$ or $(r, \theta + 360°)$. In general, if a point P has polar coordinates (r, θ), then it also has polar coordinates $(r, \theta + k2\pi)$ or $(r, \theta + k360°)$.

C. GRAPHING POLAR EQUATIONS

1. A polar equation is expressed in terms of polar coordinates. For example, $r = \cos\theta$ is a polar equation.

2. The solution of a polar equation is the set of all points (r, θ) that satisfy the polar equation. The solution can be represented as a polar graph. For example, the graph of $r = 3$ will be a circle 3 units from the origin.

Test Tip

Graph Polar Equations on Your Calculator To graph polar equations on your calculator, first press [MODE] and select POL for polar mode. In this mode, the Y= screen will show r = instead and the [X, T, θ, n] key will input θ. When the graph is displayed, only the axes are shown and the concentric circles will have to be inferred. Following are some graphs of polar equations. Note that window settings have been changed to best view each graph.

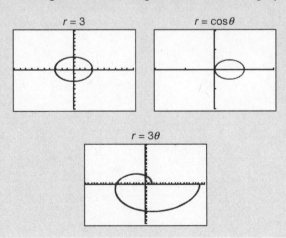

THREE-DIMENSIONAL FIGURES

KEY VOCABULARY

Cone A three-dimensional figure with a circular base and a vertex that is not in the same plane as the base.

Cross section The intersection of a solid and a plane.

Cylinder A three-dimensional figure with two congruent, parallel circular bases.

Lateral surface area The sum of the areas of the faces and side surfaces of a three-dimensional figure; sometimes lateral surface area is just called *lateral area*.

Polyhedron A three-dimensional figure whose faces are polygons.

Prism A three-dimensional figure with two congruent, parallel polygon bases connected by lateral parallelogram faces.

Pyramid A three-dimensional figure with a polygonal base, a vertex that is not in the same plane as the base, and lateral triangular faces that meet at the vertex.

Sphere The locus of all points in space that are the same distance from a single point, which is the center of the sphere.

Surface area The sum of the areas of the faces and side surfaces of a three-dimensional figure.

Volume The amount of space enclosed by a three-dimensional figure.

I. SOLID GEOMETRY

A. SOLID GEOMETRY BASICS

1. Three-dimensional figures are also called *solids*.
2. *Surface area* is the sum of the areas of the faces and side surfaces of a three-dimensional figure.
3. *Lateral surface area* or lateral area is the sum of the side surfaces of a three-dimensional figure.
4. *Volume* is the amount of space enclosed by a three-dimensional figure.
5. The surface area and lateral surface area of a three-dimensional figure is measured in square units. The volume of a three-dimensional figure is measured in cubic units.

B. POLYHEDRA

1. A *polyhedron* is a three-dimensional figure whose faces are polygons. The plural of polyhedron is *polyhedra*. Prisms and pyramids are polyhedra. On the other hand, solids with curved surfaces such as cylinders, cones, and spheres are not polyhedra.
2. *Faces* are the flat polygonal surfaces of polyhedra. *Edges* are the line segments where faces intersect. *Vertices* are points where three or more edges intersect.

C. CROSS SECTIONS

1. A *cross section* is the intersection of a solid and a plane. A cross section is a two-dimensional figure.
2. A solid can have cross sections in multiple shapes, depending on where the plane intersects the solid. For example, if a plane intersects a cube so that the plane is parallel to a face of the cube, then the cross section is a square. On the other hand, if the plane intersects a corner of a cube through three adjacent faces, the cross section is a triangle.

II. PRISMS

A. PRISM BASICS

1. A *prism* is a three-dimensional figure with two congruent, parallel polygon bases connected by lateral parallelogram faces.

2. Prisms are classified by the bases. For example, a rectangular prism has bases that are rectangles, a triangular prism has bases that are triangles, a hexagonal prism has bases that are hexagons, and so on.

Prism Classifications

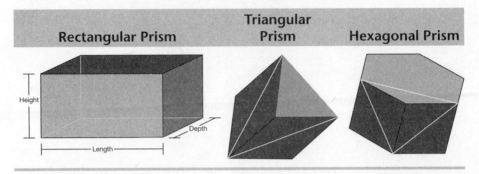

3. To find the surface area of a prism, find the area of each of its faces and add the areas. The surface area of a prism is measured in square units.

4. The volume of a prism is given by the formula $V = Bh$, where B is the area of a base and h is the height. The volume of a prism is measured in cubic units.

B. RECTANGULAR PRISMS

1. A rectangular prism has bases that are rectangles.

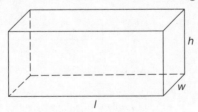

2. A cube is a rectangular prism whose bases and lateral faces are all squares.

3. The surface area *S* of a rectangular prism is given by the formula $S = 2lw + 2lh + 2hw$. The lateral surface area *L*, which is the surface area of just the lateral faces, is given by the formula $L = 2lh + 2hw$.

4. The volume *V* of a rectangular prism is given by the formula $V = lwh$.

Test Tip

> ***Longest Line Segment between Two Vertices of a Rectangular Prism*** *The longest line segment between two vertices of a rectangular prism is the segment between the opposite vertices. For example, in the following diagram, the longest segment is between points P and Q.*
>
>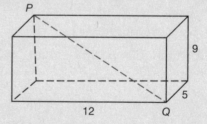
>
> *To find the distance between P and Q, you can use the Pythagorean theorem. Note that $\overline{PQ}$ is the hypotenuse of a right triangle whose legs are the height of the rectangular prism and the diagonal of the rectangular base. Also note that the diagonal of the rectangular base is also the hypotenuse of a right triangle whose legs are the length and width of the rectangular base. Since 5, 12, and 13 form a Pythagorean triple, the length of the diagonal of the rectangular base is 13. Now, use the Pythagorean theorem to find the length of a right triangle whose legs are the height of the prism and the diagonal of the base, with lengths of 9 and 13, respectively:*
>
> $$PQ = \sqrt{9^2 + 13^2} = \sqrt{81 + 169} = \sqrt{250} = 5\sqrt{10}\,.$$

III. CYLINDERS

A. CYLINDER BASICS

1. A *cylinder* is a three-dimensional figure with two congruent, parallel circular bases.

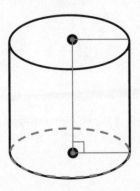

2. The *axis* of a cylinder is the line segment whose endpoints are the centers of the circular bases.
3. If the altitude of a cylinder is also the axis, then the cylinder is a right cylinder. Otherwise, the cylinder is an oblique cylinder. In a right cylinder, the axis intersects the bases at right angles.
4. If a cylinder is represented as a two-dimensional net, it is composed of two circles, which are the bases, and a rectangle whose sides are the circumference of the cylinder and the height of the cylinder.

B. SURFACE AREA AND VOLUME OF CYLINDERS

1. To find the surface area of a cylinder, add the areas of each of its circular bases and the area of the rectangle that forms its lateral area. Surface area S of a right cylinder is given by the formula $S = 2\pi rh + 2\pi r^2$, where h is the height of the cylinder and r is the radius of its base. The lateral area L of a right cylinder is given by the formula $L = 2\pi hr$, where h is

the height of the cylinder. The surface area of a cylinder is measured in square units.

2. The volume of a cylinder is given by the formula $V = Bh$, where B is the area of its base and h is its height. An equivalent formula for the volume of a cylinder is $V = \pi r^2 h$, where r is the radius of its circular base and h is its height. The volume of a cylinder is measured in cubic units.

IV. CONES

A. CONE BASICS

1. A *cone* is a three-dimensional figure with a circular base and a vertex that is not in the same plane as the base.

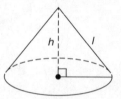

2. The *axis* of a cone is the line segment whose endpoints are the centers of the circular base and the vertex.

3. If the altitude of a cone is also the axis, then the cone is a right cone. Otherwise, the cone is an oblique cone. In a right cone, the axis intersects the base at a right angle.

4. In a right cone, the height h of a cone is the same as its altitude.

5. The slant height l of a right cone is the measure of any line segment joining the vertex of the cone to the edge of its circular base.

B. SURFACE AREA AND VOLUME OF CONES

1. Surface area S of a right cone is given by the formula $S = \pi r l + \pi r^2$, where r is radius of the circular base and l is the slant height of the cone. Lateral area L of a right cone is given by the formula $L = \pi r l$, where r is radius of the circular base and l is the slant height of the cone. Surface area of a cone is measured in square units.

2. The volume of a right cone is given by the formula
$V = \frac{1}{3}Bh$, where B is the area of its base and h is its height.
An equivalent formula for the volume of a right cone is
$V = \frac{1}{3}\pi r^2 h$, where r is the radius of its circular base and h is
its height. Volume of a cone is measured in cubic units.

V. PYRAMIDS

A. PYRAMID BASICS

1. A *pyramid* is a three-dimensional figure with a polygonal base and a vertex that is not in the same plane as the base. A pyramid has lateral triangular faces that meet at the vertex.

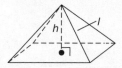

2. The *altitude* of a pyramid is the line segment from the vertex to the base that is perpendicular to the base.
3. A regular pyramid has special characteristics.
    i. The base of a regular pyramid is a regular polygon.
    ii. The altitude is the line segment whose endpoints are the vertex of the regular pyramid and the center of its base.
    iii. The lateral faces of a regular pyramid are all congruent isosceles triangles.
4. The slant height *l* of a regular pyramid is the height of each lateral face.

B. SURFACE AREA AND VOLUME OF PYRAMIDS

1. Surface area S of a regular pyramid is given by the formula
$S = \frac{1}{2}Pl + B$, where P is perimeter of the base, l is the slant
height, and B is the area of the base. The lateral area L of a
regular pyramid is given by the formula $L = \frac{1}{2}Pl$, where P is

perimeter of the base and *l* is the slant height. The surface area of a pyramid is measured in square units.

2. The volume of a regular pyramid is given by the formula $V = \frac{1}{3}Bh$, where *B* is the area of its base and *h* is its height.

VI. SPHERES

A. SPHERES

1. In space, a *sphere* is the locus of all points that are the same distance from a single point, which is the center of the sphere.

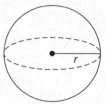

2. The radius *r* of a sphere is a segment whose endpoints are the center of the sphere and a point on the sphere.

3. When a plane intersects a sphere so that it contains the center of the sphere, the intersection is a great circle. The radius of a great circle of a sphere is the same as the radius of the sphere. Each great circle separates a sphere into two congruent halves called *hemispheres*.

B. SURFACE AREA AND VOLUME OF SPHERES

1. Surface area *S* of a sphere is given by the formula $S = 4\pi r^2$, where *r* is the radius of the sphere. The surface area of a sphere is measured in square units.

2. The volume of a sphere is given by the formula $V = \frac{4}{3}\pi r^3$, where *r* is its radius. The volume of a sphere is measured in cubic units.

3. A solid can have cross sections in multiple shapes, depending on where the plane intersects the solid. For example, if a plane intersects a cube so that the plane is parallel to a face of the sphere, then the cross section is a square. If the plane

intersects a corner of a cube through three adjacent faces, the cross section is a triangle.

> **Do Not Memorize These Formulas** *The following four formulas are printed in the directions to the SAT Math Level 2 Subject Test:*
>
> *Volume of a right circular cone with radius r and height h:*
> $$V = \frac{1}{3}\pi r^2 h$$
> *Volume of a sphere with radius r:* $V = \frac{4}{3}\pi r^3$
>
> *Volume of a pyramid with base area B and height h:* $V = \frac{1}{3}Bh$
>
> *Surface area of a sphere with radius r:* $S = 4\pi r^2$

VII. CONGRUENT AND SIMILAR SOLIDS

A. CONGRUENT SOLIDS

1. Solids are congruent if they have exactly the same size and shape.
2. Two solids are congruent if their volumes are equal and their corresponding edges, faces, and angles are congruent.

B. SIMILAR SOLIDS

1. Solids are similar if they have exactly the same shape, but not the same size.
2. Two solids are similar if the ratios of their corresponding linear measures are proportional.
3. If two similar solids have a scale factor of $a:b$, then their surface areas have a scale factor of $a^2:b^2$.
4. If two similar solids have a scale factor of $a:b$, then their volumes have a scale factor of $a^3:b^3$.

Check Surface Area and Volume Ratios *You can use your calculator to do a quick check of your answers to problems involving surface area and volume ratios of solid figures. For example, consider two rectangular prisms, one with length 15, width 9, and height 6 and the other with length 10, width 6, and height 4. The solids are similar with a scale factor of 3:2. Therefore, the scale factor for their surface areas should be $3^2:2^2$ or 9:4, and the scale factor of their volumes should be $3^3:2^3$ or 27:8.*

Now suppose you calculate surface areas of 558 for the first prism and 248 for the second prism, as well as volumes of 810 for the first prism and 240 for the second prism. Since ratios are simply fractions, you can check your answers by using your calculator to make sure the fractions $\dfrac{9}{4}$ and $\dfrac{558}{248}$ are equal for surface area, and also that $\dfrac{27}{8}$ and $\dfrac{810}{240}$ are equal for volume.

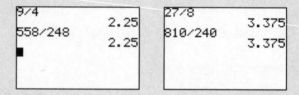

Since the quotients for each pair of ratios are equal, the answers are correct.

COORDINATES IN THREE DIMENSIONS

KEY VOCABULARY

Ordered triple Representation of a point in three-dimensional space by three coordinates (x, y, z), where x, y, and z are real numbers.

I. THREE-DIMENSIONAL COORDINATES

A. THREE-DIMENSIONAL COORDINATE BASICS

1. Three-dimensional coordinates can be used to describe points in space.
2. Points in space can be represented in a three-dimensional coordinate system with three axes: the x-axis, the y-axis, and the z-axis. The axes are perpendicular to each other.

B. REPRESENTING POINTS AND FIGURES WITH THREE-DIMENSIONAL COORDINATES

1. A point in space is represented by an *ordered triple* (x, y, z), where x, y, and z are real numbers. For example, the vertex P of the following rectangular prism is represented as P(−2, 0, 4), and the vertex Q is Q(0, 2, 0).

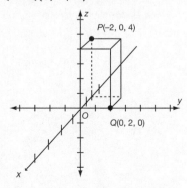

2. The distance formula and midpoint formula can be extended to find distances and midpoints between points in space.

    i. The distance between two points $P(x_1, y_1, z_1)$ and $Q(x_2, y_2, z_2)$ in space is given by the equation

$d = \sqrt{(x_2 - x_1)^2 + (y_2 - y_1)^2 + (z_2 - z_1)^2}$. For example, the distance between points $P(-2, 0, 4)$, and $Q(0, 2, 0)$ in the preceding three-dimensional coordinate system is given by the following:

$$d = \sqrt{(x_2 - x_1)^2 + (y_2 - y_1)^2 + (z_2 - z_1)^2}$$
$$d = \sqrt{(0 - (-2))^2 + (2 - 0)^2 + (0 - 4)^2}$$
$$d = \sqrt{2^2 + 2^2 + 4^2}$$
$$d = \sqrt{4 + 4 + 16}$$
$$d = \sqrt{24}$$

So, $PQ = 2\sqrt{6}$.

Reuse Expressions on Your Calculator *Using your calculator to evaluate long, complicated expressions such as the distance formula in three dimensions can be very time-consuming, especially when the same formula needs to be evaluated multiple times. To save time, you can press [2ND][ENTER] to step back through previous entries in the main window and then simply edit the numbers in a formula you just used rather than typing the formula again from scratch. The following screens show the result of first calculating the distance between P(-2, 0, 4), and Q(0, 2, 0) and then re-using the formula to calculate the distance between P(-2, 0, 4), and a different point R(-2, 2, 4), which is another vertex of the rectangular prism.*

1. *Input expression and press [ENTER] to perform the calculation.*

```
√((0--2)²+(2-0)²
+(0-4)²)
        4.898979486
```

(continued)

(continued)

2. *Press [2ND][ENTER] to display the previous entry, which is the distance calculation you just input.*

```
√((0--2)²+(2-0)²
+(0-4)²)
        4.898979486
√((0--2)²+(2-0)²
+(0-4)²)
```

3. *Edit the equation by substituting the coordinates for point R. Press [ENTER] to perform the calculation.*

```
√((0--2)²+(2-0)²
+(0-4)²)
        4.898979486
√(( -2--2)²+(2-0)
²+(4-4)²)
                  2
```

Note that when −2 is being substituted for 0, two characters are being substituted for one character. You will have to press [2ND] [DEL] to go into INSERT mode to enter the extra character. Insert mode works on a toggle basis in the same way as the Caps Lock key on your computer keyboard: each time you press [2ND] [DEL], insert mode is turned ON if it is OFF or OFF if it is ON.

Also note that checking the calculator result in decimal format for PQ against the result in radical form shows that

$PQ = 2\sqrt{6}$ *is the correct solution.*

```
+(0-4)²)
        4.898979486
√(( -2--2)²+(2-0)
²+(4-4)²)
                  2
2*√(6)
        4.898979486
```

ii. Given two points $P(x_1, y_1, z_1)$ and $Q(x_2, y_2, z_2)$ in space, the midpoint of $\overline{PQ}$ is $\left(\frac{x_1+x_2}{2}, \frac{y_1+y_2}{2}, \frac{z_1+z_2}{2}\right)$.

For example, the midpoint of the segment between $P(-2, 0, 4)$, and $Q(0, 2, 0)$ is given by the following:

$$\text{midpoint of } \overline{PQ} = \left(\frac{-2+0}{2}, \frac{0+2}{2}, \frac{4+0}{2}\right) = (-1, 1, 2)$$

So, the midpoint of $\overline{PQ}$ is represented by the ordered triple $(-1, 1, 2)$.

Two Equations to Remember *You may have already committed to memory the standard form of the equation for a circle with radius r and center at the origin: $x^2 + y^2 = r^2$. Another equation worth memorizing is the standard form of the equation for a sphere with radius r and center at the origin of the three-dimensional coordinate system: $x^2 + y^2 + z^2 = r^2$.*

TRIGONOMETRY

KEY VOCABULARY

Arccosine The inverse of the cosine function: if $y = \cos x$, then the inverse function is defined by $y = \cos^{-1} x$ or $y = \arccos x$.

Arcsine The inverse of the sine function: if $y = \sin x$, then the inverse function is defined by $y = \sin^{-1} x$ or $y = \arcsin x$.

Arctangent The inverse of the tangent function: if $y = \tan x$, then the inverse function is defined by $y = \tan^{-1} x$ or $y = \arctan x$.

Cofunctions Trigonometric functions and their reciprocals that are defined by a special relationship such that $\sin \theta = \cos(90° - \theta)$ and $\cos \theta = \sin(90° - \theta)$, $\tan \theta = \cot(90° - \theta)$ and $\cot \theta = \tan(90° - \theta)$, and $\sec \theta = \csc(90° - \theta)$ and $\csc \theta = \sec(90° - \theta)$.

Cosecant For an acute angle $\sin \theta$ in a right triangle, cosecant θ is the reciprocal of sine θ: $\csc \theta = \dfrac{1}{\sin \theta}$ or $\dfrac{\text{hypotenuse}}{\text{opposite}}$.

Cosine For an acute angle θ in a right triangle, cosine θ is the ratio of the side adjacent θ and the hypotenuse: $\cos \theta = \dfrac{\text{adjacent}}{\text{hypotenuse}}$.

Cotangent For an acute angle θ in a right triangle, cotangent θ is the reciprocal of tangent θ: $\cot \theta = \dfrac{1}{\tan \theta}$ or $\dfrac{\text{adjacent}}{\text{opposite}}$.

Secant For an acute angle θ in a right triangle, secant θ is the reciprocal of cosine θ: $\sec \theta = \dfrac{1}{\cos \theta}$ or $\dfrac{\text{hypotenuse}}{\text{adjacent}}$.

Sine For an acute angle θ in a right triangle, sine θ is the ratio of the side opposite θ and the hypotenuse: $\sin\theta = \dfrac{\text{opposite}}{\text{hypotenuse}}$.

Tangent For an acute angle θ in a right triangle, tangent θ is the ratio of the side opposite θ and the side adjacent θ: $\tan\theta = \dfrac{\text{opposite}}{\text{adjacent}}$.

 RIGHT TRIANGLES

A. RIGHT TRIANGLE BASICS

1. Right triangles contain an angle that measures 90° (a right angle). The other two angles are both acute angles (measures less than 90°) and complementary angles (the sum of their measures is 90°).
2. The hypotenuse of a right triangle is opposite the right angle and is the longest side of the triangle. The two other sides are called *legs*. When a leg is one side of one of the acute angles, that leg is said to be *adjacent* to that angle, and the other leg is said to be *opposite* that angle.

B. TRIGONOMETRIC RATIOS

1. The trigonometric ratios are the ratios of the sides of right triangles. The trigonometric ratios are defined in terms of an acute angle in the right triangle that is represented by the Greek letter θ (theta) and that angle's relationship to its adjacent side, opposite side, and hypotenuse.

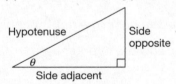

2. There are three trigonometric ratios: sine, cosine, and tangent.
    i. The *sine* is the ratio of the side opposite θ and the hypotenuse:

$$\sin\theta = \dfrac{\text{opposite}}{\text{hypotenuse}}$$

ii. The *cosine* is the ratio of the side adjacent θ and the hypotenuse:

$$\cos\theta = \frac{\text{adjacent}}{\text{hypotenuse}}$$

iii. The *tangent* is the ratio of the side opposite θ and the side adjacent to θ:

$$\tan\theta = \frac{\text{opposite}}{\text{adjacent}}$$

3. The mnemonic SOH-CAH-TOA can be used to remember the trigonometric ratios.

$$\sin\theta = \frac{\text{opposite}}{\text{hypotenuse}} \qquad \cos\theta = \frac{\text{adjacent}}{\text{hypotenuse}} \qquad \tan\theta = \frac{\text{opposite}}{\text{adjacent}}$$

4. Here's an example of how to find the trigonometric ratios for the following triangle:

$$\sin\theta = \frac{\text{opposite}}{\text{hypotenuse}} = \frac{3}{5} \qquad \cos\theta = \frac{\text{adjacent}}{\text{hypotenuse}} = \frac{4}{5}$$

$$\tan\theta = \frac{\text{opposite}}{\text{adjacent}} = \frac{3}{4}$$

Test Tip

Similar Triangles and Trigonometric Ratios *Since the corresponding sides of similar triangles are proportional, similar triangles have the same trigonometric ratios as well.*

C. RECIPROCAL TRIGONOMETRIC RATIOS

1. The reciprocal trigonometric ratios are the reciprocals of the trigonometric ratios. The reciprocal trigonometric ratios are also defined in terms of an acute angle in the right triangle that is represented by the Greek letter θ (theta). There are three reciprocal trigonometric ratios: cosecant, secant, and cotangent.

i. The *cosecant* is the reciprocal of the sine:

$$\csc\theta = \frac{1}{\sin\theta} \quad \text{or} \quad \frac{\text{hypotenuse}}{\text{opposite}}$$

ii. The *secant* is the reciprocal of the cosine:

$$\sec\theta = \frac{1}{\cos\theta} \text{ or } \frac{\text{hypotenuse}}{\text{adjacent}}$$

iii. The *cotangent* is the reciprocal of the tangent:

$$\cot\theta = \frac{1}{\tan\theta} = \frac{\text{adjacent}}{\text{opposite}}$$

2. Here's an example of how to find reciprocal trigonometric ratios:

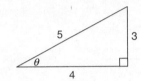

$$\csc\theta = \frac{\text{hypotenuse}}{\text{opposite}} = \frac{5}{3} \qquad \sec\theta = \frac{\text{hypotenuse}}{\text{adjacent}} = \frac{5}{4}$$

$$\cot\theta = \frac{\text{adjacent}}{\text{opposite}} = \frac{4}{3}$$

Cosecants, Secants, and Cotangents on Your Calculator
You may notice that there are no keys for cosecants, secants, and cotangents on your calculator. Since csc θ, sec θ, and cot θ are equal to $\dfrac{1}{\sin\theta}$, $\dfrac{1}{\cos\theta}$, *and* $\dfrac{1}{\tan\theta}$, *respectively, you can calculate the reciprocal trigonometric ratios by using their reciprocals:*

$$\text{cosecant}(x) = \csc(x) = \sin(x)^{\wedge}-1$$

$$\text{secant}(x) = \sec(x) = \cos(x)^{\wedge}-1$$

$$\text{cotangent}(x) = \cot(x) = \tan(x)^{\wedge}-1$$

For example, to find the cosecant of 35°, first make sure your calculator is in degree mode by pressing the [MODE] key, then moving the cursor to DEGREE and pressing [ENTER]. Then press [2nd] [MODE] to return to the home screen. Input sin(35), press the [x^−1] key to raise the entry to the (−1) power, and press [ENTER] to complete the calculation.

Test
Tip

D. TRIGONOMETRIC RATIOS IN SPECIAL TRIANGLES

1. Special triangles are $30°-60°-90°$ and $45°-45°-90°$ triangles with proportional relationships between the lengths of their sides. A $30°-60°-90°$ triangle has sides of x, $x\sqrt{3}$, and $2x$, and a $45°-45°-90°$ has sides of x, x, and $x\sqrt{2}$.

2. The trigonometric ratios for the acute angles in special triangles are shown in the following table:

Trigonometric Ratios for Acute Angles in Special Triangles

θ	$\sin\theta$	$\cos\theta$	$\tan\theta$	$\csc\theta$	$\sec\theta$	$\cot\theta$
30°	$\dfrac{1}{2}$	$\dfrac{\sqrt{3}}{2}$	$\dfrac{\sqrt{3}}{3}$	2	$\dfrac{2\sqrt{3}}{3}$	$\sqrt{3}$
45°	$\dfrac{\sqrt{2}}{2}$	$\dfrac{\sqrt{2}}{2}$	1	$\sqrt{2}$	$\sqrt{2}$	1
60°	$\dfrac{\sqrt{3}}{2}$	$\dfrac{1}{2}$	$\sqrt{3}$	$\dfrac{2\sqrt{3}}{3}$	2	$\dfrac{\sqrt{3}}{3}$

3. There are three sets of *cofunctions* in the relationships between the trigonometric and reciprocal trigonometric ratios:

   i. Sine and cosine: $\sin\theta = \cos(90° - \theta)$ and $\cos\theta = \sin(90° - \theta)$

   ii. Tangent and cotangent: $\tan\theta = \cot(90° - \theta)$ and $\cot\theta = \tan(90° - \theta)$

   iii. Secant and cosecant: $\sec\theta = \csc(90° - \theta)$ and $\csc\theta = \sec(90° - \theta)$

4. If you know the trigonometric value of an angle, but not the measure of the angle itself, you can use the inverse trigonometric functions to find the angle.

   i. The inverse of the sine is the *arcsine*. In expressions and equations, arcsine is denoted as arcsin or $\sin^{-1}$.

   ii. The inverse of the cosine is the *arccosine*. In expressions and equations, arcsine is denoted as arccos or $\cos^{-1}$.

iii. The inverse of the tangent is the *arctangent*. In expressions and equations, arctangent is denoted as arctan or $\tan^{-1}$.

E. USING TRIGONOMETRIC RATIOS TO FIND UNKNOWN MEASURES IN RIGHT TRIANGLES

1. You can use trigonometric ratios to find unknown measures of right triangles if either of the following are known:
    i. The lengths of two sides
    ii. The length of one side and the measure of one acute angle
2. You can use trigonometric ratios to find an unknown length of a side. For example, you can use the sine ratio to find *x* in the following triangle.

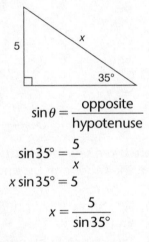

$$\sin\theta = \frac{\text{opposite}}{\text{hypotenuse}}$$

$$\sin 35° = \frac{5}{x}$$

$$x\sin 35° = 5$$

$$x = \frac{5}{\sin 35°}$$

3. You can use trigonometric ratios to find an unknown angle measure. For example, you can use the cosine ratio to find *x* in the following triangle.

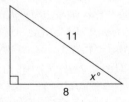

$$\cos\theta = \frac{\text{adjacent}}{\text{hypotenuse}}$$

$$\cos x = \frac{8}{11}$$

$$x = \cos^{-1}\left(\frac{8}{11}\right) \approx 43.3$$

So, the measure of the angle is about 43.3°.

F. SOLVING PROBLEMS WITH ANGLES OF ELEVATION AND DEPRESSION

1. Trigonometric ratios can be used to solve problems involving angles of elevation and depression.

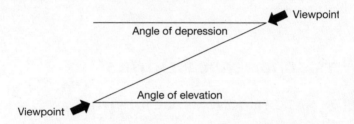

  i. An angle of elevation is the angle between a horizontal line and the line of sight of an observer looking upward at an object at a higher level.

  ii. An angle of depression is the angle between a horizontal line and the line of sight of an observer looking downward at an object at a lower level.

  iii. In any given situation, the angle of elevation and the angle of depression have the same measure because they are alternate interior angles of parallel lines.

2. Angles of elevation and depression can be used to find the heights of objects and determine distances. For example, suppose you want to find how far from the door to start building a ramp with a 10° angle of elevation so that the ramp rises 2 feet.

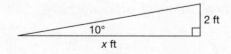

Let x be the distance you want to find. Note that you know the measure of an angle and the length of its opposite side. You want to find the length of the adjacent side. Since the tangent is the ratio of opposite side to adjacent side, you can use the tangent ratio to solve this problem.

$$\tan\theta = \frac{\text{opposite}}{\text{adjacent}}$$

$$\tan 10° = \frac{2}{x}$$

$$x\tan 10° = 2$$

$$x = \frac{2}{\tan 10°} \approx 11.3$$

So, the start of the ramp should be about 11.3 feet from the door.

II. TRIGONOMETRIC IDENTITIES

A. BASIC TRIGONOMETRIC IDENTITIES

1. Trigonometric identities are true for all values of the variables for which the expressions are defined.

2. Relationships between reciprocal trigonometric ratios are reciprocal identities. The following identities are true for all values of θ for which the identity is defined:

$$\sin\theta = \frac{1}{\csc\theta} \qquad \csc\theta = \frac{1}{\sin\theta}$$

$$\cos\theta = \frac{1}{\sec\theta} \qquad \sec\theta = \frac{1}{\cos\theta}$$

$$\tan\theta = \frac{1}{\cot\theta} \qquad \cot\theta = \frac{1}{\tan\theta}$$

3. Relationships involving quotients between trigonometric ratios are quotient identities. The following identities are true for all values of θ for which the identity is defined:

$$\frac{\sin\theta}{\cos\theta} = \tan\theta \qquad \frac{\cos\theta}{\sin\theta} = \cot\theta$$

4. The Pythagorean theorem is used to derive the following identities. Therefore, they are called the *Pythagorean identities*. The following identities are true for all values of θ for which the identity is defined:

$$\sin^2 \theta + \cos^2 \theta = 1 \quad \tan^2 \theta + 1 = \sec^2 \theta \quad 1 + \cot^2 \theta = \csc^2 \theta$$

5. Symmetry identities give general rules for sines and cosines. The following identities are true for all values of θ and for all integers k:

$$\sin \theta = \sin(\theta + 360k°) \qquad \cos \theta = \cos(\theta + 360k°)$$

$$-\sin \theta = \sin(\theta + 180°(2k - 1)) \quad -\cos \theta = \cos(\theta + 180°(2k - 1))$$

$$-\sin \theta = \sin(\theta + 360k°) \qquad -\cos \theta = \cos(360k° - \theta)$$

$$\sin \theta = \sin(180°(2k - 1) - \theta) \quad \cos \theta = \cos(180°(2k - 1) - \theta)$$

6. The symmetry identities $-\sin \theta = \sin(360k° - \theta)$ and $-\cos \theta = \cos(360k° - \theta)$ can be written as opposite angle identities when $k = 0$. The following identities are true for all values of θ:

$$\sin(-\theta) = -\sin \theta \qquad \cos(-\theta) = \cos \theta$$

B. SUM AND DIFFERENCE IDENTITIES

1. Sum and difference identities can be derived for two angles whose measures are represented by α and β. The following sum and difference identities are true for all values of α and β:

$$\cos(\alpha \pm \beta) = \cos \alpha \cos \beta \mp \sin \alpha \sin \beta$$

$$\sin(\alpha \pm \beta) = \sin \alpha \cos \beta \pm \cos \alpha \sin \beta$$

$$\tan(\alpha \pm \beta) = \frac{\tan \alpha \pm \tan \beta}{1 \mp \tan \alpha \tan \beta}$$

2. The minus–plus ($\mp$) sign used in the sum and difference identities for the cosine and tangent function is used in conjunction with the plus–minus sign ($\pm$) to indicate that a negative value is to be used when a positive value is indicated by the plus–minus sign, and vice versa.

III. LAW OF SINES

A. LAW OF SINES BASICS

1. The law of sines can be used to solve triangles that are not right triangles.
2. For any triangle $\triangle ABC$ where a, b, and c represent the measures of the sides opposite the angles with measures A, B, and C, the law of sines says the following is true:

$$\frac{a}{\sin A} = \frac{b}{\sin B} = \frac{c}{\sin C}$$

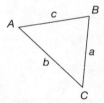

B. SOLVING TRIANGLES USING THE LAW OF SINES

1. If you know the lengths of two sides of a triangle and the measure of an angle opposite one of them, you can use the law of sines to find the measure of the angle opposite the other side. Also, if you know the measures of two angles of a triangle and the length of a side opposite one of them, you can use the law of sines to find the length of the side opposite the other angle.
2. To use the law of sines, substitute the known measures into the equation and solve for the unknown value. For example, here's how you can use the law of sines to solve a triangle when you know the measures of two angles of a triangle and the length of a side opposite one of them:

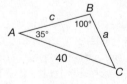

First, find the measure of $\angle C$: $180° - (35° + 100°) = 45°$

Next, use the law of sines to find the lengths of sides a and c:

$$\frac{a}{\sin A} = \frac{b}{\sin B} \qquad\qquad \frac{c}{\sin C} = \frac{b}{\sin B}$$

$$\frac{a}{\sin 35°} = \frac{40}{\sin 100°} \qquad\qquad \frac{c}{\sin 45°} = \frac{40}{\sin 100°}$$

$$a = \frac{40\sin 35°}{\sin 100°} \qquad\qquad c = \frac{40\sin 45°}{\sin 100°}$$

$$a \approx 23.2969911 \qquad\qquad c \approx 28.72060172$$

So, the solution of this triangle is $C = 45°$, $a \approx 23.3$, and $c \approx 28.7$.

3. You can also use the law of sines if you know the lengths of two sides of a triangle and the measure of an angle opposite one of them, and you want to find the length of the side opposite the other angle. However, it is possible that the measures of two sides and a nonincluded angle do not define a unique triangle. It is possible that there may be no solution, one solution, or two solutions. The case of two solutions is called the *ambiguous case*.

    i. To determine the number of solutions for a triangle with sides a and b and angle A, you can use the following rules:

    a) If $A < 90°$ and $a < b$, there are no solutions if $a < b\sin A$, one solution if $a = b\sin A$, and two solutions if $b > a > b\sin A$.

    b) If $A < 90°$ and $a \geq b$, there is one solution.

    c) If $A \geq 90°$ and $a \leq b$, there is no solution. If $A \geq 90°$ and $a > b$, there is one solution.

    ii. Here's how you could use the law of sines to solve the following triangle: $\angle A = 30°$, $AC = 15$, $BC = 10$. Determine the other two angle measures.

    First, determine the number of solutions. Since $A < 90°$ and $a < b$, find the value of $b\sin A$ for $b = 15$ and $A = 30°$: $15\sin 30° = 7.5$. Since a is 10, this means $a > b\sin A$ and there are two solutions.

Next, use the law of sines to find B:

$$\frac{a}{\sin A} = \frac{b}{\sin B}$$

$$\frac{10}{\sin 30°} = \frac{15}{\sin B}$$

$$\sin B = \frac{15 \sin 30°}{10}$$

$$\sin B = 0.75$$

$$B = \sin^{-1}(0.75)$$

$$B \approx 48.6° \text{ or } 131.4°$$

Since angles measuring approximately 48.6° and 131.4° both have sines of 0.75, there are two possible solutions. Here are the two possible diagrams.

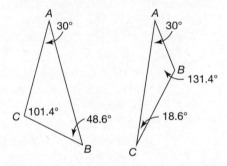

If $B = 48.6°$, then the angle measurements for $\triangle ABC$ are 30°, 48.6°, and 101.4°. If $B = 131.4°$, then the angle measurements for $\triangle ABC$ are 30°, 131.4°, and 18.6°. The law of sines can be used to determine the length of side c for both cases.

IV. LAW OF COSINES

A. LAW OF COSINES BASICS

1. The law of cosines can be used to solve triangles that are not right triangles.

2. For any triangle $\triangle ABC$ where a, b, and c represent the measures of the sides opposite the angles with measures A, B, and C, the law of cosines says the following is true:

$$a^2 = b^2 + c^2 - 2bc \cos A$$
$$b^2 = a^2 + c^2 - 2ac \cos B$$
$$c^2 = a^2 + b^2 - 2ab \cos C$$

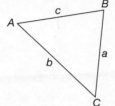

B. SOLVING TRIANGLES USING THE LAW OF COSINES

1. If you know the lengths of two sides of a triangle and the measure of their included angle, you can use the law of cosines to find length of the third side. Also, if you know the lengths of three sides of a triangle, you can use the law of cosines to find the measure of an angle.

2. To use the law of cosines, substitute the known measures into the equation and solve for the unknown value. For example, here's how you can use the law of cosines to solve the following triangle:

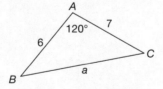

i. First, use the law of cosines to find a:

$$a^2 = b^2 + c^2 - 2bc \cos A$$
$$a^2 = 7^2 + 6^2 - 2(7)(6) \cos 120°$$
$$a^2 = 127$$
$$a \approx 11.3$$

ii. Next, use the law of sines to find the measure of $\angle B$:

$$\frac{11.3}{\sin 120°} = \frac{7}{\sin B}$$

$$\sin B = \frac{7 \sin 120°}{11.3}$$

$$B = \sin^{-1}\left(\frac{7 \sin 120°}{11.3}\right)$$

$$B \approx 32.44405972$$

So, $B \approx 32.4°$

iii. Finally, find the measure of $\angle C$: $180° - (120° + 32.4°) = 27.6°$. So, $B \approx 32.4°$, $C \approx 27.6°$, and $a \approx 11.3$.

3. Suppose you know that a triangle has sides with lengths of 5, 11, and 14 inches and you want to find the measure of its largest angle. Here's how you could use the law of cosines to solve the problem:

i. Since the largest angle of a triangle is opposite it longest side, let $a = 14$ and A be the largest angle.

ii. Use the law of cosines to find A:

$$14^2 = 5^2 + 11^2 - 2(5)(11)\cos A$$

$$196 = 25 + 121 - 110\cos A$$

$$50 = -110\cos A$$

$$\cos A = \frac{50}{110}$$

$$A = \cos^{-1}\left(-\frac{50}{110}\right) \approx 117.0°$$

V. TRIGONOMETRIC EQUATIONS

A. TRIGONOMETRIC EQUATION BASICS

1. You can solve trigonometric equations by using trigonometric reciprocals, cofunctions, and identities, as well as basic strategies such as factoring.

2. Due to the periodic nature of trigonometric functions, trigonometric equations can have infinitely many solutions if not restricted.

B. SOLVING TRIGONOMETRIC EQUATIONS

1. Here are some strategies for solving trigonometric equations.

   i. The quotient identity $\dfrac{\sin\theta}{\cos\theta} = \tan\theta$ can be very useful when solving trigonometric equations. For example, here's how you could use the quotient identity to solve the trigonometric equation $\sin x = 5 \cos x$ for $0° \leq x \leq 360°$:

$\sin x = 5\cos x$	Original equation
$\dfrac{\sin x}{\cos x} = 5$	Divide both sides by cos x.
$\tan x = 5$	Quotient identity $\dfrac{\sin\theta}{\cos\theta} = \tan\theta$
$x = \tan^{-1} 5$	Inverse of tangent
$x \approx 78.7°$	Use a calculator.

   Note that since the specified interval is $0° \leq x \leq 360°$, the $78.7° + 180° \approx 258.7°$ is also a solution. So, the solution is $x \approx 78.7°$ or $x \approx 258.7°$.

   ii. Factoring is another strategy you can use to solve trigonometric equations. For example, here's how you could use factoring to solve the trigonometric equation $8 \cos^2 x = 1 - 2 \cos x$ for $0° \leq x \leq 360°$:

$8 \cos^2 x = 1 - 2\cos x$	Original equation
$8 \cos^2 x + 2\cos x - 1 = 0$	Set equation to 0.
$(4 \cos x - 1)(2 \cos x + 1) = 0$	Factor.
$\cos x = \dfrac{1}{4}$ or $\cos x = -\dfrac{1}{2}$	Set each side to 0 and solve.
$x = \cos^{-1}\left(\dfrac{1}{4}\right) \approx 75.5°$	Use your calculator.
$x = \cos^{-1}\left(-\dfrac{1}{2}\right) \approx 120°$	

   Since the specified interval is $0° \leq x \leq 360°$, the possible solutions are $x \approx 75.5°$, $x = 120°$, $x = 240°$, or $x \approx 284.5°$

Using Radians Note that you can also define trigonometric identities, find unknown triangle measures, and solve trigonometric equations using radians instead of degrees. The following table shows equivalent measures in degrees and radians.

Degrees	30°	45°	60°	90°	120°	135°	150°	180°
Radians	$\frac{\pi}{6}$	$\frac{\pi}{4}$	$\frac{\pi}{3}$	$\frac{\pi}{2}$	$\frac{2\pi}{3}$	$\frac{3\pi}{4}$	$\frac{5\pi}{6}$	π

Degrees	210°	225°	240°	270°	300°	315°	330°	360°
Radians	$\frac{7\pi}{6}$	$\frac{5\pi}{4}$	$\frac{4\pi}{3}$	$\frac{3\pi}{2}$	$\frac{5\pi}{3}$	$\frac{7\pi}{4}$	$\frac{11\pi}{6}$	2π

Remember to set your calculator to DEGREE mode when working with degrees and RADIAN mode when working with radians.

VI. DOUBLE-ANGLE FORMULAS

A. DOUBLE-ANGLE FORMULA BASICS

1. Double-angle formulas allow you to find the value of the sine, cosine, and tangent of twice an angle.
2. The double-angle formulas for sine and cosine are the following:

$$\sin 2\theta = 2\sin\theta\cos\theta$$
$$\cos 2\theta = \cos^2\theta - \sin^2\theta$$
$$\cos 2\theta = 2\cos^2\theta - 1$$
$$\cos 2\theta = 1 - 2\sin^2\theta$$
$$\tan 2\theta = \frac{2\tan\theta}{1-\tan^2\theta}$$

B. USING DOUBLE-ANGLE FORMULAS

1. If $\sin\theta = \frac{3}{5}$ and θ is in Quadrant I, you can use a double-angle formula to find the value of $\cos 2\theta$ as follows:

   i. If $\sin\theta = \frac{3}{5}$, then $\cos\theta = \frac{4}{5}$.

ii. Use the double-angle formula $\cos 2\theta = \cos^2\theta - \sin^2\theta$:

$$\cos 2\theta = \cos^2\theta - \sin^2\theta$$

$$\cos 2\theta = \left(\frac{4}{5}\right)^2 - \left(\frac{3}{5}\right)^2$$

$$\cos 2\theta = \frac{7}{25}$$

2. Double-angle formulas can help you simplify trigonometric expressions. For example, if you want to simplify $2\sin 5x \cos 5x$, you can use the double-angle formula $\sin 2\theta = 2\sin\theta\cos\theta$ to rewrite $2\sin 5x \cos 5x$ as $\sin 2(5x) = \sin 10x$.

MEAN, MEDIAN, AND MODE

KEY VOCABULARY

Mean The average of a set of numbers.

Median The middle number of a list of ordered numbers.

Mode The most frequent value in a data set.

I. MEASURES OF CENTRAL TENDENCY

A. MEASURES OF CENTRAL TENDENCY BASICS

1. Measures of central tendency can be used to find average values, middle values, and most frequent values.
2. Mean, median, and mode are the three statistics used to measure central tendency.

B. MEAN

1. The *mean* is the average of a set of numbers.
2. The mean is calculated by finding the sum of the terms and dividing the sum by the number of terms. For example, consider the following data set:

$$3 \quad 7 \quad 10 \quad 8 \quad 12 \quad 3 \quad 6$$

The mean is $\dfrac{3+7+10+8+12+3+6}{7} = \dfrac{49}{7} = 7$.

3. In statistics, the mean is often represented as $\overline{X}$.

C. MEDIAN

1. The *median* is the middle number of a list of ordered numbers.

2. The process for finding the median of a list of ordered numbers depends on whether the number of terms is even or odd.

    i. If the number of terms is odd, then the median is the middle number in the list. For example, consider the following data set:

       3   7   10   8   12   3   6

       To find the median, first order the numbers in the list:

       3   3   6   7   8   10   12

       The median is 7, the middle number in the list.

    ii. If the number of terms is even, then the median is the average of the two middle numbers. For example, suppose one more value is added to the previous data set:

       3   3   3   6   7   8   10   12

       The median is now the average of 6 and 7, which is 6.5.

Test Tip

*Avoid a **Common Median Mistake** Remember to make sure the list of numbers is ordered before identifying the median.*

D. MODE

1. The *mode* is the most frequent value in a data set. For example, consider the following data set:

   3   3   3   6   7   8   10   12

   The mode is 3.

2. A data set can have more than one mode. For example, consider the following data set:

   3   3   6   7   8   8   10   12

   The modes are 3 and 8.

3. If each number occurs only once, there is no mode. An example of a data set with no mode is: 3, 4, 6, 7, 10.

USING MEAN, MEDIAN, AND MODE

A. CHARACTERIZING A DATA SET

1. The mean, median, and mode can provide a general characterization of a data set. For example, suppose salaries for 10 employees at a small business are the following:

   $15,000 $18,000 $20,000 $20,000 $22,000

   $25,000 $25,000 $26,000 $28,000 $199,000

   i. The mean is calculated by adding the 10 salaries and dividing by 10. To save space, you can just add the thousands:

   $$\frac{15+18+20+20+22+25+25+26+28+199}{10} = 39.8$$

   So, the average salary is $39,800.

   ii. Since there is an even number of salaries and the list is already ordered, the median is determined by finding the average of the middle two salaries:

   $$\frac{\$22,000 + \$25,000}{2} = \$23,500$$

   So, the median salary is $23,500.

   iii. The mode is the most frequent data value. This data set has two modes: $20,000 and $25,000.

   iv. Note that the median and the mode are more accurate representations of most of the salaries since the median and the mode are not affected by extreme values in the way that the mean is affected.

2. Measures of central tendency are used to obtain other statistics. For example, the mean is used in the calculation for standard deviation.

B. SOLVING PROBLEMS

1. You can also write equations to solve problems involving measures of central tendency. For example, suppose the mean math test score for 13 students was 73 points. When a new score is added after a student takes a make-up test, the mean increases to 74. What is the new score?

To find the new score that was added, you can write an equation to model the situation. Let x be the new score. Before the new score was added, the mean was determined as follows:

$$\frac{\text{total of 13 scores}}{13} = 73$$

Therefore, the total of the 13 scores before the new score was added is $13 \cdot 73 = 949$. When the new score x is added to 949 and the sum is divided by 14, the quotient increases to 74. This situation can be modeled by the equation $\frac{949 + x}{14} = 74$. To find the additional score, solve for x:

$$\frac{949 + x}{14} = 74$$
$$949 + x = 14(74)$$
$$949 + x = 1036$$
$$x = 87$$

So, the additional test score was 87.

2. Sometimes, as in the preceding problem, it is not necessary to know each individual score in order to solve a problem involving means. Note, however, that although you knew the total of the original 13 scores, there is no way to determine the individual scores with the given information.

Test Tip

Mean, Median, and Mode on Your Calculator *Here's how to use your graphing calculator to find the mean, median, and mode of the following data set:*

55   72   43   85   65   72   81   61   70   72

First, input your data into a list. Press [STAT] and select EDIT to get the list screen. Input the data into L1. Press [2ND][MODE] to return to the home screen.

L1	L2	L3	1
55	------	------	
72			
43			
85			
65			
72			
81			
L1(1)=55			

(continued)

(continued)

*To find the mean, press [2ND][STAT] and MATH, then choose
3 for mean. When the home screen prompts for the list, press
[2ND] and 1 for L1. To find the median, repeat the process, but
choose 4 for median after pressing [STAT] and MATH.*

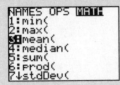 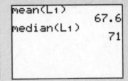

*An alternate way to find mean and median is to use the statis-
tics functions. Press [STAT], then select CALC and 1 for 1–Var
Stats. When the home screen prompts for the list, press [2ND]
and 1 for L1. The mean, represented by $\bar{X}$, is the first statistic
listed and is 67.6. To see the median, use the arrow to scroll
down. The median is 71.*

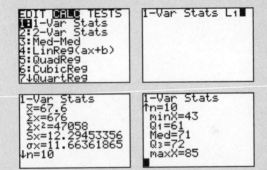

*To find the mode, you can sort the data into ascending or descend-
ing order and then find the value(s) that occurs most frequently.
Press [STAT] and choose 2 for SortA to sort the data in ascending
order. When the home screen prompts for the list, press [2ND] and
1 for L1, then [ENTER]. To see the sorted list, press [STAT] and select
EDIT to get the list screen. The mode is 72, which occurs three times.
Note that after the data has been sorted, it will stay in this order.*

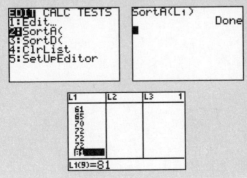

RANGE AND INTERQUARTILE RANGE

KEY VOCABULARY

Interquartile range The difference between the first quartile and the third quartile of an ordered set of numbers.

Quartiles The three values that divide an ordered set of numbers into four equal groups.

Range The difference between the greatest and least data values in a set of numbers.

I. MEASURES OF DATA SPREAD

A. MEASURES OF DATA SPREAD BASICS

1. *Measures of the spread of data* describe the dispersion of data about some central tendency.
2. Range and interquartile range are two statistics used to measure the spread of data.

B. RANGE

1. The *range* is the difference between the greatest and least data values in a set of numbers.
2. The range is calculated by subtracting the least data value from the greatest data value. For example, consider the following data set:

$$53 \quad 27 \quad 10 \quad 78 \quad 12 \quad 31 \quad 96$$

The greatest value is 96. The least value is 10. The range is 96 − 10 or 86.

C. INTERQUARTILE RANGE

1. *Quartiles* of a data set are the three values that divide an ordered data set into four equal groups.

   i. The first or lower quartile, often denoted by Q_1, is the value that marks off the lowest 25% of the data.

   ii. The second quartile or median, often denoted by Q_2, is the value that divides the data in half.

   iii. The third or upper quartile, often denoted by Q_3, is the value that marks off the upper 25% or lower 75% of the data.

2. The *interquartile range* is the range of the middle 50% of the data, which is between the first and third quartiles.

3. The interquartile range is computed by first finding the three quartiles of an ordered data set. For example, consider the following data set:

$$53 \quad 27 \quad 10 \quad 78 \quad 12 \quad 31 \quad 96$$

   i. Arrange the data in ascending order:

$$10 \quad 12 \quad 27 \quad 31 \quad 53 \quad 78 \quad 96$$

   ii. Find the median of the entire data set. The median is the middle value, which is 31.

   iii. Find the lower quartile by finding the median of the data to the left of the median, 31. The lower quartile is 12.

   iv. Find the upper quartile by finding the median of the data to the right of the median, 31. The upper quartile is 78.

   v. Find the interquartile range by subtracting the lower quartile from the upper quartile. For this data set, the interquartile range is $78 - 12$, or 66.

Different Methods for Finding Quartiles *Note that there are two methods for finding the lower and upper quartiles, based on whether or not the median value is included in the data set when these are found.*

1. *Method 1: The median is not included in the upper and lower halves when the upper and lower quartiles are determined. This method is used by the TI-83 calculator for the "1-Var Stats" and boxplot functions.*

2. *Method 2: If the data set contains an odd number of values so that the median is an actual data value, then the median is included in the upper and lower halves when the upper and lower quartiles are determined. If the data set contains an even number of values so that the median is the average of the two middle values, as opposed to being an actual data value, then the median is not included in the upper and lower halves when the upper and lower quartiles are determined.*

Method 1 is used for all examples in this Crash Course.

II. USING THE RANGE AND INTERQUARTILE RANGE

A. USING THE RANGE

1. The range can be used to characterize a data set by providing information about how far the data is spread out. For example, consider the following ordered set of 13 test scores:

   25   62   64   66   68   70   72   73   75   75   79   81   99

   The range is the difference of the greatest and least values: $99 - 25$, or 74.

2. Note that the range is affected by the extreme values of 25 and 99. The range tells you that the scores fall within a 74-point range, but it does not tell you that most of the scores fall within a much smaller range of values.

B. USING THE INTERQUARTILE RANGE

1. The interquartile range can also be used to characterize a data set by providing information about how far the data is spread out. Again, consider the following set of 13 test scores:

   25   62   64   66   68   70   72   73   75   75   79   81   99

To find the interquartile range, first find the three quartiles. Note that the data is already in ascending order.

    i. Find the median of the entire data set. The median is the middle value, which is 72.

    ii. Find the lower quartile by finding the median of the data to the left of the median, 72:

$$25 \quad 62 \quad 64 \quad 66 \quad 68 \quad 70$$

Since the number of data values is even, the median is the average of the two middle values: $\dfrac{64+66}{2} = 65$. The lower quartile is 65.

    iii. Find the upper quartile by finding the median of the data to the right of the median, 72:

$$73 \quad 75 \quad 75 \quad 79 \quad 81 \quad 99$$

Since the number of data values is even, the median is the average of the two middle values: $\dfrac{75+79}{2} = 77$. The upper quartile is 77.

    iv. Find the interquartile range by subtracting the lower quartile from the upper quartile. For this set of test scores, the interquartile range is $77 - 65$, or 12.

2. The interquartile range tells you that 50% of the test scores are between 65 and 77. This also means that 50% of the test scores fell within a 12-point range.

3. Unlike the range, the interquartile range is not affected by the extreme values of 25 and 99.

Range and Interquartile Range on Your Calculator *Here's how to use your graphing calculator to find the range and interquartile range for the following data set:*

55   72   43   85   65   72   81   61   70   72

First, input your data into a list. Press [STAT] and select EDIT to get the list screen. Input the data into L1. Press [2ND][MODE] to return to the home screen.

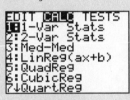

You can find the range and interquartile range by using the statistics functions. Press [STAT], then select CALC and 1 for 1–Var Stats. When the home screen prompts for the list, press [2ND] and 1 for L1. To see the minimum, maximum, median, Q₁, and Q₃, use the arrow to scroll down.

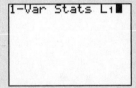

The range can be found by subtracting the minimum value from the maximum value: 85 − 43 = 42. The first quartile, also called the lower quartile or Q_1, is 61. The second quartile, which is the same as the median, is 71. The third quartile, also called the **upper quartile** *or Q_3, is 72. The interquartile range can be found by subtracting the first quartile from the third quartile: 72 − 61 = 11.*

PART V:

DATA ANALYSIS, STATISTICS, AND PROBABILITY

STANDARD DEVIATION

KEY VOCABULARY

Standard deviation The square root of the average of the squared deviations from the mean.

Variance The average of the squared deviations from the mean.

I. MEASURES OF VARIABILITY

A. VARIANCE

1. *Variance* is a measure of how far the numbers in a data set are spread out. It is the average of the squared deviations from the mean.
2. Variance is represented by σ^2.
3. The variance is calculated by finding the mean of a data set, then subtracting each data value from the mean and squaring the difference, and finally finding the average of those squared differences. For example, here's how to find the variance for the following data set:

$$5 \quad 7 \quad 9 \quad 11 \quad 12 \quad 16$$

i. Find the mean: $\dfrac{5+7+9+11+12+16}{6} = \dfrac{60}{6} = 10$

ii. Find the deviation of each score from the mean by subtracting the mean from the score. Then square each deviation. Finally add the squared deviations and find their average:

$$\sigma^2 = \frac{(5-10)^2 + (7-10)^2 + (9-10)^2 + (11-10)^2 + (12-10)^2 + (16-10)^2}{6}$$

$$\sigma^2 = \frac{(-5)^2 + (-3)^2 + (-1)^2 + 1^2 + 2^2 + 6^2}{6}$$

$$\sigma^2 = \frac{25 + 9 + 141 + 4 + 36}{6}$$

$$\sigma^2 = \frac{76}{6}$$

$$\sigma^2 \approx 12.667$$

4. Note that if the deviations from the mean were not squared, the sum of the deviations would be zero.

B. STANDARD DEVIATION

1. *Standard deviation* is also a measure of how far the numbers in a data set are spread out. It is the square root of the average of the squared deviations from the mean.

2. Standard deviation is represented by σ.

3. The standard deviation σ of a data set is the square root of the variance σ^2. For example, the standard deviation of the preceding data set is $\sigma = \sqrt{12.667} \approx 3.559$.

4. In general, standard deviation is calculated as follows:

$$\sigma = \sqrt{\frac{\text{sum of the squared deviations from the mean}}{\text{number of data}}}$$

Standard Deviation on Your Calculator *Here's how to use your graphing calculator to find the standard deviation for the following data set:*

55   72   43   85   65   72   81   61   70   72

First, input your data into a list. Press [STAT] and select EDIT to get the list screen. Input the data into L1. Press [2ND][MODE] to return to the home screen.

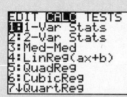

You can find the standard deviation by using the statistics functions. Press [STAT], then select CALC and 1 for 1–Var Stats. When the home screen prompts for the list, press [2ND] and 1 for L1.

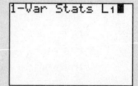

The mean $\bar{x}$ is 67.6 and the standard deviation is $\sigma = 11.66361865$ or about 11.7. This means that the numbers that fall within one standard deviation of the mean are between 67.6 − 11.7 and 67.6 + 11.7, or between 55.9 and 79.3; that the numbers that fall within two standard deviations of the mean are between 67.6 − 2 • 11.7 and 67.6 + 2 • 11.7, or between 44.2 and 91; and that the numbers that fall within three standard deviations of the mean are between 67.6 − 3 • 11.7 and 67.6 + 3 • 11.7, or between 32.5 and 102.7.

II. USING STANDARD DEVIATION

A. STANDARD DEVIATION BASICS

1. You can characterize a data set by identifying the data values that fall within one, two, and three standard deviations of the mean. For example, in a normal distribution of data, about 68% of the data falls within one standard deviation of the mean, about 95% of the data falls within two standard deviations of the mean, and over 99% of the data falls within three standard deviations of the mean.

2. Standard deviation is greater for data sets where numbers are more spread out and less for data sets that are closer together. For example, consider the following two sets of numbers:

$$3, 4, 5 \qquad\qquad 1, 4, 7$$

Although both data sets have a mean of 4, the standard deviation will be less for the data set containing 3, 4, and 5 than for the data set containing 1, 4, and 7. This is because the numbers 3, 4, and 5 are less spread out than the numbers 1, 4, and 7, which can be confirmed by the following calculations:

$$\sigma = \sqrt{\frac{(3-4)^2 + (4-4)^2 + (5-4)^2}{3}} \qquad \sigma = \sqrt{\frac{(1-4)^2 + (4-4)^2 + (7-4)^2}{3}}$$

$$\sigma = \sqrt{\frac{(-1)^2 + 0^2 + 1^2}{3}} \qquad \sigma = \sqrt{\frac{(-3)^2 + 0^2 + 3^2}{3}}$$

$$\sigma = \sqrt{\frac{2}{3}} \qquad\qquad \sigma = \sqrt{\frac{18}{3}}$$

$$\sigma \approx 0.8165 \qquad\qquad \sigma \approx 2.449$$

So, the standard deviation for the numbers in the first data set is about 0.8, and the standard deviation for the numbers in the second data set is about 2.4.

Test Tip

The Smallest Standard Deviation *The smallest possible standard deviation is 0, which is the standard deviation for a data set where all the numbers are identical. If all the numbers in a data set are not identical, then the standard deviation will always be greater than 0.*

B. INTERPRETING STANDARD DEVIATION

1. Standard deviation can be used to represent the typical variation for numbers in a data set. For example, consider the following set of 13 test scores:

   25 62 66 66 68 70 72 73 75 75 79 81 99

   i. First calculate the mean:

   $$\bar{x} = \frac{25+62+66+66+68+70+72+73+75+75+79+81+99}{13}$$

   $$\bar{x} \approx 70.1$$

   ii. Next, calculate the variance:

   $$\sigma^2 = \frac{(25-70.1)^2 + (62-70.1)^2 + \cdots + (81-70.1)^2 + (99-70.1)^2_2}{13}$$

   $$\sigma_2 \approx 248.5$$

   iii. Finally, calculate the standard deviation:

   $$\sigma = \sqrt{248.5}$$

   $$\sigma \approx 15.8$$

   Note that these calculations can be done more quickly and accurately with your calculator.

2. The data scores that fall within one standard deviations of the mean are those scores that fall between 70.1 − 15.8 and 70.1 + 15.8, or between 54.3 and 85.9. All but one of the scores in the data set are within two standard deviations of the mean.

GRAPHS AND PLOTS

Chapter

29

KEY VOCABULARY

Bar graph Represents frequency of data by length of bars.

Box-and-whisker plot Summarizes data based on the median, first and third quartiles, and minimum and maximum values of a data set.

Circle graph Represents parts of a whole as sectors of a circle.

Histogram Shows data frequencies within certain intervals.

Line graph Represents changes over time.

Scatter plot Displays information about two variables for a set of data.

Stem-and-leaf plot Shows data frequencies within certain intervals as well as individual data values.

I. BASIC DATA DISPLAY GRAPHS

A. BAR GRAPHS

1. *Bar graphs* make it easy to compare data by comparing the bars. For example, in the following bar graph, it is easy to see that more students prefer summer to the other three seasons.

283

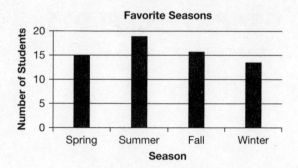

2. Bar graphs can be misleading when the scale does not start at 0. For example, in a revised version of the previous graph, there seems to be a much greater difference between the number of students who prefer summer and those who prefer the other seasons.

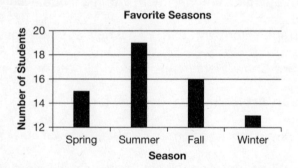

B. LINE GRAPHS

1. *Line graphs* make it easy to see changes over time. For example, in the following line graph, it appears that sales are generally decreasing.

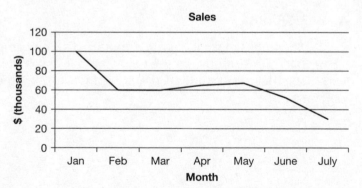

2. Line graphs can be misleading when partial data is shown. For example, by showing only the data for March through May, a revised version of the previous line graph gives the impression that sales are generally increasing.

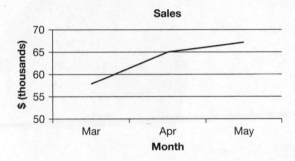

C. CIRCLE GRAPHS

1. *Circle graphs* make it easy to compare parts to the whole. For example, the circle graph below shows how a weekly budget of $500 is spent.

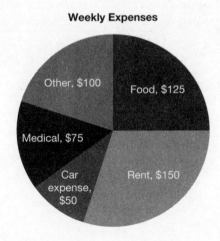

2. If percentages are shown for the sectors of a circle graph, the percentages must add to 100%.

Weekly Expenses

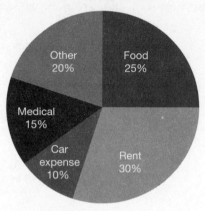

II. OTHER GRAPHS AND PLOTS

A. HISTOGRAMS

1. *Histograms* show data frequencies within certain intervals. For example, consider the following data set:

   1, 2, 4, 12, 16, 20, 21, 22, 22, 22, 34, 35, 38, 45, 49, 51, 55, 61, 61, 61, 63, 67, 70, 71, 79, 79, 90, 94

   A frequency table can be constructed showing frequencies for intervals.

   Frequency Table

Interval	Frequency
0–19	5
20–39	8
40–59	4
60–79	9
80–99	2

   The histogram shows a bar for each frequency interval. Note that there are no spaces between the bars.

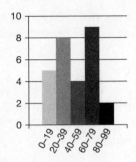

2. When data is displayed in a histogram, individual data values can no longer be determined.

B. STEM-AND-LEAF PLOTS

1. *Stem-and-leaf plots* show data frequencies within certain intervals as well as individual data values. Again, consider the following data set:

   1, 2, 4, 12, 16, 20, 21, 22, 22, 22, 34, 35, 38, 45, 49, 51, 55, 61, 61, 61, 63, 67, 70, 71, 79, 79, 90, 94

   In a stem-and-leaf plot, the "stem" is the left column, which in this plot represents the tens digit. The "leaves" are in the right column, showing the ones digit for each data value with the corresponding tens digit.

   Stem-and-Leaf Plot

Stem	Leaf
0	1 2 4
1	2 6
2	0 1 2 2 2
3	4 5 8
4	5 9
5	1 5
6	1 1 1 3 7
7	0 1 9 9
8	
9	0 4

2. When data is displayed in a stem-and-leaf plot, individual data values can still be determined.

C. BOX PLOTS

1. *Box plots*, also called *box-and-whisker plots*, summarize data based on the median, first and third quartiles, and minimum and maximum values of a data set. For example, consider the following data set:

25   62   66   66   68   70   72   73   75   75   79   81   99

The median is 72, the first quartile is 66, the third quartile is 77, the minimum is 25, and the maximum is 99. The box-and-whisker plot is constructed using these values.

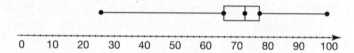

2. In a box-and-whisker plot, the box represents the interquartile range.

Box Plots on Your Calculator *You can create box plots on your graphing calculator. Suppose L1 contains the data values 1, 5, 9, 11, and 15. Press [2ND][Y=] for the STAT PLOT screen. Then select 1 and press ENTER to turn on the plot. Use the right arrow key to select the box plot as the plot type (the fifth graph option). Input L1 for Xlist and 1 for Freq. Then press [GRAPH] to see the box plot. You may have to press [ZOOM] and select 9 to adjust the window so the box plot can be seen.*

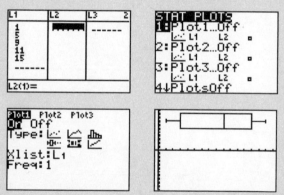

Note: To turn off the box plot, press [2ND][Y=] for the STAT PLOT screen. Select the plot and use the right arrow to select OFF, then press ENTER to turn the plot off.

D. SCATTER PLOTS

1. *Scatter plots* display information about two variables for a set of data. For example, the following table shows data relating the number of hours studied and test scores for 20 students.

Scatter Plot Data for Hours Studied and Test Scores

	1	2	3	4	5	6	7	8	9	10
Hours	1	1	1	2	3	3	3	4	4	5
Score	50	65	82	55	44	72	78	75	87	61
	11	12	13	14	15	16	17	18	19	20
Hours	5	5	5	6	6	7	8	8	9	10
Score	71	78	83	83	97	87	61	92	95	96

Data points are plotted in the same way that points are plotted in the coordinate plane, with one variable represented on the horizontal axis and the other variable on the vertical axis.

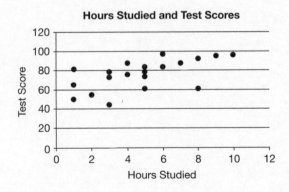

The patterns of the plotted points provide a visual representation of how the data values are related. For example, this scatter plot shows a trend where an increase in the number of hours studied corresponds to an increase in test scores.

2. Relationships between variables in a data set can be determined simply by looking at a scatter plot representing the data. For example, the following scatterplots show relationships between variables where there are positive, negative, and no correlations.

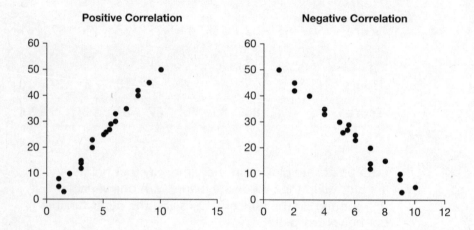

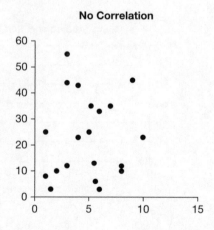

Scatter Plots on Your Calculator *You can create scatter plots on your graphing calculator. For example, consider the following pairs of data values:*

2	5	10	8	1	3	9	6	7	4
9	4	2	1	8	6	3	6	3	4

Input the top row of values as L1 and the bottom row of values as L2. Then press [2ND][Y=] for the STAT PLOT screen. Then select 1 and press ENTER to turn on the plot. Use the arrow keys to select the scatter plot (the first graph option) as the plot type if it is not already selected. Input L1 for Xlist and L2 for Ylist. For Mark, select the symbol you want. Then press [GRAPH] to see the scatter plot. You may have to press [ZOOM] and select 9 to adjust the window so the scatter plot can be seen.

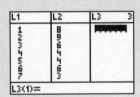

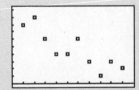

Note: To turn off the scatter plot, press [2ND][Y=] for the STAT PLOT screen. Select the plot and use the right arrow to select OFF, then press ENTER to turn the plot off.

LEAST SQUARES REGRESSION

KEY VOCABULARY

Exponential regression Using an equation of the form $y = ab^x$ to model a set of data.

Line of best fit The line that best models a set of data; same as a *regression line*.

Linear regression Using an equation of the form $y = ax + b$ to model a set of data.

Quadratic regression Using an equation of the form $y = ax^2 + bx + c$ to model a set of data.

Regression line The line that best models a set of data; same as a *line of best fit*.

Residual The offset of a point from a line.

I. UNDERSTANDING REGRESSION

A. REGRESSION BASICS

1. *Regression* is an approach to modeling the relationship between two variables in a set of data.
2. Three types of regression models are included in the SAT Mathematics Level 2 test.
    i. Linear models are of the form $y = ax + b$. The equation represents a *regression line*, also called a *line of best fit*.

ii. Quadratic models are of the form $y = ax^2 + bx + c$.

iii. Exponential models are of the form $y = ab^x$.

B. LEAST SQUARES REGRESSION

1. *Least squares regression* is a technique for finding a line or curve that models the relationship between two variables.

2. The least squares regression technique finds the best-fitting line or curve for a set of data points by minimizing the sum of the squares of the *residuals* of the points from the line or the curve. For example, consider the following set of points:

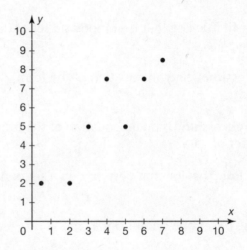

It can be seen from the graphs on the next page, that line *m* models the data better than line *l* because the sum of the squares of the residuals from line *m* would be less than the sum of the squares of the residuals from line *l*.

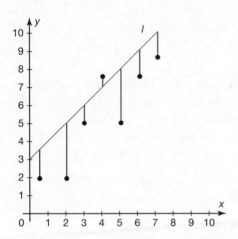
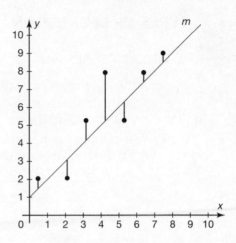

3. Because of the extensive calculations required to find the line of best fit, regression analysis is usually performed using technology such as a graphing calculator or computer program.

Your Calculator Can Help You Choose a Model *Before deciding whether to use linear, quadratic, or exponential regression for your model, use your calculator to create a scatter plot of the data. First, enter the data into L1 and L2. Press [2ND][Y=], then select 1 and press ENTER to turn on the plot. Select the scatter plot and input L1 and L2 for Xlist and Ylist. Press [GRAPH] to see the scatter plot. Press [ZOOM] 9 to fit the window to the data.*

If the scatter plot approximates a line, use linear regression. If the scatter plot approximates a parabola or a gradually rising and/or falling curve, use quadratic regression. If the scatter plot approximates a steeply rising or falling curve, use exponential regression.

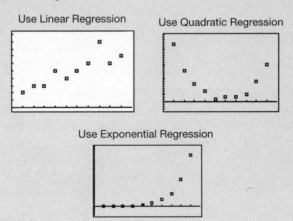

Use Linear Regression

Use Quadratic Regression

Use Exponential Regression

TYPES OF REGRESSION

A. LINEAR REGRESSION

1. If the data shows a constant increase or decrease in values and the scatterplot approximates a line, a linear model can be used to describe the data.
2. You can use your calculator to find the linear model that best fits the data. For example, consider the following data.

x	1	2	3	4	5	6	7	8	9	10
y	2	3	3	5	4	5	6	9	6	7

    i. Press [STAT][ENTER] and input the data into L1 and L2.

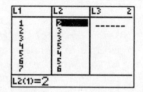

    ii. If you are not sure if a linear model is right for the data, display a scatter plot. The scatter plot approximates a line, so a linear regression model will work.

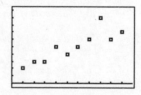

    iii. To find the equation of the line that best models the data, press [STAT] and use the right arrow to select CALC. Then select 4 LinReg (ax + b) and press ENTER.

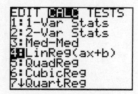

iv. When prompted for the lists, input L1, L2, then press ENTER.

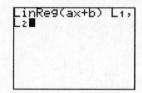

v. Use the results to write the equation that models the data by substituting the *a* and *b* values into the equation $y = ax + b$. In this case, the coefficients can be rounded, resulting in the equation $y = 0.6x + 1.67$ or, using fractions, $y = \dfrac{3}{5}x + \dfrac{5}{3}$.

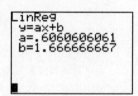

vi. To see how the line fits the data, create the scatter plot if you have not already done so, then press [Y=] and enter the equation. Press [GRAPH] to see the data points and the line that best models them.

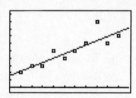

B. QUADRATIC REGRESSION

1. If the data shows a gradual increase and/or decrease in values and the scatterplot approximates a parabola or a gradually rising and/or falling curve, a quadratic model can be used to describe the data.

2. You can use your calculator to find the quadratic model that best fits the data. For example, consider the following data.

x	1	2	3	4	5	6	7	8	9	10
y	26	14	8	5	1	2	2	3	9	17

    i. Press [STAT][ENTER] and input the data into L1 and L2.

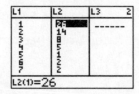

    ii. If you are not sure if a quadratic model is right for the data, display a scatter plot. The scatter plot approximates a parabola, so a quadratic regression model will work.

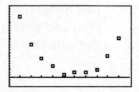

    iii. To find the equation that best models the data, press [STAT] and use the right arrow to select CALC. Then select 5 QuadReg and press ENTER.

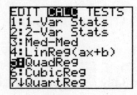

iv. When prompted for the lists, input L1, L2, then press ENTER.

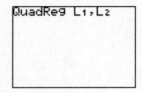

v. Use the results to write the equation that models the data by substituting the *a*, *b*, and *c* values into the equation $y = ax^2 + bx + c$. In this case, the coefficients can be rounded, resulting in the equation $y = x^2 - 12x + 35$.

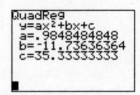

vi. To see how the line fits the data, create the scatter plot if you have not already done so, then press [Y=] and enter the equation. Press [GRAPH] to see the data points and the line that best models them.

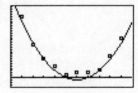

C. EXPONENTIAL REGRESSION

1. If the data shows a sharp increase and/or decrease in values and the scatterplot approximates a sharply increasing or decreasing curve, an exponential model can be used to describe the data.

2. You can use your calculator to find the exponential model that best fits the data. For example, consider the following data.

x	1	2	3	4	5	6	7	8	9	10
y	3	5	14	22	50	93	195	380	775	1510

i. Press [STAT][ENTER] and input the data into L1 and L2.

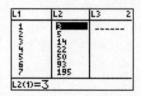

ii. If you are not sure if an exponential model is right for the data, display a scatter plot. The scatter plot is a steeply rising curve, so an exponential regression model will work.

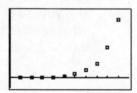

iii. To find the equation that best models the data, press [STAT] and use the right arrow to select CALC. Then, using the arrow key to scroll down, select 0 ExpReg and press ENTER.

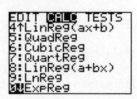

iv. When prompted for the lists, input L1, L2, then press ENTER.

v. Use the results to write the equation that models the data by substituting the a and b values into the equation $y = a \cdot b \wedge x$. In this case, the coefficients can be rounded, resulting in the equation $y = 1.5 \cdot 2 \wedge x$.

vi. To see how the line fits the data, create the scatter plot if you have not already done so, then press [Y=] and enter the equation. Press [GRAPH] to see the data points and the line that best models them.

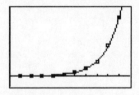

Test Tip

Find the Line of Best Fit *In a regression problem on the SAT Mathematics Level 2 test, you may be given either a table of values or a scatter plot along with a choice of equations that could model the data. Since time is limited, first try to use what you know about graphing equations to identify the line of best fit. If you still need help, use your calculator to create a scatter plot representing the data and then try the different equation to see which line fits best.*

PROBABILITY

KEY VOCABULARY

Compound event An event comprised of two or more simple events.

Dependent events The outcome of one event affects the outcome of the other event.

Event One or more of the possible outcomes when something is done.

Experimental probability Type of probability based on the results of an experiment that is repeated many times: $\frac{\text{number of times desired event occurs}}{\text{total number}}$.

Inclusive events Events that can occur at the same time.

Independent events The outcome of one event does not affect the outcome of the other event.

Mutually exclusive events Events that cannot occur at the same time.

Probability The likelihood that an event will occur.

Theoretical probability The number of ways an event can occur divided by the total number of outcomes: $\frac{\text{number of favorable outcomes}}{\text{total number of possible outcomes}}$.

I. PROBABILITY OF SIMPLE EVENTS

A. PROBABILITY BASICS

1. *Probability* is the mathematical representation of the likelihood that an event will occur.

2. An *event* is a one or more of the possible outcomes when something is done. For example, when tossing a coin, getting heads would be an event and getting tails would be another event.

3. *Theoretical probability* is the number of ways an event can occur divided by the total number of outcomes:

$$\frac{\text{number of favorable outcomes}}{\text{total number of possible outcomes}}.$$

4. *Experimental probability* is based on the results of an experiment that is repeated many times:

$$\frac{\text{number of times desired event occurs}}{\text{total number}}.$$

Each performance of the experiment is a *trial*. As the number of trials increases, experimental probability gets closer and closer to theoretical probability.

5. *Probability* can be expressed as a fraction, decimal, or percent.

6. The greatest value for a probability is 1, which represents total certainty that an event will occur. The least value for a probability is 0, which represents an event that cannot happen.

7. Probability is sometimes represented as odds.

   i. Odds in favor of an outcome is given as the ratio of the number of favorable outcomes: number of unfavorable outcomes. For example, the odds of rolling a three on a die are 1:5.

   ii. Odds against an outcome is given as the ratio of the number of unfavorable outcomes: number of favorable outcomes. For example, the odds against rolling a three on a die are 5:1.

8. The notation for probability is a capital *P* followed by the event in parentheses: *P*(event). For example, the probability of getting heads in a coin toss is represented as *P*(heads), and the probability of rolling a three on a die is represented as *P*(3).

B. CALCULATING PROBABILITY OF A SIMPLE EVENT

1. To calculate the probability of a simple event, write a fraction with the total number of possible outcomes as the denominator and the number of favorable outcomes as the numerator. For example, to calculate the probability of

getting heads when tossing a fair coin, determine that the total number of possible outcomes is 2 (heads or tails) and the number of favorable outcomes is 1 (heads). So, P (heads) $= \frac{1}{2}$, 0.5, or 50%.

2. The complement of an event is the opposite of an event. For example, when rolling a die, the complement of rolling a three is *not* rolling a three. The probability of the complement of an event is equal to 1 minus the probability of the event. So, if the probability of rolling a three on a die is $P(3) = \frac{1}{6}$, then $P(\text{not } 3) = 1 - \frac{1}{6}$, or $\frac{5}{6}$.

II. PROBABILITY OF COMPOUND EVENTS

A. COMPOUND EVENT BASICS

1. A *compound event* is comprised of two or more simple events. For example, getting heads in a coin toss is a simple event and rolling a three on a die is another simple event. If you toss a coin and roll a die at the same time, getting heads *and* rolling a three is a compound event.

2. Compound events can be classified as *independent events*, *dependent events*, *mutually exclusive events*, or *inclusive events*.

B. INDEPENDENT EVENTS

1. Events are *independent* when the outcome of one event does not affect the outcome of the other event. For example, getting heads in a coin toss and rolling a three on a die are independent events because the result of a coin toss does not affect the result of rolling a die.

2. If A and B are independent events, then the probability of both A and B occurring is the probability of A multiplied by the probability of B: $P(A \text{ and } B) = P(A) \bullet P(B)$. For example, since the probability of getting heads in a coin toss is $\frac{1}{2}$ and the probability of rolling a three on a die is $\frac{1}{6}$, the probability of getting heads *and* rolling a three is the product of $\frac{1}{2}$ and $\frac{1}{6}$: $P(\text{heads and } 3) = \frac{1}{2} \bullet \frac{1}{6} = \frac{1}{12}$.

C. DEPENDENT EVENTS

1. Events are *dependent* when the outcome of one event affects the outcome of another event. For example, randomly selecting a card from a standard deck of cards and then randomly selecting another card without replacing the first one are dependent events because the probability of selecting the second card depends on what card was selected first.

2. If *A* and *B* are dependent events, then the probability of both *A* and *B* occurring is the probability of *A* multiplied by the probability of *B* after *A* occurs:
   $P(A \text{ and } B) = P(A) \bullet P(B \text{ following } A)$. For example, the

   probability of selecting an ace from a standard deck of cards is

   $\dfrac{\text{number of aces}}{\text{total number of cards}} : \dfrac{4}{52} \text{ or } \dfrac{1}{13}.$

   The probability of selecting another ace if the first card is not

   replaced is $\dfrac{\text{number of aces remaining}}{\text{number of cards remainin}} : \dfrac{3}{51} \text{ or } \dfrac{1}{17}.$

   So, $P(\text{ace, ace}) = \dfrac{1}{13} \bullet \dfrac{1}{17} = \dfrac{1}{221}.$

Test Tip

Selecting Two Things at the Same Time Selecting two items at the same time is often equivalent to selecting one item and then selecting another item without replacement. For example, the probability of selecting two aces from a standard deck of cards is equivalent to selecting an ace and then selecting another ace without replacing the first one.

D. MUTUALLY EXCLUSIVE EVENTS

1. Events are *mutually exclusive* when they cannot occur at the same time. For example, rolling a three on a die and rolling a four on the same die are mutually exclusive since you cannot roll a three and a four on a die at the same time.

2. If *A* and *B* are mutually exclusive events, then the probability of either *A* or *B* occurring is the probability of *A* plus the probability of *B*: $P(A \text{ or } B) = P(A) + P(B)$. For example, the probability of rolling a three on a die is $\dfrac{1}{6}$ and the probability of rolling a four on a die is $\dfrac{1}{6}$. So, $P(3 \text{ or } 4) = \dfrac{1}{6} + \dfrac{1}{6} = \dfrac{2}{6} = \dfrac{1}{3}.$

E. INCLUSIVE EVENTS

1. Events are *inclusive* when they can occur at the same time. For example, selecting an ace from a standard deck of cards and selecting a heart from a standard deck of cards are inclusive because a card can be both an ace and a heart.

2. If A and B are inclusive events, then the probability of either A or B occurring is the probability of A plus the probability of B minus the probability of both A and B: $P(A \text{ or } B) = P(A) + P(B) - P(A \text{ and } B)$. For example, the probability of selecting an ace from a standard deck of cards is $\frac{4}{52}$ or $\frac{1}{13}$ and the probability of selecting a heart is $\frac{13}{52}$ or $\frac{1}{4}$. So,

$$P(\text{ace or heart}) = \frac{1}{13} + \frac{1}{4} - \left(\frac{1}{13} \cdot \frac{1}{4}\right) = \frac{4}{52} + \frac{13}{52} - \frac{1}{52} = \frac{16}{52} = \frac{4}{13}.$$

Probability Simulation App on the TI-83 and TI-84 *The Probability Simulation app shows animations for tossing coins, rolling dice, picking marbles, spinning spinners, and drawing cards. To access the Probability Simulation app, press [APPS] and then use the down arrow to scroll down to 0:Prob Sim and press ENTER.*

Following is the main menu for the app.

Note that the Probability Simulation app will help you find experimental probability, not theoretical probability. Since problems on the SAT Mathematics Level 2 test will most likely involve either theoretical probability or situations where experimental probabilities are already given to you, the Probability Simulation app will probably not help you solve problems on the test. However, as you study for the probability component of the Level 2 test, the Probability Simulation app can be an effective and fun tool for exploring and gaining a deeper understanding of probability concepts.

INDEX

Notes

Notes

Notes

Notes

Notes

Notes

Notes

Notes

Notes

Notes

Notes

Notes